About ᴛ

Clive Hart lives in the m.
spends as much time as ......our
on horseback. He is a sma ...international
community dedicated ι ..creating medieval
mounted combat as close as it originally was.

The horse on the cover is Squire, the
author's palomino warhorse.

For information on other books, please visit
www.clivehart.net

Also by Clive Hart:

The Rise and Fall of the Mounted Knight

The Legend of Richard Keynes series:
Book One: Golden Spurs
Book Two: Brothers in Arms
Book Three: Dogs of War
Book Four: Knight Errant **OUT SOON**

This book is dedicated to Sharon & Colin who were
responsible for showing the author that it was possible
to recreate history in the modern world, and without
this introduction, this book would not exist.

Contents

THE LITTLE LORD

Normandy, Early Autumn, 1167

Over the road from the Flying Monk, two armies confronted each other across barren ground. On the road, Richard sat on his horse next to Bowman and his half-brother Nicholas. Eva and her dozen Irishmen followed behind them. Richard wore one of his mail shirts, the other in a bag tied to the back of his saddle next to his helmet. The cool air of the day did nothing to temper Richard's rising temperature as his eyes fell on the armies.

'God help us,' he said, 'I'd hoped I was wrong.'

'Afraid not,' Bowman swung his shield around from his back to his side.

Richard felt his mouth dry up. 'I hope the Little Lord is here, maybe we can end this today.'

'If Lord Tancarville is here, he might end us instead. Although I don't see his personal banner,' Bowman said.

Richard did recognise de Cailly's banner flying above the other force. Both sides looked evenly matched.

'Is this your village?' Nicholas asked.

'At the moment,' Bowman laughed.

Richard frowned.

Two riders faced each other between the two armies, their horses nose-to-nose. Behind them their bannermen held their fluttering flags. On the left, the red banner of Tancarville flew, and on the right fluttered the green, yellow and blue banner of Sir Roger de Cailly.

Richard pushed his horse on to reach the two riders quicker. Solis snorted but obeyed. He cantered past the partially rebuilt inn that was the Flying Monk, wooden scaffolding covered it and planks of wood lay in piles all around. Richard turned off the road and onto the open and unused ground between the two sides. He broke into a gallop and grass and mud flew up from Solis's hooves. Richard halted him when he reached the two men, who ceased their conversation.

'Richard,' de Cailly nodded, 'it is fitting that you are here.'

'Richard?' The other man said in a growling voice from beneath the Tancarville banner.

'Sir John,' Richard said to him.

Sir John peered at him down his nose. 'It is you. I remember the scar on your face from the last time I was here, but you look older. I recognised your horse first, truth be told.'

'Where is Lord Tancarville?' Richard asked.

'At home,' Sir John replied, 'he had little interest in this venture.'

'Just go home, John,' de Cailly said.

'I would like nothing more,' the Tancarville knight replied.

The wind picked up and caught the banners. They snapped and billowed above Richard's head.

De Cailly looked at the Tancarville army. 'What do we have, maybe four hundred lives on this field?' He said.

'You do not have to preach peace to me,' Sir John said, 'I have no desire for any blood to be spilt for the sake of this patch of dirt.'

Richard glared at the knight. 'Speak for yourself,' he said.

'Now, Richard, calm yourself,' de Cailly said.

'I can't let you through,' Sir John said, 'so it will be well if you wait here. It will be even better if you turn around and go home.'

'You should probably know,' de Cailly said, 'that the Little Lord has gone into the village.'

'What?' Richard's eyes widened.

'They arrived before us, that's why they are blocking our way in,' de Cailly replied.

Sir John sighed. 'He is a hard youth to follow, let alone like. But the fact remains that his father sent me to keep him safe,' he said, 'so I can't let you go in and harm him.'

'I don't need to harm him,' Richard said, 'I just need get him away from my wife and my village.'

'Then we'll have to fight and stain this unremarkable soil with the blood of good Norman men,' Sir John looked over to de Cailly, 'and some others.'

Richard flexed his right arm but it still felt numb where the tower door at Castle Josselin had dented it. If the Little Lord had already gone through though, that was a problem. Maybe the King's squires garrisoning the castle had at least kept the gate closed to the young Tancarville.

'I cannot be blocked from entering my own village,' Richard said.

'You have been,' Sir John backed his horse up, 'and shall continue to be.'

'My men have come from a campaign,' de Cailly said, 'they are tired and impatient to go home. They are seasoned, too. Your men look nervous and untested, their faces are fresh and clean.'

'You shall have to find out, for I have my duty,' Sir John replied.

'Very well,' de Cailly backed his horse up and away from Sir John, 'we decide it by force of arms.'

Both knights began to turn back to their armies.

'Wait,' Richard cried.

The knights stopped and looked back.

'We might have no choice to settle this by force of arms,' Richard said, 'but we don't have to kill anyone who isn't involved.'

Sir John faced Richard and his banner whipped around in the air above his head. 'You surprise me, boy. Most would hide behind the mail shirt of Sir Roger and his army, and hope they claimed a victory for them.'

'Richard, don't do it,' de Cailly said, 'Sir John is a famous horseman and he will not have any qualm about striking your face with his lance.'

'I will fight the single combat,' Richard nodded, 'if we lose any battle fought here, I might as well be dead, anyway.'

De Cailly coughed. 'And I thought the youth of today were made of weaker stuff than us,' he said.

'I accept your proposal,' Sir John said, 'if I win you will remain outside of the village until the young Tancarville leaves it.'

'But if I win, we go through,' Richard said.

Sir John nodded and waved away his bannerman.

'Good luck, Richard,' de Cailly rode back to his lines, leaving Richard and Sir John alone.

'This is a legal combat,' Sir John said, 'so first to die or yield loses. If anyone else lays a blow on either of us, their side forfeits.'

Richard nodded and realised that Sir John had been holding his lance the whole time. Richard hadn't held a lance since they'd arrived at Castle Josselin in Brittany. 'I need a lance,' he said.

'The combat begins,' Sir John spurred his horse towards Richard.

The soft ground barely slowed Sir John's black Italian warhorse at all.

Richard didn't have time to swing his shield around to the front, he chose to draw his sword instead. Sir John's lance lowered and pointed at Richard's face. Richard swatted the lance aside and pushed Solis on into a canter. Richard raced away from Sir John and used the time to shift his shield around to his front. Sir John turned his warhorse almost on the spot and charged again.

Richard knew he would have to out-ride his opponent to get close enough to use his sword. Richard slowed his horse before Sir John reached him, and started to turn just as the knight raced by. His lance skated harmlessly off Richard's shield. Richard used everything he had to turn Solis. The palomino grunted but turned so fast that he could see Sir John's back. Richard urged his horse on as fast as he could go, and the beast bounded after his prey. Sir John pulled his horse up and started to turn. Richard reached him and struck out with his sword. The blade caught Sir John on his back, but the metal rings of his mail shirt kept the slicing attack out. As his opponent finished his own turn, the two horses collided into each other. Richard's sword-arm jammed into Sir John and the sword fell from his hands. The two horses jumped apart and untangled their legs.

'Inexperience,' Sir John turned towards Richard.

Now weaponless, Richard clamped his legs onto his horse and started to gallop over to de Cailly and his army.

'You flee, boy?' Sir John didn't bother to chase him.

Richard slammed to a halt and held his open hand out towards de Cailly. He nodded and one of his knights rode forwards and pressed his lance into Richard's grip.

Richard turned. 'I'm not fleeing,' he shouted to Sir John, 'but now the contest is level.'

Sir John laughed and approached Richard, faster and faster.

Solis leapt into a canter as foam trailed from his mouth. Richard could smell him as he heated up, a warmth he could also feel through his legs.

Richard lowered his lance and locked it in place under his arm, the point aimed at Sir John's face. The old knight's face set in a scowl, his sharp lance bounced up and down in time with his horse's stride as they closed on each other.

The two lances clashed together and the sound echoed between both armies. The wooden shafts tangled and both men nearly dropped them as they separated at speed.

The two armies cheered at the impact, even though both men failed to make a clean hit.

Richard turned Solis and clenched his jaw as he attacked again. This time Richard leant his entire bodyweight into the lance. When Sir John tried to attack him, Richard pushed his lance into his opponent's weapon and shoved it down and out of the way. Richard's lance caught the leather shield strap of his enemy and wrenched Sir John over and backwards. His horse cantered on, but Sir John was too out of balance and he toppled slowly from his saddle. He tumbled onto the earth head first and gouged a long mark in the soil.

De Cailly's army cheered. Richard stopped Solis and struggled to catch his breath as he faced his dismounted enemy.

Sir John pushed himself up onto his hands and knees and spat out some mud.

Richard walked his horse over. 'Do you yield?'

'Yield?' Sir John got back up to his feet, 'do I look finished to you?'

Richard thought about running him down and ending the matter under Solis's hooves. Instead he rested the lance on the ground and got out of his saddle.

'Stay,' he said to his horse, who rubbed his nose on Richard's mail shirt. That patch would rust now. Richard took the lance in two hands and neared Sir John.

The knight drew his sword but his shield lay far away, the neck strap snapped in two.

'When you yield,' Sir John said, 'I'll set the ransom to be Yvetot itself, then it will be mine and I can ban you from it.'

Richard thrust with the lance point. Sir John used his sword to push it aside and charged. Richard stepped backwards and ran to keep his distance. Sir John had been quicker than he'd looked.

'Running again?'

Richard regained his distance and pointed the spear at Sir John. He knew if the older knight got past the blade of his weapon, he would be dead. Sir John knew it too, and ran at him. Richard jinked sideways and the Tancarville knight followed. Richard kept circling until the older man started to puff.

When Sir John lunged again, Richard tried to turn his point at Sir John's chest. Instead, he slipped on the loose earth and went down onto one knee. Richard could see Sir John's mouth turn up into a smile. The veteran knight's sword raised. Richard rolled over and brought the back end of the lance up at Sir John to knock the smile out. The wooden butt smashed into his jaw and his two front teeth flew from his mouth. Richard scrambled to his feet as Sir John reeled back with his sword held up to his face.

Richard decided against calling for him to yield, and instead swung the sharp end of his lance around. Sir John looked up just in time to see it, but Richard's blade pushed his own hand, sword still in it, back into his face.

Sir John back-pedalled as blood poured from his mouth and nose. He spat and looked over to Richard. 'You've learnt well since you left Castle Tancarville,' he said.

Richard gripped the spear tightly and readied for his opponent.

Sir John however, stood and tried to get air into his lungs.

Men from both sides shouted and jeered, plenty had laid bets, too.

Sir John closed his eyes and shook his head, and Richard recognised his chance. He went to swipe the man's legs away with the shaft of the spear. Sir John saw it quick enough to jump one leg over the spear, but the other tripped him up and he fell over onto Richard. They collapsed into the earth together and Richard lost the spear. Sir John's face looked down on him and blood dripped onto Richard's. He tried to push Sir John's sword away with his left hand, and with his right he reached down Sir John's mail shirt until he reached leather. Richard traced his hand along the belt until it reached a scabbard.

Sir John's sword-hilt thumped into the side of Richard's head as he drew the man's own dagger against him. His head rang from the blow and he fought to focus his vision.

Richard dragged the dagger up between their bodies and jammed the hilt up into Sir John's chin. It collided with his upper jaw with a great crack and he slumped. Richard pushed him away, scrambled on his knees in the mud, and jumped on top of his opponent, dagger to Sir John's throat.

'Are you done now?' Richard howled into his face.

Sir John winced from the sharp point that pricked his neck. 'Yes,' he gulped.

'Louder, so they can hear,' Richard said.

'I yield,' Sir John said. His men groaned, except for the few who had bravely bet against him.

Richard rolled off the man and pushed himself up onto his feet. He wiped down some mud from his woollen legs. 'I'm keeping the dagger,' he said.

Sir John waved at him, for he was more concerned with his mangled face and missing teeth.

'I didn't want to do that,' Richard said.

His fallen opponent spat red onto the brown earth. 'God has signalled his will. Go on, go into your dammed village,' he said.

Richard looked around for his horse, who hadn't stayed put. He spotted Solis next to de Cailly, his yellow head trying to eat its way into de Cailly's leather bag. The knight tried to swat him away but the stallion didn't care.

'Solie,' Richard shouted. The horse's ears pricked up. He abandoned the bag and trotted over back to Richard, who remounted.

De Cailly followed and looked over at Sir John. 'Our time is fading,' he said, 'it is the time of the young.'

'Will you come with me into the village?' Richard asked.

De Cailly nodded. 'No. We'll stay here to stop them coming in to help the Little Lord,' he said.

'Thank you, and thank you for coming to Yvetot,' Richard made his way back over towards the Flying Monk.

Bowman and Nicholas waited by it.

'You need to learn to keep a hold of your sword,' Nicholas said.

Bowman laughed. 'Don't bother. It's not even worth him having one,' he said.

Richard glanced over at the building site around his inn. 'One day I want to have a drink in there, but we need to find the Little Lord before he gets near my wife,' he said.

Bowman nodded and followed Richard into Yvetot.

The orchard that lined both sides of the road still bulged with apples, although some of the older leaves had begun to yellow. When they reached the village itself, the first thing Richard saw was the fallen lump of masonry that half-blocked the church entrance. He frowned and decided he needed to move it whether or not the Priest agreed. The graveyard had holes in it with piles of fresh dirt all around, although what any bodies there had worth robbing, Richard couldn't imagine. Sir Arthur's wooden cross had been snapped in half, and the roof of the church he noticed had partially caved in. Or at least, had not yet been repaired from the village's burning earlier in the year. Some rebuilding had happened though, as some of the villager's houses stood tall and clean, and a new barn's wooden frame was nearly complete.

'Where is he?' Richard said when they reached his castle and found no one at all standing guard outside the wooden palisade.

'He must be inside,' Bowman said.

Richard felt a mix of anger and apprehension creep into his stomach. 'Why is the gate open?'

Richard didn't wait for an answer, instead he cantered Solis towards it and left everyone else behind. Solis tore through the gate and into the lower bailey. The horse snorted as Richard reached the stone wall around his keep and almost threw himself from his saddle. Richard pushed the wooden gate open and looked around. One of the King's squires looked down at him from the wall.

'Why aren't the rest of you on the front gate?' Richard asked.

'They're all ill, my lord,' the young man replied, 'I'm the only one who can stand.'

'How ill?'

'We don't know, a pestilence, the others said.'

'Is the Little Lord here?' Richard asked.

'Who?'

Richard started to run towards the keep. 'Has anyone come in?'

'Oh yes,' the young squire said, 'two of them.'

Richard drew Sir John's dagger from his belt and rushed up into the hall. He burst in through the door. The fire burnt away on the other side of the room, the air dense with woodsmoke, but not one person was inside. Richard turned and ran up the stone staircase until he reached the door of his chamber, in front of which stood a man.

'You can't come in,' the man said in a gruff voice.

In the near darkness of the staircase Richard couldn't make out his features, but he was short and squat.

'Let me through,' Richard said.

The squat man squared up to him, and a sword-shaped shadow shifted in the gloom.

Richard thought what argument he could use to get him to step aside.

A cry rang out from the chamber. A woman's cry. Sophie's cry.

Richard forgot about negotiating and lunged.

A second scream flooded through the closed door, but this time it was a man's.

Richard thrust the dagger up into the squat man's core, up inside his ribs. It pushed the air out of his lungs with a sucking noise. Richard felt the man's last breath against his cheeks and for a moment regretted his haste.

The male screams from his chamber hadn't stopped, if anything they grew louder and more intense. Richard heaved the squat man's body off himself and ran for the door. He flung it open, burst in, then froze in his tracks.

The Little Lord stood in front of Richard's bed in his white linen underwear, with his hands over his groin. A dark red patch grew there as he howled in agony.

Sophie's long blue dress had gashes down it, and a flap hung torn from the back. In her hand, and still aloft, a small knife pointed at the Little Lord. The blade had blood on it.

Sophie, motionless but breathing heavily, had her eyes set on the young Tancarville. Her hair was a mess and Richard thought she looked like a wounded wolf.

The Little Lord held his hands up to look at them for a moment, but had to clamp them back down between his legs.

'What is this?' Richard asked.

Sophie didn't move.

'She's crazy,' the Little Lord said, 'the devil is in both of you. She'll hang for this.'

Sophie raised her knife hand towards the young Tancarville.

'Don't,' Richard walked over to her.

His wife slowed and turned her head. 'Richard?'

'I'm here,' Richard closed on her and put one hand gently on hers. He carefully unpicked the knife from her fingers, which released only reluctantly. He put his other arm around her and held her tightly. 'I'm back now.'

'Who cares,' the Little Lord shouted, 'she attacked me, I'm bleeding to death.'

Richard glanced over at him, and he had lost a fair amount of blood. 'I think you deserved it, you'll find no help here.'

The young Tancarville peered down at himself and his face paled.

'Get out of my chamber and out of my castle,' Richard said.

The Little Lord scrambled his hands down into his underclothes, his eyes wild and pleading under his red hair.

'What did you do to him?' Richard asked.

Sophie clenched her teeth but kept her eyes on her attacker.

Richard ran his hand around the bump that was his wife's stomach.

'She cut me, I've never hurt like this,' the Little Lord started to cry.

'Did you stab him? Once? Twice?'

Sophie's body began to relax. 'I don't know.'

'Why are you still here?' Richard said to the injured man.

'Help me.'

'Get out,' Richard said.

The Little Lord fumbled around his groin. 'I don't know if it's still there.'

Richard choked laughter. 'Did she cut it off?'

'He tried to force me,' Sophie whispered in Richard's ear.

Richard didn't need to be told that. He pointed the confiscated red knife at the Little Lord. 'Don't make me throw you out. But if she's sliced it off, it would give a new meaning to your name, wouldn't it?'

The Little Lord looked at Richard with blank eyes.

'Maybe we should call you the Very Little Lord now?' Richard wondered.

The young Tancarville's face flashed anger for a moment. He shuffled off in the direction of the door.

'I know I shouldn't find it funny,' Richard said to Sophie as the Little Lord slipped away.

'He deserved it,' she said.

'He did,' Richard said, 'you shouldn't feel any guilt.'

'I don't,' she turned her eyes up to Richard's, 'but had you been here.'

'Yes I know,' Richard said, 'I'm sorry, but we had to ransom Sir Wobble before he rotted. Not that he was very grateful about it.'

'You should look to your lands before your friends, even if you care little for your wife,' Sophie said.

'Don't say that.'

'I am not a foolish little girl,' Sophie said, 'I know how and why marriages are crafted. But if a knight wishes to be respected, he must care for the foundation of his reputation. And you nearly let that foul boy steal it all from you.'

'He won't be trying that again though, will he?'

Sophie frowned and stepped away from Richard. She noticed the body slumped in her stairwell. 'His father might not take kindly to what just happened.'

'Lord Tancarville abandoned the King's army in Brittany, the night before we were attacked. To the King that is not a coincidence, and to him Tancarville committed treason. I think Tancarville has far more to worry about than our little village.'

'I hope you're right, but promise me that you'll stay until we know.'

Richard nodded. 'I need to rest, a crossbow bolt broke one of my ribs,' he rubbed the rib, which had increased in soreness since his joust by the Flying Monk.

'What happened to your finger?'

'That happened at the same time. On the walls of Castle Josselin. Someone said it's because I tried to block an axe with my finger,' Richard grinned.

'I am not one of your friends to show off to,' Sophie said, 'you can't lose a piece of yourself every time you go away. Soon there'll be nothing left of you.'

'A bit like the Very Little Lord,' Richard's grin widened, 'the Little Lord has lost his sword.'

Sophie stared at her husband for a moment before bursting into laughter.

'Bowman will like that one,' Richard said.

Sophie pointed over to their bed, where the Little Lord's actual sword and belt lay propped up against the frame. 'He has actually left his sword.'

'I think I'll keep it,' Richard said, 'or you should, as you are the one that bested him.'

Sophie raised her eyebrows and Richard looked at her blonde hair. Then her belly.

'If you have to ask if the baby is yours,' she said, 'I'll find another knife.'

Richard shook his head. 'How long?'

'It will come in the spring. The Priest found some charms to lay on me while I sleep to ensure it is a boy.'

Richard narrowed his eyes. 'If you trust him to use the right ones.'

Sophie shrugged. 'Who else can I trust, no one else here knows the proper things to do.'

'If the baby is a girl, I'll poke the Priest's eyes out,' Richard still occasionally had the dreams where he did just that. They were his better dreams of late.

Bowman appeared in the doorway and stepped over the body. 'I just saw the most curious thing outside.'

'The Little Lord has lost his sword,' Richard laughed.

'Stop it,' Sophie said.

'What? It's right there,' Bowman pointed to the sword by the bed.

'You saw his blood?' Richard asked.

'Aye, and if you stabbed him in the balls then his father might take that personally.'

'That was me,' Sophie's eye's glanced down.

Bowman stopped. 'Oh, really? That might save us. You should have finished the job, though.'

Richard looked at his friend. 'I think he's been punished enough, the Little Lord might have lost two swords. I'm thinking of calling him the Very Little Lord.'

Bowman's eyes pulsed in recognition. 'She cut it off?'

'We don't know,' Richard said.

'We're going to need a new inn, just to call it the Very Little Lord,' Bowman smiled.

'Children, enough,' Sophie said, 'I don't need any more children around here, having the Red Baby in the village has been bad enough.'

'Looks like you'll be having another, soon,' Bowman walked up and nudged Richard, 'congratulations.'

'Thank you. Have Sir John's men stayed outside?'

'So far as I know, both armies are where we left them.'

'Armies?' Sophie gasped.

'Fear not,' Bowman said, 'our young modern-day Roland here fought Sir John in a duel and battered him into a bloody pulp. I'd pay good coin to see Lord Tancarville's face when Sir John and the Little Lord arrive before him, both covered in blood, both bested by you two warriors.'

Richard's fingers ran over the hilt of Sir John's dagger in his belt. He didn't even remember putting it there. 'I think I need to go and check that Sir John is leaving and taking the Little Lord with him.'

Bowman nodded.

As Richard left the chamber, Sophie coughed deliberately. 'Can the two of you at least move that body first.'

NIGHTMARES

Richard woke up with a start. A cold sweat coated his back and his heart thumped in his chest. The first hint of morning came in through the eastern window of his chamber, and painted a faint yellow splash of light on the ceiling. Sophie snored softly beside him. Far in the distance he heard the first birdsong of the day so he pushed himself out of bed and threw his blue tunic over himself. He belted the Little Lord's sword around his waist and went downstairs to his hall.

The hearth had been well tended overnight and roared away, although its popping and sizzling was drowned out by the snoring of the dozen men who slept crammed together across the floorboards.

'Good morning, you're up early,' de Cailly said from the table in the centre of the room. He was the only other man awake.

Richard yawned and sat down opposite him. He found a pottery jug of something to drink and poured some for himself. 'I didn't sleep well.'

'I can't sleep for long anymore,' de Cailly said.

Richard thought of the nightmare that had violently thrown him from sleep. He had been back in the alleyway that wasn't an alleyway, where he'd first met Bowman, and first spilled another man's blood.

'I thought I'd sleep better once I got back here,' Richard said.

'Well, it wasn't exactly the welcome you'd expected,' de Cailly grinned.

'I can't decide if it went well or badly.'

'Everyone on that field will speak of your joust with Sir John as long as they live. And none will forget the sight of the Little Lord walking his horse out of the village on foot, in his underclothes, and with his manhood in tatters.'

'In tatters?'

'That's what they're all saying,' de Cailly said.

'But they don't know for sure?'

'Do you?'

'No, but there was a lot of blood,' Richard said.

The older knight grinned. 'I remember what that little runt tried to do to my daughter. If your wife saw to it that he can never do it to anyone else's daughter again, then I am a very happy man.'

'Even if Lord Tancarville comes after us?'

De Cailly nodded. 'I regret nothing. Even watching you turn Sir John's face into a mess was not a bad sight. He will wear his defeat for all to see until the day he dies. My knights and squires speak of you, and they have done so all the way through Brittany. Not as much as Lord Mandeville or the other famous knights, mind, but you are on the edge of fame.'

Richard felt his cheeks warm.

De Cailly laughed. 'But you are still but a boy.'

Richard drank what turned out to be slightly stale cider.

'You need to build a real hall,' de Cailly cast his eyes around the mass of sleeping men, 'if you wish to gather men around you, you need somewhere for them to sleep. Indoors.'

'I'm sorry your army is stuck outside,' Richard said.

'Nonsense, they've been sleeping outside since we crossed the Breton frontier. But if you wish to grow your household to match your burgeoning fame, you need somewhere to put them. I am going to leave for home this morning, but I will sell you some farmers and tradesmen. Your village does not even have a blacksmith. You also need a few carpenters to finish what has been started here, and expand the village. You can pay me for them in a year or two.'

'You'd help me with all that? I can't afford it.'

De Cailly nodded. 'No, you can't. But I'm investing in you and this castle to keep Lord Tancarville away from me. Besides, Cailly is full. Refugees from the east have flooded us, so I'm only proposing to send them on to you.'

'It would still be of a great help,' Richard said, 'half the village still lies in ruins. If it became more productive we could man our own walls instead of relying on the King's men.'

'I heard they are all ill, lying in your cellar apparently,' de Cailly said, 'which is another reason we're leaving now.'

Richard frowned, he'd forgotten about the potential plague locked down in his cellar.

'Keep the sick ones down there until they die or recover. Keep them away from your wife.'

Richard nodded.

'I pray you have a son,' de Cailly stood up and grinned, 'I'm going to ready my horse. I'll shame the rest of them into waking up.'

Richard watched him leave. The clink of the iron spurs on his heels that used to be Richard's echoed off the stairway.

In the corner of the hall closest to the hearth, Bowman sat up in his bedding. 'It's a bit early for you, isn't it?' He asked.

'I dreamt about the alleyway.'

'I'd forgotten about that,' Bowman got out of bed and packed it up against the wall, 'it seems like such a long time ago, young lord.'

'Where's your brother, we should introduce him to Sophie when she wakes.'

'Half-brother,' Bowman said, 'and just because I didn't want to kill him, doesn't mean I trust him. He's still at least half Martel, remember.'

More birds chirped outside and new light penetrated the horn slats that covered the windows.

'We also need to introduce Eva,' Richard said.

Bowman's face woke up. 'Of course, she agreed to go hunting with me today,' he said.

'Hunting?'

'We need more food if her and her Irishmen will be here for a few days.'

'Why does it need to be the two of you?' Richard asked.

'Why not,' Bowman grinned.

'Have you seen Sarjeant yet?'

Bowman shook his head. 'Odd really, not sure where he could be. Maybe he's in town?'

'I'm going to ask around,' Richard got up and left the keep.

The air outside was fresh and the trees in the distance had a brown tinge to their green. Richard found a cloak to wrap himself in and made his way out of his inner bailey. The single King's squire had gone and he grimaced at his undefended gate. At least it was closed, although Richard couldn't lock it behind him once he'd gone through and down into the lower bailey. Some of de Cailly's men had been asleep there with their horses, but the knight himself had half prepared his horse already. The rest of his men were awake and beginning to do the same, making the yard much busier than the hall.

Richard went to Solis's stable and rubbed his yellow and white nose. The stallion whinnied back at him but looked bleary eyed.

'You and me both,' Richard patted him and decided to walk into the village on his own two feet.

Unlike the sleeping warriors in his keep, the villagers of Yvetot were already at work. The autumn ploughing looked half complete, and as Richard approached the village he saw the village plough being carried out of the church, where ploughs were commonly stored. The farmers regarded him only in passing as they took the plough, Richard assumed because they had forgotten who he was. He reached the church with its damaged roof and lump of masonry jammed into the ground in the doorway. He walked around it and entered.

Sarjeant snored in a corner while the Priest was nowhere to be seen.

'Wake up,' Richard walked over and prodded his steward with his foot.

Sarjeant rolled over and Richard smelt cider in the air.

'Have you been drinking?'

His steward looked up at him and blinked. Richard looked down on the man he had seen as proud and wise before, and wondered if he'd been wrong about both.

Sarjeant rubbed his eyes, groaned, and propped himself up. He coughed roughly. 'Of course, my boy, it's the only safe thing to drink around here.'

'I mean have you drunk too much?' Richard asked.

Sarjeant's blue eyes shone out in the gloom of the unlit church. The eyes reflected the single shaft of light that beamed through the hole in the roof.

'I suppose I did. I heard what happened, I am so very glad

Lady Sophie was unhurt.'

'Physically unhurt,' Richard crossed his arms, 'I expected my steward to at least try to put up some resistance to someone attacking my wife.'

Sarjeant got up to his knees but paused and held a hand up to his forehead due to dizziness.

'How long has this been going on? The steward can't sleep in the church, at least not this church. It doesn't even look like the Priest sleeps in this church.'

'Yesterday was the first and only night this has happened,' Sarjeant pushed himself all the way up.

Richard looked up at him once he stood on his feet. 'Why didn't you try to stop the Little Lord?'

'I was on my way back from the Miller, reached the castle and the squire told me who had gone in. He informed me that there were two of them who entered.'

'There were two of you,' Richard said.

Sarjeant looked down at the floor. 'That squire has never lowered his lance in anger, what chance would him and I have had against two men hardened in battle?'

'My wife isn't hardened in battle,' Richard said, 'and she managed to deal with one of them just fine. Your duty was to defend the lady of the castle. You failed her. You failed me.'

Sarjeant's eyes welled up. 'If the squires had all been healthy, all would have been well.'

'But they weren't, where they?'

'I know I failed. That's why I ended up here, too ashamed to see you. I said I was too old for soldiering.'

'I remember,' Richard said, 'you told me that up on Yvetot's very walls the night before the villagers came to kill us. The first time.'

A tear rolled down the older man's cheek and Richard's expression softened. He sighed. 'I left you as my steward, not my castellan. Maybe I'm being too harsh.'

'It will never happen again, you have given me a great position and I will not let you down.'

Richard sighed. He could taste damp in the air. 'I was trying to give you what you wanted, but it hasn't exactly been easy for you here. Sir Roger is going to send us villagers and craftsmen to expand Yvetot. If we can prosper we can better man our walls. That is the sort of thing I wanted you to help me with. There were a dozen King's men to help keep the Little Lord from my wife, it wasn't your job.'

'More villagers? We could expand the orchard or even sell more than one type of cider,' Sarjeant's eyes twinkled.

Richard chuckled softly. 'That's what you can do. Make sure that the new arrivals build where we want them to, what we want them to. They will be your responsibility.'

'I won't fall into sin again,' Sarjeant said, 'the pain in my head has reminded me of all the wrongs I have done in my life.'

Richard believed him.

Sarjeant coughed. 'There is another matter we need to discuss.'

Richard raised his eyebrows.

'The Reeve.'

Richard's heart sank. 'What now? Has that petty little fat man been skimming from the villagers again?'

Sarjeant's face scrunched up.

'Worse than that?' Richard asked.

'Do you remember that the Templars in their farm to our north had moved the boundary fences into your land?'

Richard nodded. He remembered what Sarjeant's first solution to the problem had been, too. 'You haven't been fighting with them again, have you?'

'No, well, only a little,' Sarjeant said, 'I have not come to blows with them. They moved the fences further along this time.'

Richard groaned. He didn't care about the Templars on his border, although he knew he couldn't let them get away with it.

'I asked them to move it back,' Sarjeant said, 'they ignored me so I threatened to take the matter to the church court in Rouen.'

'Did that work?'

'What do you think?'

'Why do the Templars have to be such a nest of thieves, are they not rich enough already?'

Sarjeant scratched his jaw. 'The Templars are not rich, my boy, I've told you this before. They live as monks with nothing of value save church-silver. Even their swords and mail are old, some wear helms that our grandfathers would scoff at as old fashioned. No secular knight would degrade himself with such things, but the Templars wear them without complaint. The Templars here commit a crime, but they commit it for the right reason. Since the Crusade of Kings failed a dozen or so years ago it is harder for them now to beg coin from people.'

'You're siding with them?' Richard stepped back.

Sarjeant laughed, a smooth laugh that soothed. 'Everything they do is done to send shipments of coin and fighting men to the Holy Land. But these Templars act like common knights squabbling over land.'

'Are you calling me a common knight?

Sarjeant grinned. 'Are you not?'

Richard shrugged. 'I wouldn't say common, myself. What has all this excuse-making got to do with my land, and my Reeve?' Richard asked.

Sarjeant frowned. 'Treacherous swine.'

'What has he done?'

'It is what he plans to do that is hard to believe. He made a deal with the Templars,' Sarjeant said.

'To let them move the fences?' Richard asked.

'No. The fence-moving has ceased.'

'What's the problem then?'

'The Reeve has agreed to join the Templars, and hand them Yvetot in it's entirety.'

'What?' Richard clenched his fists, 'why would he do that? He's already the Reeve, he can't rise any higher.'

'You'd have to ask him that,' Sarjeant said, 'the deal is that the Reeve continues to act in his current role after the takeover.'

Richard couldn't feel the chill in the air anymore. He wanted to find the Reeve and crush him like the vermin he was.

'How did you find out about it?' Richard asked.

'I went onto their property. Only to speak with them, of course.'

'Of course.'

Sarjeant grinned. 'I saw the Reeve inside with their clerk, he knelt down and kissed a cross the clerk held out. I heard what they plotted, from their own mouths.'

'The people will need to see some proof before we can accuse him publicly of his misdeeds,' Richard said.

'Why?' Sarjeant scrunched up his face, 'you are lord and judge in Yvetot. If you judge the Reeve to be guilty, then guilty he is.'

'I need to think about that,' Richard looked around the church. Dew from the roof dripped in through the hole, accompanied by a gentle breeze.

'You know what you need to do,' Sarjeant said.

'We'll see. There are some things I need to attend to first,' Richard replied.

Hoof beats floated through the air from the road out of the village, so Richard left Sarjeant and went outside.

The blue, yellow, and green de Cailly banner shone through the branches of the trees that lined the graveyard. Richard walked over to the treeline as the column of horsemen rode by. Some nodded down to Richard, others grinned. One or two even turned their heads away and pretended not to have seen him. The last of the squires went by and they were followed by a string of packhorses. Once they too disappeared into the orchard and out of the village, quiet again descended over Yvetot.

Richard walked back up the track towards the castle. He wanted to write a letter to his sister and have a messenger take it to England. He thought he could at least warn her that Uncle Luke might be on his way.

'Where are you going?' Richard spotted Bowman riding towards him.

'To fill our table, remember,' he replied with a large smile on his face.

Behind Bowman, Eva and her Irishmen also rode, spears in hand.

Richard noticed the bow that Bowman held across his saddle. 'Hunting?'

Bowman nodded and looked back towards Eva. 'I'm going to show her around,' he said.

'Really.'

Eva stopped by Richard. 'I don't want my party to be a burden on your hospitality,' she said, 'the least we can do is feed ourselves.'

Richard frowned. Tired or not, Solis would have quite enjoyed a hunt. 'Next time, I wouldn't mind going,' he said.

'We'll be sure to invite you, young lord,' Bowman nodded back to the Irish and walked his horse on.

Richard watched them go with his hands on his hips. Invite him? When he got a moment alone with Bowman, he'd remind him that Eva was a princess. In the meantime, he had a letter to write and a wife he wanted to feel safe, so he returned to the hall.

Once the ink on the parchment had dried, he found the squire who wasn't sick and entrusted the letter to him.

'Ride through the town first,' Richard told him, 'and ask them to send a healer to tend to your friends.'

The young man had nodded and scurried off, Richard thought him glad to be away from the sickness afflicting those in his cellar.

Richard spent the rest of the day in the hall by the fire with Sophie, who mostly dozed.

He heard Bowman return, and peered out of the keep window to see him in the lower bailey. A deer lay across the back of Bowman's horse, his triumphant voice so loud Richard could hear it echo around the palisade walls.

That night the hall filled with people, the smell of roasted venison, the roar and heat of the fire, and laughter. Richard fell asleep in his chair and prayed that every night could be like this one. That night, the first for a long time, he didn't dream of alleyways or burning villages.

In the morning however, Eva left.

'Already?' Bowman asked as she vaulted up onto her small chestnut horse.

Eva nodded and her brown hair rippled in the autumn wind. 'I must ride east and find the King of the French,' she said, 'but we shall return here. This is the first place we have been welcomed and not treated like barbarians.'

'There are other places we can hunt,' Bowman said.

'Grow up,' Richard said, 'she said they'd be back.'

As the small horses walked off down the road, Bowman sighed. He turned to Richard. 'Not a word.'

Richard laughed. 'How are things with your brother?'

'Half-brother,' Bowman replied.

'Fine, half-brother. What do you make of him?'

Bowman tipped his head from side to side. 'I haven't thought about it much,' he said.

Richard glanced at the blonde man. 'Been too busy thinking about someone else?'

Bowman shrugged. 'You'll ransom him and then he'll leave. I may never see him again.'

Richard hadn't even thought about sending a ransom note. He cursed himself for having already sent his only messenger off to England with his letter for Adela.

'Until a squire recovers enough to travel, Nicholas is not going anywhere,' Richard said, 'so you might as well learn to get along with him.'

'He did try to kill me.'

'But you did take a risk to save him,' Richard added.

'It felt like the right thing to do at the time,' Bowman said, 'I didn't put much thought into it.'

'He could be useful to have on our side, he is part Martel.'

'Doesn't that make him dangerous?' Bowman asked.

Richard nodded. 'Or he could be an opportunity. He could help us to overcome Luke and Eustace.'

Bowman laughed. 'You want to go and take them on now, do you? You win one joust against an old Norman knight, and now you think you can fight anyone.'

'You're forgetting that I captured Eustace once before,' Richard said.

'Next time he could just as easily kill you,' Bowman said, 'and Nicholas tried to kill me once already.'

'You have mentioned that,' Richard frowned.

'I will ask him about my mother tonight.'

'Good, see if there is evil in him,' Richard said.

A pair of crows circled overhead in a noisy stand-off. Richard knew what they meant and it made him think about the Reeve.

Richard had a flash of inspiration and his eyes lit up. 'We could test him.'

'Who?'

'Your brother.'

'Half-brother.'

'Whatever,' Richard said, 'but I have a problem that he could help me with. If he does, maybe it will show that we can trust him.'

'What can he possibly help you with?' Bowman asked.

'My vermin problem.'

Sarjeant entered the hall with his old brown mantle in his hands. 'Moths have eaten some holes in a corner,' he said, 'but you can wrap it around your shoulders just the same.'

Richard grinned. 'This might work.'

Bowmen tossed an apple core into the fire.

'You could have given that to a horse,' Richard said.

Bowman shrugged.

'Do you have any red material?' Richard asked his steward.

Sarjeant shook his head.

Sophie looked up from her chair. 'You can use my red dress.'

'That's your best dress,' Richard said, then realised he hadn't seen his wife in it since the Red Baby had been born.

She looked over to Richard.

'Oh,' Richard said, 'yes, we can cut a cross from that.'

Sarjeant laid the brown mantle down on the smaller of the two tables in the hall.

Bowman sighed. 'You could at least get a new table to match either one of them, you can't blame a lack of coin for uneven tables.'

'I'm a bit busy with more important things,' Richard picked up the mantle and examined it. 'I haven't seen this in what, nearly two years?'

Sarjeant nodded. 'I had no wish to see it again, but if it can be useful, then very well.'

The tall slender frame of Nicholas Martel sat opposite Richard. 'Are you sure this is going to work?' He asked.

Richard chuckled. 'No.'

'It's a stupid idea,' Bowman pushed himself up and left the hall.

'What's his problem?' Nicholas asked, 'is it me?'

Sophie laughed. 'Don't be so centred on yourself. He is sulking because the Irish have left.'

'Oh, good,' Nicholas replied.

'Are you ready for this?' Richard asked him.

The Martel Bastard gulped and nodded.

Richard worried he might be too young for the task, but put the thought aside.

Later that day, and with Bowman dragging the Priest by his cloak, they walked over to the mill. Its waterwheel turned behind the building with a regular splashing noise and the sun hung just above the woods to the west. Soon the cloud cover would make walking slow in the deteriorating light.

When they reached the mill, Nicholas Martel knocked on the Miller's door. He wore Sarjeant's old Templar mantle, a new and bright red cross sewn onto it.

Richard motioned to Bowman and Sarjeant to back away, and they retreated back towards the village until Richard thought they'd be unseen from the doorway.

'What are we doing out at this hour?' The Priest pulled his arm free from Bowman.

'Quiet,' Richard whispered, 'you're here to listen, not speak.'

'I can't hear anything from here.'

Nicholas entered the mill and the door closed behind him.

'Exactly, now he's in we get close enough,' Richard said.

'What are you expecting them to be doing in there? Our village is innocent and free from sin.'

Bowman grabbed the Priest's arm and marched him towards the building.

An owl hooted in the distance and Richard made the sign of the cross.

'A bad omen,' the Priest said, 'it is certain that someone will die.'

Bowman raised his fist. 'If you don't shut up, it'll be you.'

The churchman recoiled and Bowman nodded. 'Just follow me,' he whispered.

Richard walked up to the mill's window and sat down under it.

'Why did we hide from your captive friend when he entered?' The Priest whispered.

'That's nothing to do with you,' Bowman elbowed him in the ribs.

The Priest gasped and kept quiet.

Sarjeant sat down beside Richard and they strained to hear

the words from inside. Richard could make out the Reeve's voice. He spoke quickly and his words were lively.

'It is always an honour to meet a Templar,' he said.

'I am but a young sarjeant,' Nicholas replied.

'Any man from such a holy order is welcome in my village,' the Reeve said.

Richard bristled.

'Your village?' Nicholas asked, 'I thought it belonged to Sir Richard.'

The Reeve chuckled.

'What sort of man is your lord?'

'Absent,' the Reeve said, 'he is cruel and meddling, too. He is but a boy, barely older than yourself. What does he know of crop rotation and the lives of peasants?'

'Do you trust him?' Nicholas asked.

'Of course not,' the Reeve replied, 'he's English.'

Richard groaned. Not that again.

'Has he ever had a captive knight or squire here before?'

'That's a curious question.'

'What's he doing?' Richard hissed towards Bowman.

'Just curious,' Nicholas said, 'I heard Sir Richard took a prisoner in the south and I was wondering how he treats such men.'

'My half-brother is scared of you,' Bowman tried to suppress a laugh.

'There was a prisoner here before, but I don't know if our English boy took him captive,' the Reeve said, 'he was a tall, great man they all feared. He had green eyes like yours.'

'What was his name?'

'Eric,' the Reeve said, 'or maybe Eustace, I can't remember.'

'What happened to him?'

'He escaped during a wedding. Killed a man on his way out, too,' the Reeve said.

'That was not a good day,' Bowman mumbled.

'Had he not escaped, would Sir Richard have ransomed him and treated him well?'

'Don't ask me. I think the boy is scared to dispense justice, so maybe he would have been scared to harm the big man, too. For all his faults, I expect he would have gone through with the ransom. If only because he is poorer than me.'

Sarjeant started to laugh but stopped when Richard glared at him.

'Would the Templars smuggle a man out of Yvetot?' Nicholas asked.

'So the Martel blood does run though him,' Richard whispered.

'Another odd question, young sarjeant.'

'Merely trying to get the measure of the lord here,' Nicholas said, 'before he is replaced.'

'Ah, so you know of the plan.'

'Got him,' Richard said.

'What plan?' The Priest asked, 'and I'm cold, can we go now?'

'If you try and leave, I'll cut your toes off,' Bowman said.

The Priest folded his arms and turned his head away from Bowman.

'I have come with a message about the plan,' Nicholas said.

'From the Master?'

'No, from a preceptory south of Rouen.'

'That explains your accent,' the Reeve said, 'I could tell you aren't from around here.'

'Indeed. My preceptor has dealings with the farm to the north of Yvetot, and wishes to confirm trading arrangements once you rule here.'

Richard nodded. Maybe Nicholas had heard enough about Richard to trust him after all.

'I see,' the Reeve said. He walked somewhere within the mill and Richard couldn't hear what he said next.

'Very well,' Nicholas responded.

'What are they talking about?' The Priest asked, 'and why am I here?'

'To hear the Reeve confess his crime from his own mouth,' Richard said.

'When is the plan due to happen?' Nicholas asked.

'Saint Cecilia's day,' the Reeve said.

'Not long, then,' Nicholas said, 'how is it going to work? Do you kill Sir Richard or do you have a plan to remove him another way?'

'The English boy has to go,' the Reeve answered.

Richard went to get up but Sarjeant caught his arm. 'Patience, my boy. There is no harm in letting him dig a deeper grave for himself,' he said.

Richard slid back down the wooden wall, which ripped his cloak on a splinter.

'The Templars have condoned murdering an innocent Christian?' Nicholas asked.

'Of course not, that part of the plan is mine. Their involvement only begins once I have cleared the way for them.'

'I'm not sure I can condone murder,' Nicholas said.

'You don't have to, speak to your brothers in the farm and then go back to Rouen,' the Reeve said, 'this is none of your business.'

'Very well,' Nicholas said, 'thank you for your hospitality.'

The door creaked open. Richard got up and beckoned the others to follow him. He walked around to the front of the mill and straight into Nicholas.

They bumped into each other and Nicholas blinked in the dark of the night. 'Who's that?' He asked.

'Me, watch where you're going,' Richard said.

'It's too dark,' Nicholas stepped aside.

'Who is that?' The Reeve appeared in the glow of the open doorway.

'Get him,' Richard said.

The Reeve's eyes locked onto Richard's and his oval face froze.

Bowman and Sarjeant jumped into the doorway and latched onto the startled man's arms. They dragged him out of the light and into the blackness.

'What is this?' The Reeve asked.

'We heard all of it,' Richard said.

'All of it?' Nicholas scratched his chin.

'Don't worry,' Richard grinned at him, 'I think you proved yourself.'

'I don't like being spied on,' he replied.

'What did you hear?' The Reeve stuttered.

'You were going to kill me,' Richard pointed to the Priest, 'and he heard every word.'

'Well, not every word,' the Priest said.

Richard arched his eyebrows. 'You heard the part about him

plotting to kill me on Saint Cecilia's day, though?'

The churchman nodded slowly.

'No, I meant no such thing,' the Reeve said, 'I simply meant to remove you, my lord, from the property so the Templars could visit it.'

'You can protest as much as you like, but your words damn you,' Richard said.

'He probably didn't mean it,' the Priest said.

'He meant it,' Bowman punched the Reeve in the stomach to wind him.

'Why did you do that?' Richard asked.

'I'm tired of his excuses.'

'So am I,' Richard said, 'we'll throw him in the cellar and the Priest here can tell the villagers what he was plotting.'

'I don't know what he was plotting,' the Priest said, 'you can't be sure of anything.'

'I am sure of what he said, and you can be too,' Richard walked towards the Priest and looked him in the face. Richard could feel the anger in his own eyes and the Priest saw it too.

'Maybe I do know what he said,' the Priest nodded.

'Good, tomorrow morning you will tell the village, word by word. And I'll be standing at the back to make sure you don't lie.'

'I would never lie,' the Priest stuck his chin out.

Richard laughed. 'I believe you, you wouldn't even know you were doing it. But he'll be there, too,' he pointed at Bowman.

Bowman flexed his fist as the Reeve gasped for air.

The Priest nodded quickly and bowed to Richard. 'It will be done,' he said.

'Throw him in the cellar and lock the door,' Richard said.

'Not the cellar,' the Reeve sucked in short bursts of air, 'sickness is in there.'

'I don't much care,' Richard said, 'you should have thought before you planned to murder me.'

Richard let the Reeve rot in the cellar for a lot longer than he'd planned. He'd intended on dealing with the issue and moving on within a day or two, but he kept finding ways of putting it off.

'I'd half hoped he'd just catch the plague in the cellar and die by himself,' Richard looked down into his cup.

Rain pelted down onto the horn windows outside.

'He's not going to go away on his own,' Sophie put a hand on his shoulder.

Richard put his hand on hers as he sat in his hall, looking into the flickering flame of a candle. 'It looks that way.'

'Justice must be done,' Sophie walked away and sat down. She ran a hand over her belly, which lay under a blue dress with extra fabric sewn into it to make it larger.

'What if the villagers don't believe me,' Richard said.

'The Priest already told them,' she said, 'and you watched him relay it as it was. They know the Reeve has committed a serious crime, there is no reason to delay. The longer you wait, the worse it is, not the other way around.'

The flames flickered as the door opened and Bowman and Nicholas entered. They hung their sodden cloaks up and left watery footprints on their way to the table.

'It rains worse here than in England,' Bowman wiped water off his face.

'That's not true,' Nicholas said, 'and from what you tell me, you spend less time stuck out in it on this side of the sea, so I don't know what you're complaining about.'

'Maybe I'll go east, it never rains in the Holy Land.'

'It must rain sometimes,' Richard said, 'how else would anything grow?'

'When are we going east?' Bowman asked.

'Not until I let him,' Sophie said.

Richard looked between the two. 'I'll go when I should,' he said.

'I noticed the cross on your tunic,' Nicholas said, 'but it is so faded I thought your vow may have been forgotten.'

'I think of it every day,' Richard said.

'Why? Why go east to disease, suffering and death?' Nicholas asked.

'My father died there, and some say badly. I must find the truth,' Richard said, 'and I owe the Lord for it more than once.'

'And the archbishop made him,' Bowman said.

'He made you, too. Or have you forgotten?' Richard said.

'Not forgotten,' Bowman said, 'just put aside. We need the silver first.'

'Silver?' Nicholas asked.

Richard looked at Bowman with strong eyes.

'We have it with a bank, of sorts,' Bowman said.

'Really.'

'That's not the point,' Richard said, 'the point is that we aren't going yet.'

'No, you're not,' Sophie stared at him.

'How are the squires?' Richard asked Bowman.

'Three are walking again, they'll be able to ride in a couple of days,' Bowman said.

Nicholas relaxed into his chair and found some cider. 'We buried one more, though.'

'The grave pooled with water,' Bowman said, 'so we just had to roll him into it. He splashed us. I'm thinking of burning my clothes.'

'The Priest said you can't catch it from touching the bodies,' Richard said.

'And you believe him?'

Richard drummed his fingers on his armrest. 'We only have five squires left, then?'

Bowman nodded. 'One is ready to travel.'

'Good,' Richard said, 'I can send your brother's ransom note.'

'Half-brother,' Bowman and Nicholas said at the same time.

'Whatever you want to call him, I'll send a squire off first thing in the morning,' Richard said.

'We do need the money,' Sophie said.

'You don't need to remind me,' Richard said, 'and if Sir Roger sends us say, a blacksmith, what if they don't come with any tools? Who is going to build them a forge, buy an anvil?'

'You,' Bowman said.

'Exactly, so I need him,' Richard pointed to Nicholas, 'to fetch a decent price.'

'Glad I can be of service,' the Martel Bastard drank from his cup and put it down with a thud.

'It's nothing personal,' Richard said.

Nicholas grunted.

'It isn't personal with the Reeve, either,' Sophie said, 'why can't you deal with that as quickly as a ransom?'

'I'm getting to it,' Richard replied.

'Get to it tomorrow.'

Richard didn't get to it tomorrow. He dreamt he was inside the flaming abbey where Sir Wobble's father had lost an eye from falling molten lead. The flames licked Richard's feet and the heat pressed into his skin. Smoke choked his lungs and the taste of ash covered his tongue. When molten lead fell from the roof, he woke up in a sweat.

While Richard did send the ransom request off to England, he found excuses and things to do for another week before he decided to act on the Reeve. He eventually wrote a letter to the sheriff at Rouen and started proper proceedings.

One afternoon, and still waiting for the reply, Richard stood on his stone wall as Eva returned, leading her Irishmen back into Yvetot. He went down to greet her as her men slid off their horses and went to put them away in a paddock.

'How was your journey?' Richard asked.

Eva groaned. 'Wasted,' she handed her horse to a comrade, 'the King of the French was not anywhere to be found. He is probably too far east for us to travel, at least not at this time of year.'

The sun had already dipped and Richard didn't think it had yet been up that long.

'You are welcome to winter here,' he said.

Eva smiled and slid the brown hood off her head. 'That is very kind of you, I fear the Irish Sea will already be far too rough to cross, so your offer is a welcome one.'

'Bowman will be glad to see you,' Richard grinned.

'He seemed very keen on hunting,' she paused for a moment, 'I fear he will not let me rest over the cold months.'

'I think you're more right that you know,' Richard laughed.

'I don't mind him, it is a distraction from the mission I am failing to accomplish,' she said.

'Did a single knight join your cause?'

She shook her head. 'We found some mercenary companies, but their men are fat and slow. They were happy to take our coin readily enough, but they surely would be unable to earn it.

It seems that this land is full enough of its own troubles, no one here dares leave home if they can avoid it.'

'You sound like my wife.'

'She's wise, you should listen to her more,' Eva said.

'That's why I'm still here,' Richard said, 'despite the fact I'm growing bored of disobedient tenants and arguments over whose cow it was that trampled someone or other's fence.'

The woman laughed. 'You boys grow up thinking being a lord is all battles, glory and names being sung across crowded halls. All men find out the end it's about the small things that need fixing to keep the circle of life turning.'

'Well, there's more here to fix than I'd feared,' Richard replied, 'and I can barely afford any of it.'

'We met the sheriff,' Eva said, 'he gave us his response to your troublesome Reeve.'

'Really?'

'He didn't want to waste a messenger on you. Had we not found him, his message would still sit on his table.'

Richard put his hands on his hips. 'Waste a messenger? One could get here in a day.'

Eva shrugged. 'He was a rude man. And very fat.'

'What was his message for me?'

'Try the Reeve. Stick to the law.'

'What is the law?'

'I asked that too,' Eva said, 'if a groups of his peers finds him guilty, trial by water. Trial by fire is illegal now.'

Both of Richard's hands clenched and unclenched without thought. He looked down at the palms, and because he knew where to look, saw the burn scars.

'Interesting,' Eva said.

He closed his hands. 'Water it'll be, then,' Richard said.

The next morning Richard stood outside the church next to the Priest and the masonry that had fallen from its doorway during his wedding.

'Can't you just let me move it,' Richard looked at the now weathered stone.

The Priest pursed his lips. 'It was the Lord's will,' he said.

'As is this,' Richard looked at the twelve villagers lined up before them. The Reeve stood near the graveyard, his arms held by Bowman and Sarjeant.

'Everyone heard the Priest's words in this church,' Richard said loudly, 'he heard the Reeve commit a great crime. You are gathered, as his peers, to judge him.'

A layer of fog hung around the trunks of the trees in the orchard beyond the churchyard.

The Reeve whimpered. His face had lines in it where before there were none, but somehow his weight had not dropped off during his incarceration.

'Bless them and let's get on with it,' Richard said to the Priest.

The churchman held a bowl of water and walked towards the twelve jurors. They bowed their heads and made the sign of the cross as holy water sprinkled over them. The Priest retreated and put the bowl away.

'Raise you arm if you think the Reeve is guilty,' Richard said.

'Which arm?' One of the jurors, an old man with one leg shorter than the other, asked.

'It doesn't matter,' Richard replied, 'any arm.'

The jurors discussed the matter amongst themselves.

Richard sighed. 'Just raise your right arm if he's guilty,' he said.

The jurors nodded and chimed in agreement, then raised their arms.

As the twelfth arm raised, the Reeve's legs gave way and Bowman and Sarjeant let him crumple to the ground.

'I thought it would be harder than that,' Richard said.

'A good congregation listens to its priest,' the Priest said proudly.

'I know, that's how they ended up setting fire to my palisade,' Richard glowered at the churchman.

'The judgement is clear,' the Priest turned to the Reeve, 'do you accept your guilt and punishment, or deny it and choose ordeal by cold water?'

The accused started to sob.

'Well?' Richard asked.

The Reeve shivered. 'I have done nothing, everything is lies.'

The Priest leant in to Richard's ear. 'Can you not just take a finger from him?'

'He denied his guilt, what can I do?' Richard replied.

'There is a good man inside the Reeve, he can change his ways.'

'If there were any hope for that, he would have knelt before us in humility and begged for forgiveness,' Richard said.

'If you won't settle for a finger, take a hand, but let him live.'

Richard sighed again. 'The sheriff told me to follow the law, so I'm going to.'

The Reeve's tears flowed and he threw himself to the ground. 'Spare me, please, I've done nothing wrong.'

'The water will show us what you have done,' the Priest said.

'I'm not so sure about that,' Richard thought back to the red-hot iron bar in Castle Tancarville.

'The accused will remain in the church until Sunday. He shall eat nothing but unleavened barley bread with salt and watercress, and drink only water. He shall hear mass and be stripped.'

The Reeve howled. 'Not in front of everyone,' he cried.

'Completely stripped,' the Priest continued, 'and taken in a procession to the pool of cold water. If the water accepts him, he is innocent and shall be hauled from the water. However, if the anointed water rejects him and he floats, the Lord reveals true guilt.'

'Put him back in the cellar,' Richard waved the prisoner away.

The villagers shuffled off, leaving Richard to stare into the morning mist alone with the Priest and the fallen masonry. 'Would you like the Reeve to sink or float?' The Priest asked.

'It isn't my choice to make,' Richard said.

'What if it was?' The Priest said, 'for the sake of my curiosity only, of course.'

'He wanted to kill me.'

The Priest nodded.

'I'm not telling you to find a way to cheat the trial, just to be clear,' Richard said.

'Of course not, that would be a crime.'

'Just do everything properly,' Richard said.

'All will be well,' the Priest nodded, 'guilty men float.'

The entire village turned out on Sunday to the pit that had been dug between the church and the pond. Sarjeant and the healthy squires had laboured for two days to dig it. It was as long and wide as a man, but twice as deep. They cut a channel from the pond towards it, and the dank stale water ran in and filled it.

The Priest threw a cup of holy water into the hole and said something in Latin.

'Can you swim?' Bowman asked Richard.

'My father could but I never did,' he replied, 'I was too busy riding.'

'I used to, until someone drowned in a river,' Bowman said.

'I'd rather swim in a river than be plunged into that,' Richard peered down into the pit.

'Then it's a good thing it's not you that's going in there.'

The Reeve quaked in the cold air of the Sunday morning. The sun's rays lit up the east side of the church but couldn't yet take the edge off the cold.

Richard folded his cloak over himself and felt glad that he wasn't the Reeve.

The accused stood naked and shivering, his eyes stuck on the freezing hole in the grass.

'How does it feel to be on this end of it?' Bowman asked.

'Much better,' Richard said, 'although I'm not exactly enjoying this.'

'Bring him,' the Priest pointed to the Reeve.

Richard tried not to look at the exposed man, and felt very glad that no women were permitted to witness the ordeal.

The squires held him over the pit. The Reeve looked down and his legs buckled under him. 'Please, please don't.'

Richard felt a twinge of pity. Then he remembered how smug the Reeve had been in the mill, bragging of his plan to murder Richard.

'Throw him in,' he commanded.

The two squires picked the Reeve up and lowered him into the water. He gasped. Once it reached his ankles he started to scream.

'All the way,' the Priest said, then sung in Latin.

The Reeve squirmed and tried to climb out of the pit. The squires pushed him back in.

'If he won't hold still, we are supposed to bind his hands,' the

Priest said, his voice quick and excited.

'I didn't think you'd enjoy this so much,' Richard said.

'I'm not enjoying it,' the churchman said, 'although I had always wanted to hold an ordeal by cold water.'

Richard squatted down by the pit as the Reeve's head breached the surface and he gasped for air.

'Look,' Richard said, 'they're going to tie you up, and then you'll float to the surface and die with no dignity left. Hold still and at least show them you could find some dignity deep within yourself at the end.'

The Reeve's big brown eyes looked up at him. They were round and full of terror, but for a moment they connected and the Reeve ceased his struggle. He took a deep breath and put his head under the water. His body bobbed straight back up, his back surfaced and he floated for a moment.

'Guilty,' the Priest opened his arms to the crowd of onlookers, 'the Lord has shown us the truth.'

The villagers cheered.

Richard frowned. 'I thought that he was one of them, I expected the Priest to fight just a little for the Reeve.'

'Don't mind the villagers, they just love some excitement. As for the Priest, well, he's a priest,' Bowman said.

The Reeve's bulbous body floated until he ran out of breath and pushed his head back above the water. Water splashed out onto the grass and he gulped down air.

'Did I sink?' He asked.

Richard raised his eyebrows. 'What do you think?'

'No, no, I'm not guilty.'

'Everyone here thought you were guilty already,' Richard said, 'and now the Lord has proved it. Your words only condemn you further.'

The Priest sighed. 'A sentence of death should not be down to mortal men to give, but the trial by ordeal ordains the punishment and cannot be ignored. You must die.'

The Reeve screamed and Richard again almost felt pity for him. 'Drag him out,' he said to the squires.

They hauled him onto the grass and puddles formed around his naked body.

'I see no reason to prolong this,' the Priest said to Richard, 'hang him now and be done with it.'

Richard could barely look at the pathetic image the Reeve cut on the grass by the watery pit. He had at least submitted himself to divine judgement with some sort of honour in the end.

Bowman stepped closer to Richard. 'Remember Simon the Quiet.'

'I can hardly forget,' Richard replied and stepped towards the villagers. He studied their faces, a few men were older than him but most looked more like his own age.

'The Reeve committed a crime that mortal men cannot forgive. We have followed the letter of the law and now he shall be submitted for his final, divine, judgement.'

The condemned man sobbed again.

'The law sentences him to be hung,' Richard sighed, 'but for the glory of Christ I will show him mercy and use the axe instead.'

The villagers exchanged hush words.

The Priest had a genuinely surprised look on his face. 'Being the target of his murderous scheme yourself, I expected you to find the harshest punishment.'

'Do not mistake it for weakness,' Richard's face darkened. He turned to a squire and asked for an axe. Then Richard spoke so everyone could hear. 'Justice will always be served in Yvetot. Burn my palisade again, and everyone who didn't try to stop it will be hung.'

That silenced the onlookers.

The squire returned from the village with a wood splitting axe. He handed it to Richard who turned it over in his hands. The edge wasn't quite as sharp as he'd have liked.

'I need a block,' Richard told the squire, 'find me a cutting stump.'

The Reeve, his skin pale and his exposed body shaking with cold, curled up into a ball and cried.

'I tried to be nice to all of you,' Richard continued, 'I tried to help you, to forgive those of you who harmed me. But then this one saw my kindness as weakness.'

The Reeve put his hands over his head.

The squire returned with a small tree stump and placed it

down in front of the Reeve.

'Put his head on it,' Richard said, 'and you'll probably have to hold him there.'

Two squires dragged the weeping man into place, his head on its side jammed down onto the stump. He continued to cry as a squire's hand stretched over his face and held him still.

Richard moved into position. 'In Yvetot the law will be followed. If you are loyal to me, I will be fair to you. If you cross me, I will punish you. My patience has run out. Look closely at him as he cries naked on the floor, look into his eyes. Do you want that to be you? Remember that face, see it in your nightmares, for if anyone steps out of line, that is what I will be to you, a nightmare.'

Richard raised the axe and the Reeve yelled out. Richard put all his force into the blow and the axe flew down. It rammed into the Reeve's neck exactly where he'd aimed, but it sunk into bone and stopped.

The Reeve, his neck only half severed, gasped and gurgled, his eyes bulged and the crowd winced. Richard tried to pull the axe out but it was stuck.

'Pull his head over so I can get it out,' Richard said.

The squire holding the Reeve's head down tilted it and Richard wrenched the axe free. He quickly flung the weapon down for a second blow. This time cut through the spine, although still not the whole neck. Some of the onlookers looked away, but others cheered. Richard pulled the axe free.

The Reeve's eyes blinked on his severed head for much longer than Richard had expected, then finally stilled.

Blood dripped from the axe's blade.

Richard dropped it and walked over to the Priest, who shook from head to toe.

'My God,' he said.

'Do you know what will happen if you incite another riot?' Richard asked.

The Priest looked down to the axe on the grass and meekly nodded.

'Good,' Richard said, 'you know, I really tried to be generous and fair to all of you.'

The Priest nodded quicker and turned to his congregation.

'Begone, think on what you have seen,' he said in a voice that cracked and wavered, 'my dreams will be full of this day for the rest of my years, do not cross our master.'

'You didn't have to put it quite like that,' Richard said.

The Priest looked into his eyes and Richard saw real fear.

'I'll play the Devil's Englishman if you like, then,' Richard said, 'as long as it keeps the peace.'

He glanced down at the Reeve's body and the head that had rolled away from it. Richard knew that this scene would add itself to the growing list of his own nightmares, but at least justice had been done.

ARRIVALS

Richard kicked a stone along the track and thought back to the Reeve's execution.

'I shouldn't complain,' he said to Bowman, 'but nothing interesting has happened since the Reeve died.'

Bowman laughed. 'No, you really shouldn't complain.'

'I know, I spent the whole of Christmas last year wondering if the King was going to execute me. It's funny how things circle around,' Richard said.

'Earl Patrick certainly knew how to host over the winter,' Bowman nodded.

'I can't really remember, I was too worried,' Richard patted his stomach, 'but now I think I'm just too fat.'

The blonde man chuckled. 'This past one was a better winter than many, I'll grant you that. But there are fresh shoots growing through now and the sun rises at a more useful hour.'

Richard kicked another stone into the ditch by the side of the track. It didn't splash into water, rather it thudded into black mulch. 'We need to clean those out, all the ditches are like that one, again,' he said.

'Then you need more farmers to owe you labour,' Bowman said.

'Sir Roger promised more, and when they come they can start work.'

'And what will you pay them with, apples?'

'Do you think they'd take apples?' Richard asked.

Bowman shook his head with a smile on his face. 'Would you?'

The sound of hooves was followed out of the castle gate by Eva and her six remaining Irishmen. They still rode their smaller horses without saddles.

Bowman frowned.

'Don't worry, she'll be back,' Richard said.

'I don't know why she's even bothering,' Bowman said, 'no one in the whole of the French-speaking world wants to go to Ireland.'

'I don't think she has any choice,' Richard said as the group met them on the track.

'Thank you for your hospitality,' Eva said, 'I have a mind to make this our last attempt, so that we shall not be a burden on you next winter.'

'Nonsense,' Richard said, 'I've never eaten so well. Between you and Bowman I think I'm actually getting sick of venison.'

Eva laughed. 'The boar here are bigger than in Ireland, hunting here is more of a contest. I cannot believe they roam around here the size of my horse,' she patted her chestnut horse on its hairy neck.

'It is a small horse,' Richard smiled.

Eva walked her horse on. 'Have a good spring,' she said and rode away towards the orchard.

Richard looked at Bowman. 'You should be grateful for what you've had. Just being able to go hunting with a princess all winter is more than most men could ever dream of. It isn't as if you're going to marry her.'

'How do you know?' Bowman crossed his arms.

'You always tell me real life isn't like I read in a romance,' Richard said.

Bowman kicked another stone into the clogged ditch.

'Don't sulk all spring,' Richard said.

Bowman sulked for most of the spring. He only went hunting when Richard made him, and he largely avoided his half-brother. Richard watched the villagers clean the ditches and watched his wife's belly grow.

'This baby is bigger, bigger than,' Sophie started and then stopped.

'The last one?' Richard said.

'That wasn't a baby,' she replied.

'It has nearly made it to a year,' Richard said, 'and the King called him Henry.'

'I'm not calling it by a name.'

'Have you thought about names for our son?'

'It might be a girl,' Sophie yawned. She looked up into the blue sky as a pair of pigeons flew overhead.

Richard kept his eyes away from the dark circles under her blue eyes. He'd learnt to avoid mentioning anything like that as her pregnancy had gone on.

'We used all the charms the Priest suggested,' Richard said, 'it will be a boy.'

Sophie yawned again. 'I'm choosing the name. The baby is my concern. The adult children are yours.'

'What adult children?'

'Those two,' Sophie nodded towards Bowman and Nicholas, who stood by the well drawing water for the stabled horses.

'What do you want me to do?' Richard asked.

'Something, anything, just stop Bowman brooding for he is beginning to annoy me. The Martels haven't sent any word back about his brother's ransom, either.'

'So?'

'They could be stuck here together for a long time. I'm fed up of their depressing moods,' Sophie said.

'I don't know how to cheer someone up.'

'Think of a cheerful person you know, and do what they would do.'

Richard rubbed his forehead. 'The happiest person I know, or knew, was Sir Wobble.'

'Can't you call him William?' Sophie asked.

'There are too many Williams.'

'Suit yourself. What would he do?'

Richard groaned. 'He'd go swimming, or for a run, or throw rocks. Bowman hates running, and there's no river right here, so I suppose we'll try rocks.'

He collected the five surviving King's squires and ordered them to find a collection of good-sized stones. Richard had them start to throw them and mark their furthest attempts.

'Come on,' he said to Bowman, 'someone needs to show those youngsters how to do it.'

Bowman raised his eyes to Richard. 'It's throwing stones, are we back at Castle Tancarville again?'

45

'Just do it,' Richard said, 'I'll have a go, too.'

Bowman set down the empty bucket he'd been holding and walked over to the centre of the bailey where the squires hurled the stones.

Richard beckoned Nicholas over too. 'We're throwing stones.'

'I can see that,' Nicholas said, 'still no word from my father?'

'No, I'm sorry.'

The Martel Bastard picked up an awkwardly shaped white stone and hurled it with one hand. It dug into the turf beyond the squire's markers and rolled.

Bowman folded his arms.

'You do better, then,' Richard nudged him.

'I'm not Sir Wobble,' Bowman said, 'you can't entertain me with games for squires.'

Richard waited and looked down at a rock by Bowman's foot.

'Are you saying a Martel can throw further than, well, whatever you are?'

Bowman grunted and squatted down to pick up the stone. He took a run up and threw the stone through the air. It landed on top of Nicholas's stone, cracked it in half, bounced off, and came to a rest beyond it.

Bowman clapped the dust off his hands and turned to walk away. 'There,' he said.

Nicholas looked at Richard and shrugged. 'Not a bad throw.'

Richard turned to see Sophie's reaction, but her face had nothing but horror across it.

'The throw wasn't that bad,' Richard said to her.

'Richard,' Sophie had two hands on her stomach.

'What?'

'Richard,' she repeatedly louder.

Bowman walked over. 'It's time, young lord,' and put a hand on Richard's shoulder.

'Oh,' Richard said, 'now?'

Bowman nodded. 'The squires will need to warm some water.'

They helped Sophie back inside, fetched the Priest and waited in the hall. Richard looked up to where his chamber and wife were, while Bowman poured him a drink.

'There's nothing you can do now,' Bowman said.

A moan filtered down from upstairs.

'What if the baby dies?' Richard said.

'Chances are it will,' Sarjeant said from opposite the table, 'most do, you know that.'

Richard felt tension in his stomach as it tightened up. 'What if she dies?'

No one answered. Nicholas went to the fire to jab at it with an iron poker.

Bowman poured himself a drink and downed all of it.

Sarjeant pulled a sad face but ran his fingers around a knot in the table.

'None of you are helping,' Richard said, 'she gave birth once and survived that. And that was for the Red Baby, so this should be fine. Shouldn't it?'

Sarjeant made the sign of the cross and whispered a prayer to himself.

Richard felt sick, a bitter burning taste rose up in his throat. 'I want to be up there.'

A louder moan echoed down through the ceiling.

'Maybe not,' he said and looked out of the window where the sky was blue and the day peaceful. 'I think I'd rather go for a ride.'

'If you aren't here to receive the child,' Sarjeant said, 'I don't think you will survive your wife.'

Bowman chuckled, but stopped when Richard whirled round to him. The blonde man poured himself another drink, but this time held the cup out to Richard.

Richard considered the cup. He reached out and drank the cider. The drink had aged badly since it had been made, and was only slightly better tasting than water now.

'Will you send the Red Baby to a foster family?' Sarjeant asked, 'he is nobly born after all.'

Richard thought for a moment. 'If everyone thinks he is the King's son they might be honoured to be given him. And he would be away from Sophie.'

Sarjeant nodded. 'I know you were not fostered, but it is the normal way,' he said.

Richard nodded back. 'I can't afford to give my own son a horse, a mail coat and a sword, let alone Red Henry as well.'

'Is that what you're calling it?' Bowman said.

'Him,' Richard said as a wail cut through the air from his bedchamber.

Richard went down to the cellar to find the last barrel of wine he knew was down there. He filled a jug but couldn't help notice that there was half as much wine as he'd expected. He shivered at the thought of the squires who had died down in the cool depths, and quickly went back up to the warmth of his hall.

He drank and ate and found his copy of Eric and Enid to read, while Sophie screamed and shouted above. He told Nicholas and Bowman to go and hunt together so Sophie could eat well once ready to, and then spent the rest of the day with his eyes in the fire and his wife's shouting in his ears.

As dark began to descend outside, raindrops started to spatter onto the horn windows. Bowman returned and told of a huge boar that now roasted in the kitchen, and how that was an omen for the birth of a strong warrior.

Sarjeant inclined his head to the window as a crow squawked. 'And we know what crows mean.'

Richard made the sign of the cross.

'A great warrior who will bring death,' Bowman nodded solemnly.

Richard didn't know if that was a good or bad thing. The fire that roared in the hearth danced and struggled, but Richard's eyes saw the flames of Fallencourt.

He snapped himself away from those thoughts. 'At least it will be a boy,' he said.

Sarjeant yawned. 'I should mention that Lady Sophie has been walking with her left foot first. This is a sure sign of the baby being carried on her left side, which being the weak side means the baby is a girl.'

'I hadn't noticed that,' Richard put his head in his hands, 'I wish it would just come out so I'd know.'

The Priest burst into the hall, a bundle of white, blood-stained linen in his arms. He held up his free hand, in which he held a mass of flesh and blood.

'What's that?' Richard grimaced.

'The birth cord,' the Priest said, 'you must burn it to cleanse all sin transmitted through conception.'

'Conception?'

'Yes,' the Priest said, 'the sins you passed to the child. Which are many, so be quick about it.'

Richard went over and looked into the bundle of linen. 'Is that?'

'Your daughter,' the Priest looked away, 'I'm so sorry.'

Richard felt his heart drop. A girl meant trying again, staying at home again, and another year of grinding poverty.

The Priest held out the gory cord. 'Quickly. Each moment you waste transmits more of your sin into her. And as a girl she has quite enough already.'

Richard held his hands out and the Priest poured the stomach-churning contents into Richard's. It squelched as it landed in his scarred palms. Richard went to the fire and tipped it into the blaze. He wiped his hands on a cloth and felt very bad when the smell from the fire started to make him hungry and sick at the same time.

Richard overcame both urges and walked back to his daughter. He looked down at the small human and his anger and worry faded. 'She's beautiful.'

'Here we go,' Bowman said, 'every baby is ugly except your own. Keep your womanly fawning to yourself, young lord.'

Richard ignored him. He had made this baby girl. Richard raised his face up to the Priest's. 'How is my wife?'

'Perfectly well,' he smiled.

Richard thought it was the first time the irritating man had smiled.

A scream from his chamber wracked Richard's ears. 'Sophie?' He said.

The Priest threw the baby at Richard and ran upstairs.

Richard peered down at the child. 'What do I do with it?'

'Hold it, speak to it, and don't drop it,' Sarjeant said.

Sophie cried out a second time and Richard felt nerves bite into him. 'Is that normal?'

Sarjeant pursed his lips and retraced the knot on the table.

Bowman poured Richard the last of the wine and held the cup up for him.

Tears welled up in Richard's eyes. He wasn't going to say it, and sometimes she nagged him too much, but he was quite fond of his wife.

A gust of wind blew in through all of the windows and the fire flickered and roared back.

The Priest returned soon after and Richard winced in anticipation.

A second bundle lay in his arms.

'Another one?' Richard asked, and immediately wondered how he would afford to feed two children.

The Priest had a large grin across his face. 'My lord,' he said, 'it is a boy.' He held out another birthing cord and this time Richard performed the ritual without hesitation. He retrieved the boy from the churchman and sat in his chair with a new baby in each arm.

Richard looked up at the Priest. 'Sophie?'

'Sleeping.'

Richard breathed a sigh of relief.

'Congratulations,' Sarjeant said, and both Bowman and Nicholas got up to say the same.

Richard felt like his body melted into his chair as the stress drained from it.

'Don't be too happy so soon,' Sarjeant said, 'you know how many babies do not live long enough to speak.'

Richard did, but at that moment he didn't care. He had a son, and as soon as he had lived beyond the age of greatest danger, Richard would be free to leave Yvetot.

Both of the children and their mother survived their first full day, then their first full week, then their first month. Sophie recovered her strength and a new wet-nurse was found within the village, for the woman who had performed the duty for the Red Baby was not allowed to do the same for the new twins. Bowman annoyed Richard with his grumpy mood, and Richard wondered how much of it was Eva, and how much was boredom. He himself looked over into the woods around Yvetot and yearned to go somewhere new. After the second month, Richard's nightmares came back. After the third, Nicholas's mood darkened to match Bowman's when no response ever came regarding his ransom. Richard sent a follow-up message but his hopes for a good payday sunk ever lower as the summer came.

A messenger did eventually arrive. Richard supervised a work party clearing the orchard of weeds when the horseman appeared before him. The messenger lacked an eye, and Richard gazed up into the empty socket as the man leant down to pass him the rolled up parchment from his bag.

'Have a good look,' the messenger said, 'everyone else does.'

'What's it like?' Richard asked.

'The same as before, except now I no longer have to ride into battle,' he grinned, 'you only need one eye to deliver things, so losing an eye will keep me alive far longer than you.'

Richard found himself feeling oddly jealous of the messenger and his travels. 'Just give me the letter,' he said.

The messenger passed it over and kept his now empty hand held out.

Richard stared at it.

'Nothing for my troubles?'

'Oh,' Richard sighed, 'I have literally no coin to give you. You're welcome to some old cider in our inn, or to stay the night for free, but that is all I have to offer.'

The messenger's mouth curled downwards. He looked down his nose at Richard and turned his horse around. 'Some knight you are.'

Richard realised his face had reddened, but he ignored the man and opened the letter instead. It began, 'Dear Brother,' which made Richard's heart skip a beat, for Adela was alive. Uncle Luke, she wrote, had not yet returned to England. Adela believed that he wouldn't dare attack anyone in her abbey himself, and told Richard not to worry. He lowered the letter. Abbey? He remembered his sister as living in a nunnery. Richard tucked the letter into his belt and went back to the boring work of keeping an eye on the villagers.

The next two things to arrive at Yvetot came as one. Eva rode back from the east with three Irishmen and one Norman, a singer, who sang for them that night in exchange for food and a fire to sleep beside.

The young man turned the events of the world into song as they ate their evening meal, where Bowman sat opposite Eva and almost forgot to eat.

'Did you find the French King?' Richard asked her.

She nodded but her face didn't smile. 'He wouldn't even see us. We were sent away like an unwanted dog.'

'Did you find any knights willing to help your father get his kingdom back?'

Eva shook her head. 'This entire venture has been in vain.'

'I don't know about that,' Bowman said.

The singer sang a song about King Henry crowning his eldest son, also called Henry, as a junior king and heir to the throne of England. That was boring and Bowman shouted at him to liven it up.

There followed a song about a Flemish knight called Anton who murdered someone, which Bowman enjoyed a lot more.

'Are you going back to Ireland now?' Richard asked.

'We will go back this season,' she replied, 'but surely I need something to show for my considerable troubles.'

'I could do with a heap of gold myself,' Richard laughed.

'I had noticed the church looks a little forlorn,' Eva said, 'you need a mason and a carpenter.'

'I can pay neither,' Richard said.

The singer's next tale was about an English knight called William who had roved around the tournament circuit, winning countless ransoms and great fame.'

'You could enter a tournament,' Bowman said to Richard, 'take a few knights prisoner and ransom them back.'

Richard looked at Nicholas. 'I think the gathering of ransom money isn't as easy as everyone thinks it is. Besides, you can't take part with your iron spurs, so how would I manage by myself?'

'Find Sir Wobble and ride as a pair,' Bowman shrugged, 'while I hate to admit it, the two of you together would be hard to beat.'

Richard laughed. Bowman must be feeling better.

Nicholas however, gazed into the fire. 'If my father doesn't ransom me, I could join you on the field to earn my own ransom. Apparently, I can't rely on family.'

Bowman snorted. 'Not that family.'

Richard thought about it. A tournament could make a man,

but he'd heard plenty of stories about them breaking men, too.

The singer's tournament knight was presented with a large fish, a pike, as the prize for being judged the best knight of a tournament, and Richard had to laugh.

'I can imagine if Sir Wobble won a pike, he'd eat it there and then.'

The knight in the tale didn't eat his prize, but he did eat the post-match banquet out of food.

Richard and Bowman exchanged a look.

'What was this knight's name?' Richard asked the singer.

'William.'

'I know that, William of what?'

'William the Marshal,' the singer said and continued his story.

Richard felt a pit of intense jealousy open up before him.

'The Marshal? He's added a "The" to his name,' Bowman laughed, 'sometimes I think he has designs to be King.'

'What?' Nicholas asked.

'Sir Wobble,' Richard said, 'is the knight he is singing about.'

'Sir Wobble? He seemed very bitter,' Nicholas said, 'but I only saw him once, when he left Castle Lusignan.'

'He is seemingly fine now,' Richard pressed his lips together. Sir Wobble was winning tournaments and having his name spoken across the halls of Normandy, while Richard was stuck at home being nothing more than a glorified steward.

'Can we hear a different song?' He asked.

'This is my best one,' the singer said.

'Exactly,' Richard said, 'I don't want to hear about him. Not unless he's losing.'

'He hasn't lost since his first few tournaments.'

'Then change the story.'

The singer looked disappointed but started a song about a lady who became a blacksmith and robbed a merchant.

Richard turned to Bowman. 'We do have the silver. I think it might be time to retrieve it.'

Bowman's eyes lit up.

'Come on, tell me about it,' Nicholas said.

'Not him,' Bowman said.

'What are you talking about?' Eva asked.

'She can know, she might help, seeing as it is under a nunnery,' Bowman answered.

Richard rolled his eyes, then thought about it. 'You might be right, maybe she can help.'

Richard allowed the morning air to fill his lungs as Solis took him east. The day was fine and Richard felt free. He hadn't left Yvetot in so long he'd started to think he was becoming Sir Arthur.

Bowman and Eva rode next to him.

'What happened to your two men who didn't return?' Richard asked her.

'One drank bad water and the other's horse threw him. Slipped right off its back. A saddle would have saved him,' she said, 'I thought they were a Norman peculiarity, but they may really be worth the expense and trouble.'

Richard nodded and wondered how it had taken her so long to reach that obvious conclusion.

'So where are we going?' She asked.

'There is a holy house being built in a forest to the east,' Richard said, 'although I suppose it might be completed by now.'

'We stashed a hoard of silver in the crypt,' Bowman's eyes gleamed, 'in the tomb of an abbot who wasn't yet dead. We only just got away with it.'

'You stole silver and hid it on church land?'

'Well, when you put it like that,' Bowman frowned.

'We'll need help to get it out, and we'll give you a share if you help,' Richard said.

Eva nodded. 'I see. As long as the silver didn't belong to the church to begin with.'

Richard shook his head. 'Our cause is better than those who had it first,' he said.

They rode along the Norman roads lined with trees until they reached Eawry Forest. The nunnery commissioned by the late Empress Matilda had changed the landscape since their last visit. No longer a building site, the nunnery crowned the hill that stretched up from the road, and woodland had been cleared far on every side. From the outside, Richard couldn't tell how to get into the crypt.

'What do we do now?' Bowman said as they looked up from the road.

'Pretend to be travellers. Spend the night and see if we can get into the crypt,' Richard said.

'Surely men can't stay here?' Eva asked.

'What do you know of nunneries?' Bowman said, 'Ireland is known to be a pagan place.'

Eva laughed. 'Ireland is more Christian than Normandy, you can be very sure of that. They may let me stay, but I'd be surprised if they let you two in.'

'We need to try,' Richard turned Solis towards the entrance doorway.

Richard knocked on the door. They waited for a while before Eva smacked her own fist into the door.

It opened and a robust middle-aged nun peered out at them. 'What do you want?'

'We'd like to stay the night,' Richard said.

The nun looked the three of them up and down. 'You can sleep in the stables if you wish, no men are to be allowed inside.'

'We are very weary,' Richard said.

'You look very fresh, to me,' the nun said.

'I would be honoured to stay as your guest,' Eva said.

'What is that accent?' The nun asked, 'I do not know it.'

'Irish.'

'Oh my poor child,' the nun stepped back, 'come inside and we shall educate you in the way of the Lord.'

Eva shot Richard a knowing look and went inside. The door slammed shut behind her and they heard a bolt slide across.

'I suppose we should find the stables, then,' Bowman said.

Richard sighed. 'Eva can't get the silver out all by herself, even if she can get into the crypt. She doesn't know where to look.'

They took their horses around the back of the nunnery and found some barely used wooden stables. They were alone and settled down for a cold and quiet night.

An owl hooted in the dead of night and Richard awoke with a start. The girl murdered because of him in Fallencourt plagued his sleep, but he awoke because Eva shook him.

'What have you found?' He rubbed his eyes.

'The crypt is open,' she said, 'but they keep the outside doors locked.'

'How did you get out, then?' Bowman asked.

Eva smiled. 'There are windows,' she said, 'I went into the crypt but I couldn't find any silver.'

'We probably should have told you where it is hidden,' Richard said.

'You think?'

'Can we get in?' Richard asked.

Eva nodded. 'They will be awake to pray again soon but we have a short time before.'

Richard got up. 'Lead the way.'

Eva led them back to the main building and to a window covered by only a heavy canvas sheet. She pushed it aside and climbed in.

Richard followed her into the dark and cool chamber, bare stone walls and a writing desk were all he could see inside it.

Eva went out of the arched door-less doorway and into a corridor. Bowman and Richard followed, walking as softly as they could. Eva walked around a corner and through another empty chamber stacked with chests and barrels.

Then Richard recognised the entrance to the crypt, a dark hole in the floor.

'We need light,' Bowman whispered.

'Where do we get that from?' Richard asked.

Bowman shrugged.

'Stay here,' Eva said, 'I may be able to find some.'

The Irishwoman disappeared into the nunnery and Richard went and sat on the steps of the crypt. Below was pitch black, and he needed light to be able to see where he was going, let along read the names above the tombs.

Bowman stood in the doorway with his head around the corner, but luckily it was Eva that he saw approach before anyone else.

She carried a small torch and handed it to Richard. 'Go and find your riches,' she said.

Richard took the wooden handle and stepped very slowly

down into the depths.

The light shone dimly around the crypt, but at least this time it wasn't full of water. It had a musty smell, but Richard remembered which way to go. He part felt his way along the cold walls until the torch revealed the wooden plaque with Abbot Anfroy's name on it. Richard looked down at the wooden panel over the entrance and ran his fingers along the nails that held it shut. He'd heard Bowman and Sarjeant hammer them in, but hadn't ever seen it for himself. They looked undisturbed and Richard smiled. Behind the wooden board lay the means with which he'd establish Yvetot and find the truth about his father. Best of all, Abbot Anfroy must still be alive, otherwise someone would have already removed their make-shift closure and looted the silver.

Bowman stomped down into the crypt. 'Richard, get out of there,' he said.

'Quiet,' Richard replied.

'Too late for quiet, get out,' Bowman ran back up out of the crypt.

Richard scrambled to get out himself and emerged back into the chamber above.

'Put that out,' Eva said.

Richard smothered the torch in his cloak, which left black charring all over it. The smell of burning wool made his nose wrinkle. 'What is it?' He asked.

'Something's happening,' Eva said, 'I think we all need to go.'

Richard stopped moving and heard a commotion somewhere deep in the convent.

'Those are men's voices,' Bowman said, 'something is wrong.'

'Shouldn't we help the nuns?' Richard wondered.

'Help them? A moment ago you were content to rob them,' Eva said.

'It was never their silver,' Richard said, 'and my sister is a nun.'

'She's here?' Eva stuck her head out into the corridor.

'Well, no,' Richard tossed the extinguished torch back down into the crypt.

'There's too many of them and they're coming this way, get back,' Eva retreated into the chamber and they all found shadows to hide in.

Richard squatted down on the corner of the room, he couldn't even see Bowman who did the same in the opposite corner.

Loud voices approached from outside the chamber.

'Find the chapel,' one shouted loudly in a man's gruff voice.

The sound of metal rings on stone echoed down the corridor, which meant the intruders wore mail leg armour.

Richard put his hand to his sword. They hadn't even brought mail away from Yvetot, so any fight would go badly.

Eva shook her head at him.

Richard could see out into the corridor as six armed men rushed by. Their torches sent rapid shadows up the wall as they went, and as quickly as they'd come, they were gone.

'We should go,' Bowman said.

Richard got up and checked the hallway was clear. 'Let's go,' he said and carefully made his way back to their window.

Eva followed close behind him. 'Did you see them?'

'Yes.'

'Do you know them?'

'I don't know everyone in Normandy,' Richard reached the window and stuck a leg out of it.

'He was yellow with two red balls,' Eva said.

Bowman laughed. Loudly.

Richard froze halfway out of the window and looked back in. The men were coming back.

'Idiot,' he said to Bowman.

'Quickly, go,' Eva pushed Richard out of the window. He tipped back outside and landed face-first onto the grass. Earthy-tasting mud pushed into his mouth and he spat it out as he scrambled to his feet.

Bowman leapt past him. 'Run.'

Richard got to his feet once Eva rushed by, and they all sprinted up the slope towards the stables. Richard threw his saddle onto Solis. 'Are they following us?' He shouted.

'No idea,' Bowman replied from the next stall.

Eva, with no saddle to attach, left the stable on top of her horse. 'I'm having second thoughts about saddles,' she said, 'you don't have very long.'

'Don't wait for us,' Richard said as he buckled up the girth and went to grab his bridle.

He heard Eva's horse canter off down the hill.

'I mean,' Bowman said, 'she could have waited a little while.'

Richard pushed the stable door open, and half jumped, half climbed, up into his white and blue saddle.

Solis grunted and Richard kicked him on straight out of the stable.

He heard Bowman's door slam open behind him as Solis cantered out into the night.

Eva's horse was already half way back to the main road, but sure enough, six men with mailed legs jogged up the hill. Except three had stopped near the bottom with their hands on their knees. The one wearing a yellow surcoat with two red balls in the middle of it stopped when he saw Richard, his face crimson.

Richard pressed his calves into Solis and the horse charged down the hill. On his way down Richard met the gaze of the knight, a portly man with red cheeks.

'Red cheeks and red balls,' Bowman shouted gleefully.

Richard looked away and followed Eva down to the road. He reached it and turned west as the forest swallowed it.

Richard caught up with Eva who had dropped down into a walk.

'Shouldn't we go quicker?' He asked.

'Did you see the state of them?' Eva said, 'those were the fattest knights I've ever seen. It will be morning before they have strength enough even to mount their horses, let alone chase us. Part of me thinks I've seen them before, men too fat to help me in Ireland.'

Bowman flew up behind them and jolted his horse back down to a walk beside them. He was out of breath. 'That was not how I expected this night to end,' he said.

'Me neither,' Richard said.

Eva swallowed and took a deep breath. 'No matter, if there are truly crates of silver in that crypt, we would need a cart to take it all home anyway.'

Richard caught his breath. 'So we can't get the silver. What am I supposed to do now?'

'Come with me to Ireland,' Eva said,

'I said no before,' Richard said, 'and I still don't want to go now.'

'Well, if you have another way to make money, then of course, stay at home,' she said.

Richard watched the shadow-like trees as they rode past them and thought. Maybe Ireland wouldn't be so bad?

DEPARTURES

When Richard rode back through his orchard at midday, Ireland suddenly seemed like quite a good option indeed.

'We've only been gone three nights,' Bowman said.

Richard halted Solis outside the church, one of the walls of which had caved in. A piece of timber jutted out from the debris and Richard worried if the plough that was stored inside would soon start to rot. He had always found it odd that ploughs were stored in churches.

'What about them, though,' Bowman pointed over to the empty land beyond the church and before the fields.

Richard groaned. 'I suppose they are de Cailly's spare villagers,' he said.

The empty land no longer lay empty. Men, women and children scurried back and forth constructing A-frame shelters from felled tree trunks. A few already had branches and fabric along their sloped sides to act as roofs.

'They've doubled the size of the village,' Richard said, 'how in God's name do we feed all of them?'

'With coin earned in Ireland,' Eva said.

'Or on the tournament field,' Richard replied.

The Priest left the church and waved frantically. 'Did you know about this?'

'Is this a good time for honesty?' Richard asked Bowman.

'Don't ask me, you're the knight.'

'Sir Roger suggested that they might arrive,' Richard answered.

The Priest stopped and put his hands on his hips. 'The villagers are angry.'

'They're always angry,' Richard said, 'if they hang on your every word as you've so often boasted, just tell them everything will be fine.'

'But it won't be fine,' the Priest said, 'they are outsiders. They bring diseases with them. And crime. Soon theft will be rampant.'

'Has anyone stolen anything yet?' Richard asked.

The Priest said nothing.

'I am really getting bored of having responsibilities,' Richard said quietly to Bowman.

Bowman laughed. 'You chose this.'

'You know I never did.'

Sarjeant stood in the middle of the new slum with three large baskets around him. The newcomers flocked to him as he handed out bread.

Richard rode in their direction while he wondered how long he could afford to be handing out that much bread.

'Richard, my boy,' Sarjeant said, 'these are Sir Roger's refugees.'

'I can see that. Can we feed them all?'

'For now.'

'Can we send some of them back?' Richard asked.

Sarjeant shook his head. 'They all belong to you now.'

'Belong?'

'Legally, they are yours,' Sarjeant said, 'so while you can send them away, morally, they can't go unless you find someone else to take them. If you dismiss them, they shall starve on the road.'

Richard frowned.

A shout erupted from the old village and a party of a dozen farmers and their wives marched towards them. The refugees left Sarjeant and formed up to face them.

Richard did not want a fight.

'We have had a meeting,' the leader of the Yvetot farmers said. He had deep lines in his face and he walked with the faintest limp. Richard would have wagered he was younger than he looked.

'And?' Richard asked.

'Those foreigners are not welcome here.'

'I can't get rid of them,' Richard said, 'you will all have to learn to get along together.'

'They are taking our bread,' a different farmer said.

'Sarjeant, where did you get the bread from?'

'The flour came from your store,' he answered.

'You see, it is my flour and ground at my mill,' Richard said, 'they are taking nothing of yours. They are not going to, either. Any of them who steal from you will face the appropriate punishment.'

The complainants spoke amongst themselves. Their leader looked up at Richard. 'We know that you are not afraid to give punishments, but you should know that we are not happy.'

'You've made that very clear,' Richard said, 'now go before you start a riot.'

The farmers skulked back into the old village but kept their eyes on the newcomers.

'Everyone will calm down in a week or two,' Sarjeant said.

'I hope so,' Richard said, 'I'm just surprised they went back so easily.'

Sarjeant laughed. 'My boy, I think these outsiders have made you seem a lot more Norman to the villagers.'

'Where are the refugees from?'

'No idea,' Sarjeant said, 'I can't understand them.'

'That's your first task, then,' Richard smiled, 'if you're equal to it.'

Sarjeant stood tall. 'You can count on me.'

Richard nodded. 'I know.'

'But you return empty handed.'

'Abbot Anfroy is still alive.'

Sarjeant scowled. 'That man is an affront to all that is good.'

'We didn't see him, but the crypt was still sealed. We were chased away by some thieving knights. Either we need to break in like they did, or find another way,' Richard said.

Sarjeant tapped his chin. 'Pretend to be a work party. It worked for you in Saint Malo.'

Richard grinned. 'That's not a bad idea, not once we've found enough tools and a cart,' he turned Solis back towards the track.

His wife walked through the old village so Richard rode to her.

'I see you are not carrying your weight in silver,' she stood in her old blue dress, the one without the extra material.

'Some men robbed the nunnery while we were there. We had to escape.'

'What is your plan to feed this rabble, then?' She asked.

Richard sighed. 'There are two ideas, and you won't like either of them.'

Sophie put her hands on her hips. 'I don't like restricting you, Richard, I really don't.'

'I know,' Richard said, 'but I need to keep the village safe, and you safe.'

'And your children.'

'Of course,' Richard looked back to Sarjeant and the happy faces of those around him.

'They think they are safe here,' Sophie said.

'Maybe Sarjeant can form a levy from amongst them. Enough to man the walls,' Richard said.

Sophie thought for a moment. 'He might have to. The King's squires left while you were failing to rob nuns.'

'I wasn't robbing anyone. Why did they go?'

'They said they had served their time,' Sophie said, 'which they had. There were only a few left anyway, and we need a dozen armed men to hold the castle.'

'We've got three or four dozen unemployed men right here,' Richard said.

'I still don't want you to leave,' Sophie replied.

'If we work the tournament circuit, we need only be absent for two or three weeks at a time.'

'Tournaments?' Sophie laughed, 'you want to make your fortune on the tournament field?'

Richard felt his face redden. 'What's so funny about that? I've taken knights captive before.'

'Have you ever seen a tourney?' She asked.

Richard shook his head.

'I have,' Sophie said, 'and it is rigged against new knights. They pummel each other with swords until their teeth fall out, and their eyes rattle in their thick skulls. They use their swords, dear, and from what Bowman tells me, you can't keep a hold of yours.'

Richard wanted to argue, but she was right so he ground his

teeth together instead. 'What should we do then?' He asked

'The newcomers owe you labour. Use it,' she said, 'make the Flying Monk larger. Build barns to store more crops. Use them to plant more demesne fields. Sell more cider.'

'You sound like Sarjeant.'

'Maybe that's because he's right,' Sophie smiled, 'this is all boring to you, isn't it.'

'No,' Richard played with his reins, 'well, yes.'

Sophie smiled a soft smile that Richard found himself liking. 'If we can man the walls, you can play the knight errant across Christendom. But only when me and my children are safe.'

'I know,' Richard put the reins down, 'I don't want any harm to come to you.'

'Then don't leave,' Sophie said, 'we are poor and we have extra mouths to feed now. We need to find more mature animals by the autumn or half of these new arrivals shall starve when the frosts come. You have two children to protect now, they come first.'

'They do come first, which is why I need to make some money.'

'You won't make it at a tournament,' Sophie said.

Richard fought the urge to argue even though he felt extremely confident he'd excel in a tournament. He had survived war, after all, how hard could a game be?

'I'm going to check on the children,' she said, 'but a letter came, it's in the hall. The messenger who delivered it is waiting. He was a very rude man and I would like him out of my castle. His presence made me feel quite unwell.'

'A letter? If it's the ransom then maybe all our troubles will be gone,' Richard walked Solis on past his wife and to the track where Bowman spoke to Eva.

'There's a letter,' Richard told them.

'What's in it?' Bowman asked.

'I haven't read it yet, I'm going to find out,' Richard said.

Bowman and Eva rode into the castle with him.

When they reached the hall, Richard found the messenger sitting down with his feet up on his table. Mud had fallen onto the wooden surface. He had long black hair, but it was wider on the right side than his left.

'Are you missing an ear?' Bowman asked.

The messenger swung his legs around. 'At last,' he said in an accent similar to Eva's.

Nicholas sat waiting beside him. 'Open the letter, he won't tell me who it's from.'

'It's not your ransom,' Richard found himself staring out of the window.

Nicholas looked up at him. 'How do you know?'

'Because he's Irish, why would he be bringing word from the Martels?'

Nicholas glanced back at the messenger. 'Oh.'

The messenger looked right past Richard when Eva entered the hall. 'About time,' he said.

'Cormac,' Eva said flatly, 'what brings you to this fine land?'

'Your father,' the messenger replied.

Eva shrugged. 'He can complain about my efforts as much as he likes, it won't make me any more successful,' she said.

Cormac held out a rolled up parchment.

Nicholas turned his back on everyone and faced the fire. 'I'm done with him,' he mumbled.

Eva took the letter and unrolled it. Her eyes followed the writing, then she carefully rolled it up and threw it into the fire.

Nicholas had to move out of her way, which he did loudly, and banged his stool down afterwards.

The fire consumed the document with a crackle.

'Well?' Richard asked.

Eva looked him in the eyes. 'It has begun.'

'What has?' Bowman said, 'are you leaving?'

Eva nodded.

'What did your father say?'

'He has found a Norman lord to invade Leinster with him. Sir Richard de Clare promised to do so years ago, but my father sent him some fine words and now he musters.'

'I expect he sent some coin, too,' Bowman crossed his arms.

'No,' Eva said, 'he has been promised something more.'

Bowman went to the table and sat down on a chair so hard that one of its legs cracked.

'Cormac,' Eva said, 'what did my father want to tell me that wasn't in this letter?'

'The site of the muster from where the fleet will set sail,' the messenger replied.

'Well then, where is it?'

'Milford Haven.'

'Where is that?' Eva asked.

Bowman choked on the old cider he'd just drunk. 'Wales,' he wiped cider from his mouth.

'You know it?' Richard asked.

'Unfortunately,' Bowman said, 'the Welsh once ambushed a raid I was on that left from Milford Haven.'

'Would you mind showing me the way, then?' Eva asked him.

Cormac sat back. 'I know the way,' he said.

Richard didn't like the way he said it.

'Do you have any knights?' The messenger asked the princess.

Eva turned her back on him and walked over to a window.

'Richard,' Bowman looked up, 'can we go to Ireland?'

Richard tapped his foot. That had been his second best idea. Which was also now his last idea. Everyone in the hall looked at him, even Eva turned back from the window.

Bowman got off his broken chair, pulled the fractured leg off and threw all of it into the fire. 'Well, seeing as I don't have a chair anymore, I might as well go to Ireland,' he said.

'That's the worst excuse to go off to war I've ever heard,' Nicholas stood up too. His eyes met Richard's. 'But my father has abandoned me, so the dogs can have him. I'll serve you if you'll have me. I'll go to Ireland and earn my own ransom.'

'Earn your own ransom?' Bowman scoffed, 'that's the stupidest idea I've ever heard.'

'Is it?' Eva said, 'Ireland is fertile, the land is rich. A knight could find a way to earn his freedom.'

Richard could hear Sophie's voice in his head. She told him to wait until next year.

Bowman pointed at Nicholas. 'You can't trust him, you can't bring him to Ireland.'

'He's your brother,' Richard said.

'Half-brother,' Bowman moaned.

Eva walked over to Richard. 'My father wrote that he sails soon, but he has to wait for me. Come with me, please. Once my father sits on his throne again, you will find the compensation very agreeable.'

Bowman and Nicholas stared at him. The little voice in his head told Richard he had two babies to care for. But, he thought, he couldn't care for them if he were destitute.

'How much are knights paid?' He asked.

Bowman threw a jubilant fist into the air.

Nicholas smiled, although Richard found his green eyes unnerving.

'Four shillings a day for a knight,' Cormac said, 'one for a squire.'

Bowman swore. 'One?'

Richard chuckled. 'We'll be sure to find some at Harfleur,' he said.

'What?'

'Some golden spurs,' Richard said.

Bowman looked blankly at Richard. 'I don't want to be a knight.'

'You want four shillings a day? Or one?'

Bowman sucked in a breath.

'You don't need to run any land,' Richard said, 'nothing changes except your pay.'

Bowman looked at Eva. 'Done.'

She smiled, something Richard had not seen her do too often. 'Three knights, then,' she said.

'Two,' Bowman pointed at his half-brother, 'he's not coming.'

'He is,' Richard said, 'three knights. He'll pay me his earnings and then he'll be free.'

'Thank you,' the Martel Bastard said, 'you won't regret it.'

Bowman snorted. 'You had better not do anything foolish.'

'We're all doing something foolish,' Richard said, 'we're going to Ireland.'

They sailed from Harfleur all the way to Milford Haven. Which was a long time for Richard to avoid thinking about his wife and how angry she was. At Harfleur, Richard made Cormac buy a pair of golden spurs for Bowman as the price of their agreement to join the venture. The Irishman had pulled a sour face, but then handed over actual gold. He also had to pay for lodgings and food for the whole party, while they sat in

Harfleur for two weeks waiting for the wind to change. As soon as the wind stopped blowing east, they boarded a cog and sailed west. Richard apologised to Solis and fed him charmed bread to stop him being angry at yet another voyage. It didn't work. They sailed close enough to Cornwall to see the English coast, then turned north and headed for the south west corner of Wales.

Richard sat in the prow of the cog with Nicholas as it gently pushed through the waves.

'I want to see Wales first,' Nicholas peered out over the boarded side.

'I expect it will look just like England did,' Richard said. Seagulls hadn't found them yet and all around, right to the horizon, were only waves.

'This is only the second time I've sailed.'

'I've never sailed this far, but it's all sailing,' Richard said, 'at least it's calmed down now.'

The first few days had been rough as the unusual wind pushed the cog westwards. The swell of the sea had pushed the ship up and down and Richard had felt sick. Everyone else apart from Nicholas had been sick too, and it was only now that any of the other passengers emerged from below.

Two men Richard hadn't noticed or seen before came up onto the deck. The leader had a pasty-white face contrasted by his red cheeks. Richard squinted at him, but lost interest and turned his head back to where the cog headed.

Footsteps sounded on the wooden deck behind him and Richard's sense of smell changed from smelling the sea, to smelling leather and sour milk. He turned around and looked up at the rosy-cheeked man.

'I know you,' the man said.

Richard swallowed. 'I doubt it,' he replied. He didn't have any interest in talking to a fat man. A fat man. Richard realised that he had seen him before and groaned.

'You were at the nunnery,' the man said.

Richard got to his feet and had to raise his eyes to meet his gaze. 'I remember you, and I have no problem with you,' he said.

'Problem? Who said anything about a problem?'

'No one, but I'm not in the mood for conversation, so I'd

prefer it if you let me be,' Richard said.

'Why were you at the nunnery?' He asked.

'Me?' Richard said, 'I was staying the night, why were you there?'

The man opened his mouth into a grin, a grin with missing teeth and breath that made Richard flinch.

'Actually I don't care, just leave me alone,' Richard said.

'You were in the nunnery, too.'

'Who are you?' Nicholas asked.

'Sir Alan of Auge.'

'That's a vague area to say you're from,' Richard said, 'that is almost like me saying I'm Richard of Normandy.'

Alan's grin flattened. 'Are you insulting me?'

'Of course not,' Richard said, 'I think I know why you were in the nunnery, so let's try a different question. Why are you on this ship?'

'A very profitable job,' Alan said.

'Oh, no,' Richard closed his eyes.

'You are contracted, too?' Alan asked.

Richard shook his head, then stopped. 'Well, actually I think we might be.'

'It is always pleasing to meet fellow dogs of war,' Alan grabbed Richard's shoulder and shook it vigorously.

'Stop that,' Richard brushed the hand away and put his own hand on his stomach to settle it.

'We shall make our fortunes together,' Alan said.

'Are you a mercenary?' Nicholas asked.

'We're all mercenaries,' Alan said, 'you say it like there is shame in it.'

'You robbed a nunnery,' Richard said.

'We didn't really find very much in the end,' the red cheeked man said, 'and how else do men of the sword earn their living when they have no lands?'

'There are better ways,' Richard said.

'If those better ways are so good, why are you here?'

Nicholas laughed. 'He's got you there, Richard.'

Alan's belly bulged under his mustard-yellow tunic and Richard's eyes were drawn to it. Alan slapped his hands on it. 'The sign of many contracts fulfilled,' he said.

Richard shivered. He walked around Alan, which took a few steps, and towards the back of the cog.

'Where are you going?' Alan shouted after him.

'Away from you.'

Bowman came up onto deck just as Richard was about to go below.

'I feel better now,' Bowman said.

'I did,' Richard looked back at the mercenary, 'but now I don't.'

'Is that?' Bowman scrunched up his eyes.

Richard groaned. 'Unfortunately.'

'Big red balls?' Bowman's eye widened.

'You know,' Richard said, 'I think you might get on with him.'

Until land appeared on the horizon, Richard hid below deck. The cog took an age to get there, tacking east and west to creep north, but under grey skies it eventually reached Wales.

Other ships sailed along the estuary they entered, and it reminded Richard of the Seine, low hills lined both banks of the narrowing waterway.

The last on deck, Richard joined everyone else in watching land approach.

'I saw it first,' Nicholas said.

'Good for you,' Richard replied, 'if you fail at being a lance for hire, at least you can always become a seaman.'

'No money in seafaring,' Alan leant on the side of the ship.

'Although judging by his waist,' Richard said quietly to Nicholas, 'it must be quite hard to fail at freelancing.'

The young Martel man laughed, a more care-free laugh than Richard had heard before.

Bowman frowned beside them. 'When we land, don't leave the town,' he said.

'How long ago was it that the Welsh ambushed you?' Nicholas asked.

'Maybe ten years.'

'I don't think we need to worry, then,' Richard said.

Their ship turned right into a river that flowed far narrower than the wide estuary.

'Pembroke River,' Alan said loudly so all could hear.

'Show off,' Richard mumbled and began to regret the decision to sail.

A castle appeared from around a bend, and its walls of stone dominated the landscape. The river split and ran either side of it, the castle itself sitting on a rock formation taller than their mast. Stone walls ran around the top of the rock with towers along its length.

'Pembroke Castle,' Alan nodded to himself.

'We guessed,' Nicholas whispered and Richard laughed.

A collection of sailing vessels lay moored around the area, their masts and furled sails bobbed calmly on the water.

They disembarked and followed Alan on foot along the riverbank and into the castle. Richard looked up at the high walls as they entered, which looked strong enough. Carts rolled in with barrels and boxes of goods while bands of armed men hung around doing nothing.

'There's something in the air,' Bowman said, 'everyone's waiting.'

Their arrival was eyed suspiciously by a large gathering of men all dressed in faded tunics and with long knives at their belts.

Bowman shuddered. 'Welshmen,' he said.

'They look like they're all waiting here with us,' Richard said as they entered the castle's bailey.

Inside the castle horses stood shoulder to shoulder, men moved everywhere, and there was nowhere free to stand. Carts rumbled in, some with cut grass for the horses, and others carrying everything else Richard could imagine. He marvelled at the money that must lie behind the expedition, as well as the organisation of putting it all together.

Richard flexed his shoulders under his two layers of mail.

'You didn't need to put even one of those on,' Bowman said.

'I'm trying to make a good impression,' Richard replied, 'and I don't think I want to leave a mail shirt lying around here unattended, either.'

'Good point,' Bowman walked around with a hand on his sword.

Alan and his six knightly companions stopped for a rest before walking towards the keep.

'Shall we keep following them?' Nicholas asked.

'Do you have a better idea?' Bowman replied.

Nicholas shrugged. 'I've never seen so many people in a castle before.'

Richard stopped and pointed to the far corner of the bailey. 'Bowman, are those my colours?'

'Aye, white with your blue line,' he replied.

'My uncle is here,' Richard swallowed, 'what's he doing here?'

'The same thing as you, I'd wager.'

'We should keep away from him,' Richard said.

Bowman chuckled. 'That didn't work in Brittany, though, did it.'

'The fat mercenary is moving again, let's just follow him,' Richard said, but kept an eye on his uncle's banner.

Alan led them to the man the invasion force was there to raise to power.

'Father,' Eva said to a man in a light yellow tunic that only reached down to his knees. He had long reddish brown hair and an extended beard of the same colour. His face shared a passing resemblance to Eva, but with deeper wrinkles. Richard thought him likely to be in his fifties or sixties.

He replied to Eva in what was presumably Irish.

'This is Dermot, my father,' Eva said to Richard.

'King Dermot,' the old man said.

Richard bowed because that seemed the right thing to do.

King Dermot inspected Richard's face. 'You have scars. That's good. What is your name?'

'Richard of Yvetot.'

'Who are your fellow knights?'

'This is Nicholas Martel, and this is,' Richard trailed off looking at Bowman.

'Sir,' Bowman said loftily, 'Robert of Shelford. Delighted to meet you, Your Majesty.'

Dermot glowed in self importance and bowed back.

Richard wondered, and not for the first time, if he was going to regret handing Bowman those golden spurs.

Dermot noticed Alan and his comrades. He leant over to Eva and asked a question in his native language.

Eva snorted and replied. Richard could tell she was not

complimenting their fellow mercenaries, but Dermot bowed slightly to them anyway.

King Dermot and his daughter turned to each other and exchanged fast words. Eva glanced at Bowman then stormed off into the castle on her own.

'Women,' Dermot said to Richard, 'they do not know their place.'

He wasn't sure how to respond. 'I hope God favours your invasion,' he said.

Dermot grimaced. 'He has favoured little else of late. But now my daughter has bothered to arrive, the expedition can begin. Stay here, I will announce our departure.'

'He seemed like a very nice king,' Bowman said as Dermot entered the tower.

'You aren't going to charm your way to being his son,' Richard folded his mail-covered arms.

Bowman looked out across the bailey. 'No harm in trying, now that I am a knight.'

'Remember that I haven't actually knighted you.'

'So?' Bowman said, 'it only matters if I look and sound the part.'

'That isn't the point,' Richard replied.

'It is the point if I'm going to earn four shillings a day.'

'Being a knight isn't about money.'

'That's easy for you to say, and keep your voice down,' Bowman checked no one stood too close to them.

King Dermot appeared at a window above them and shouted for attention. He leant out of the first floor of the tower as the various people in the bailey turned and hushed.

'Tomorrow you shall all embark on a great adventure. Glory and riches await you in Ireland, a land of plenty, wealth and culture. Together we will reclaim my right as King of Leinster. Once restored to power, rewards will be due to all of you. We sail as one mighty host, and none shall stand against us.'

A group of men pushed through the crowded bailey towards the tower. Richard stepped out of their way. They were well armed and in fine yellow surcoats, each with three red chevrons pointing upwards.

'They look serious,' Bowman nearly got pushed aside by one

of them as they brushed past.

King Dermot looked nervous in his window. Suddenly one of the men in the yellow and red chevron surcoats pushed him aside and joined him looking out over the army.

The knight had a long nose and his face looked set in a constant frown. Richard wasn't sure if his ruddy complexion was just due to him having run up to the first floor or not.

'For those who do not know me,' he shouted from the window, 'I am Richard de Clare, Lord of Striguil. I am who you are contracted to for this enterprise.'

'He looks like a hard man,' Bowman said.

Richard thought that might be a good thing for what might lie ahead.

King Dermot tried to lean back out of the window, but de Clare put a hand on his chest and pushed him out of sight.

'Not all of you will sail tomorrow,' he continued, 'two ships will leave as an advanced party to forge a beachhead on the Irish coast. The rest of the fleet will follow them shortly.'

King Dermot pushed back into view but his face had reddened. He didn't try to impose himself again.

De Clare left the window without so much as a nod to the Irish ex-king.

'They call him Strange Hose,' Nicholas said.

'Who?' Richard asked because everyone had started to talk loudly.

'Him, de Clare,' Nicholas replied, 'he doesn't wear normal hose on his legs.'

'Bit odd to name him after that,' Richard said.

De Clare and his companions left the tower and strode back the way they'd come.

'Strange bows, was it?' Bowman raised his voice, 'I didn't hear you?'

De Clare stopped by Bowman and looked at him. Bowman was just as tall as him, but de Clare was thinner. 'What did you call me?' De Clare asked.

Bowman put his hands up. 'Nothing, someone said you were called Strong Bows or something, I didn't really hear it,' he answered.

'Strong Bow?' De Clare started to laugh, 'that's much better than what they do call me.'

Bowman looked at Richard with unblinking eyes.

'I'm not helping you,' Richard took a step back.

'Strongbow sounds better than the Lord of Striguil,' de Clare said, 'everyone can call me that, now.' The lord now known as Strongbow stormed back through the crowd with his yellow and red surcoat-wearing attendants in his wake.

'What just happened?' Bowman asked.

'I think you just renamed a lord because of your bad hearing,' Richard said.

'I don't have bad hearing.'

'What now?' Nicholas asked.

'If we aren't sailing tomorrow,' Richard said, 'we best find somewhere to make ourselves comfortable overnight.'

They walked in and out of the tower and every other castle building in an effort to find somewhere to spend the next few days. Everywhere they went men sat on cloaks or blankets, spots already taken. Where men hadn't claimed patches of ground, piles of goods stood in their way. Even the stables were full, men had taken bed space on the hay alongside richer men's horses. Their own horses had been offloaded into a communal paddock outside the small town that spilled out eastwards from the castle. Solis and Bowman's horse had commandeered a huge pile of hay for themselves, and ran off any horses that dared come too close.

Richard found a barn overlooking the paddock that so far had evaded the interest of the gathering army. Richard unrolled his bedding on some straw and they piled up their saddles and shields.

'One of us stays here with those at all times,' Richard pointed to their equipment.

Bowman nodded. 'You,' he pointed at his half-brother, 'you should go and find food and drink.'

Nicholas looked to Richard who shrugged back. The young Martel knight wandered reluctantly back to the castle on his errand.

Richard lay back on the straw, put his arms behind his head, and tried to relax.

Without realising he'd ever fallen asleep, he awoke as

Nicholas returned with a basket.

'What have you got?' Bowman asked.

'Ale and some old hard bread,' Nicholas glanced over to Richard, 'and all knights directly contracted to Strongbow are to see him now. There is a council of war.'

'So?' Richard replied.

'That means you.'

'I suppose it does,' Richard got to his feet. He drank some of the ale but decided to try his luck for better food inside the castle. He left Bowman behind and walked up back to the hustle and bustle of the fortification.

Richard didn't know what a council of war looked like, but assumed if he found the men with the red and yellow surcoats he would be in the right place. A string of horses walked by Richard, led by some young men and boys, and he could smell their beasts for a while after they went. Cooking smells made his mouth water after that, for men and women boiled and grilled food around the castle bailey. He needed to ask one of them where the meat came from, but before he could, Richard spotted one of Strongbow's men. He followed the surcoat through the bailey to the far end, under the wall where knights stood in a semi-circle around King Dermot and Strongbow. He looked around for Eva but couldn't see her. He started to count men in mail and surcoats instead, and stopped halfway round the semi-circle when he reached thirty.

Strongbow read out names from a list and then the name of the ship they would sail on. Richard didn't hear his name, although he heard his brother's.

'You all sail in a week, now go and see to your men,' Strongbow said.

Knights filtered away from the semi-circle until only a handful remained. One was Alan of Auge, and Richard turned away in the hope of not being recognised.

'You, from the ship,' Alan shouted and waddled over. He had donned his mail shirt and Richard thought it probably had twice as many rings in it as his own did.

Alan tapped him on the shoulder and Richard turned to see his ugly smile. 'Oh, I didn't see you,' Richard said.

'Looks like we're in it together,' the mercenary said.

'In what?'

'I don't know, but there's only a few of us here, maybe we're special?'

'I doubt it,' Richard said, 'it's more likely we're about to be sent home as unneeded.'

'Quiet,' Strongbow shouted at them, 'gather in.'

The remaining knights came closer and Richard realised that it was only him and Alan's six, along with one other. The other knight was one of the biggest men Richard had ever seen. Taller and broader than Bowman, the knight looked like Strongbow, just bigger.

'Raymond the Large,' Strongbow shouted and the tall knight stepped forwards, 'you will have the honour of leading our advanced party.'

Raymond bowed.

Richard's heart sank. Advanced party sounded dangerous.

'Raymond will command two ships with ten knights and seventy Welshmen. His own mother is a Welsh princess, so those animals should listen to him. If you're still standing here, it is because you either don't know your own name, or you are one of the ten knights.'

'Is ten knights enough for an advanced party?' Richard asked.

Strongbow blinked and turned his head towards Richard. 'Who are you?'

'Richard of Yvetot.'

'Ah, she told me about you. I didn't know you were coming so your name wasn't down. That is why you are here.'

Raymond the Large walked up to Richard and blocked out the sun that had started to set behind the western walls. 'He has seen war,' Raymond said, 'he is scarred and missing a finger. How did you lose that?'

'An axe.'

'Where?'

'On a castle wall in Brittany,' Richard replied.

Raymond smiled. 'I will have him in my advanced party. He at least looks like he could climb a siege ladder without needing to rest for a day once he got to the top.'

Richard could see Alan and his overweight associates watching, but they gave no sign that they realised Raymond spoke about them.

'She said you had two other knights with you,' Raymond said, 'are they seasoned, too?'

Richard nodded, 'one more than me, but who told you about us?'

'The princess, of course,' Strongbow said, 'I would go to Ireland only for her.'

Every man except Richard chuckled, and Alan laughed so loudly even Strongbow shot him a questioning glance.

'Now we all know each other,' Strongbow said, 'we can speak of tomorrow.'

'Tomorrow?' Alan asked, the red balls on his creased surcoat almost as red as his face.

'Yes,' Raymond the Large replied, 'is that too soon for you?'

'No, of course not. We just,' Alan swept his foot around the grass, 'we just hoped for some more food before we left.'

'This is a serious operation,' Strongbow shouted at him, 'there will be times where none of us have food in Ireland. It will rain. It will be cold. The naked natives will swarm around us throwing spears into our ranks. The pagans will bring down curses on us. They might try to feed us poisoned food. You'll be happy with what you're given and cease complaining.'

Alan looked at the ground and said nothing.

'Your ships leave at first light, wind permitting,' Strongbow continued, 'ten knights, twenty horses and seventy Welshmen. You will fortify a promontory in a bay near Waterford, gather supplies, scout the area, and wait for us. If any Irishmen come at you with anything other than gifts, you kill them.'

'I've only got one horse,' Richard said.

Strongbow cocked an eye at him. 'Too poor for more?'

Everyone laughed.

Richard narrowed his eyes. 'No,' he lied, 'my warhorse won't let me ride any others.'

Everyone laughed even more.

'Very well,' Raymond said, 'ten knights and nineteen horses. It will leave us more room to take wine.'

The laughing carried on and Strongbow had to wipe tears from his eyes. 'I like you,' he looked at Richard, 'I hope that the natives don't cut your head off and stick it on a pole.'

'Me, too,' Richard replied.

Strongbow bent double straining for breath, and had to turn away to regain control his breathing. 'I really do like you.'

Raymond smiled at Richard. 'Are you a god-fearing man?'

Richard made the sign of the cross.

'Good, find a priest tonight and make your peace,' Raymond's grin vanished, 'for of those who land, only a few will be alive to welcome the others.'

'Then why are you coming with us?' Richard asked, and regretted it as the big man stepped closer.

'Because the Irish can't kill Raymond the Large,' the grin returned.

Strongbow chortled. 'Ten knights in wooden saddles and mail coats shall cleave their way through the naked pagans. If you fortify the promontory, then the Welsh arrows will pin their naked hides like so many sheep. You'll conquer Dublin before I even arrive.'

Richard doubted that, but everyone else laughed.

'What's the joke?' Bowman appeared next to Richard.

'What are you doing here?'

'I got hungry. Bored and hungry.'

'Well,' Richard said, 'we're leaving in the morning with just these other knights to invade Ireland on our own.'

'Sounds grand,' Bowman said, 'but where is all this roasting meat coming from? If I don't get some soon I'll have to roast a leg from the knight with two red balls.'

'You're too happy,' Richard said, 'and the knight is over there.'

'So he is,' Bowman lowered his voice, 'he looks redder than usual.'

'He's in the advanced party. Ten knights to invade Ireland. We're in it too.'

'Ten?' Bowman let out a whine, 'and six of them are too fat to sit on a horse?'

'Good thing we're travelling by ship, then,' Richard folded his arms.

Strongbow waved everyone else away and approached Raymond. 'You have a great honour, my friend,' he held a hand out to him.

Raymond grabbed the hand and they embraced. 'We will win

much across the sea.'

'To princesses and gold,' Strongbow said.

'Princesses and gold,' Raymond replied. They stepped apart and went their separate ways.

'Princesses?' Bowman watched them go.

'Don't worry about it,' Richard said, 'let's find some food, it might be last time we eat peacefully in a while.'

'Why did they both say princesses?'

'I don't know, Bowman, maybe there are plenty of princesses in Ireland.'

Richard grabbed him by his tunic and dragged him back across the bailey. They got as far as a fire with fish of various sizes sizzling over it.

'Can we have some?' Bowman asked.

'For a coin or two,' the woman tending it replied.

Bowman swore and looked elsewhere. Behind the fish, a group of Welsh archers cleared a space and set up an archery target.

'A bit late to be practising,' Richard said, 'if they're no good now, they aren't going to learn tonight.'

'New bows,' Bowman pointed to a cart with a pile of fresh staves on it, 'they are checking the new bows won't snap.'

A Welshman placed a wooden platter with a large joint of roast meat onto a table by the cart.

'And that's their prize,' Bowman walked off towards it.

'They won't give that to you,' Richard sighed then followed him.

The stout Welshman didn't speak French, Norman or English, but when Bowman picked up a bow from the cart and pointed to the target, the short man shrugged and held out three arrows to him.

Richard counted the Welshmen. Seventy. 'Bowman, don't make them angry, we're sailing with them tomorrow.'

'I don't plan on making them angry,' Bowman finishing stringing his bow, 'I plan on making them hungry.'

The Welsh all ined up and shot their three arrows into the wicker target. A set of shrinking circles had been carved onto it. The bullseye was the size of a silver coin, and the archers shot flat at a good distance. Most of the archers hit the target once or twice. The small Welshman who'd given Bowman a stave hit with all three of his arrows, including one in the bullseye.

Archers cheered and although Richard couldn't understand a word, it sounded like congratulations went to the stout man.

Bowman took his place at the line in the turf and nocked his first arrow. He raised the bow and let fly the arrow straight away. It sailed through the air and struck the target a hand's length from the centre. Welshmen nodded quietly to each other.

'In the middle,' Richard shouted.

Bowman ignored him and nocked the second arrow. He licked his lips and loosed. The shaft cut through the air and embedded itself a finger from the bullseye. This time more Welsh took notice. The short archer scratched his neck and glanced over to the joint of meat.

'Come on,' Richard's stomach rumbled.

Bowman released his final arrow. It wobbled through the air, glanced off the shaft of the second arrow, and came to a rest just outside the centre of the target.

Richard shut his eyes. He could smell the joint, too.

Bowman kept the bow, which no one argued with, and left the archery range as hungry as when he'd entered it.

'That was pretty good shooting,' Richard said.

'Not good enough, though,' he eyed the meat again.

'I don't think anyone is going to give us anything for free, either,' Richard said.

'No,' Bowman held up the bow, 'but we have this.'

'Because that always ends so well for us,' Richard replied.

'This time the uptight game-keeper will be just as eager for our success,' Bowman grinned.

'I hope you're right,' Richard said.

'Look, there's Eva,' Bowman pointed across the castle.

'Can't we just catch something to eat,' Richard asked.

Bowman was already gone. He walked to intercept her and started to talk to her before Richard caught up with them.

'I'm sorry,' she said, 'I have to stay here, I can't go off to hunt with you. Every man here is trying to force things on me.'

'All the more reason to leave here tonight,' Bowman's eyes shone even as the sun drifted below the castle wall.

'I must attend a banquet tonight,' Eva said.

'With your father and those Norman show-offs?' Bowman asked.

'Yes,' Eva said, 'with my father, who is a King, and the Norman lords who will put him back on his throne.'

'It looked to me like your father wasn't in command here,' Richard said.

Eva crossed her arms and looked at Richard. 'That is beside the point, isn't it? Better to be a King in Ireland with some overbearing Normans being rude, than a King with no lands sitting in Wales.'

'Is Ireland really rich enough to pay for all this?' Richard asked, 'I heard the Irish don't mint coins, so how does Strongbow intend to pay for it all?'

Eva looked at her feet. She looked up. 'With land.'

Bowman gasped. 'Princesses and gold, they said. You're the princess, aren't you?'

'You know I'm a princess.'

'Strongbow is promised a princess, isn't he?'

Eva started to walk towards the keep.

'How long have you known?' Bowman shouted after her.

Eva stopped and turned around. 'Leave it.'

'Come on, there's nothing you can do here,' Richard grabbed his arm.

'Like hell there isn't,' Bowman threw Richard off and walked up to Eva, 'come on, just tonight. You can't give everything to these crusty old men.'

'That crusty old man is my father.'

'I mean the Norman, you didn't pick him, have one night with someone you do pick.'

'How to do you know I'd pick you?' Eva brushed the hair out of her face.

Richard looked around, the only person watching was Cormac the messenger, who sat by a fire not far away.

'If you're both going to do something stupid, be discreet about it,' Richard said.

'Balls to discreet,' Bowman held a hand out to Eva.

She looked down at his hand. 'I am not that brave, or that stupid.'

'We're in the barn by the horse paddock,' Bowman said, 'go there soon.'

Eva answered only with angry eyes, and Bowman withdrew his hand.

Richard checked Cormac, but he had looked away and started a conversation with someone.

'Be more discreet,' Richard hissed.

Bowman ignored him. 'I'll be waiting,' he said to Eva and turned and walked out of the castle.

Eva looked at Richard. 'If you tell anyone.'

'It's not me you should be worried about,' Richard said, 'please don't come out tonight. Stay here and stay out of trouble.'

Eva winked at him. 'I will be good. Off you go, now.'

Richard wasn't sure what that meant, but he turned on his heels and walked out of the bailey anyway.

Back at their barn, Bowman had sent Nicholas out into the dusk with the bow.

'You've turned him into a poacher?' Richard asked.

Bowman nodded. 'He's as hungry as we are, and he's less self-righteous than he was the day we met him.'

'You've grown more self-righteous,' Richard replied, 'people saw you speak to her, too. You better hope she doesn't take you up on your offer.'

'If she does, you can find somewhere else to sleep,' Bowman grinned.

'It's a bad idea,' Richard sat down on the straw and folded his arms.

Bowman went to watch the street towards the castle, and Richard waited and hoped Nicholas was as good a shot as his half-brother.

It was Eva, however, that reached the barn first.

'Go, go away,' Bowman hissed to Richard, and went out to her.

Richard gathered his cloak to ward off the evening air and left the barn in the direction Nicholas had gone. He saw Eva and Bowman enter the building, so he walked away far enough that he wouldn't have to hear anything. A bat darted between the trunks of the trees that lined the paddock and flew around the outside of the barn. Richard ducked it then looked up at the sky.

Stars shone up above and the faint breeze cooled his face. He looked for somewhere to sit, saw nowhere, and decided to walk back towards the castle. Someone there might take pity on him and feed him. As he approached the track from the paddock, he noticed a figure walking towards the barn. Richard tried to focus his eyes but he couldn't make out the figure's features.

'Richard,' Nicholas shouted from far behind him.

Richard turned to look for him but couldn't see him, either. When he turned back to the street, no one was there. Deciding he must have been imagining things, he went to find Nicholas in the dark of the night.

'There you are,' Nicholas said from within the trees as Richard approached. He held a rabbit.

'I was hoping for something bigger,' Richard said.

'I can't see in the dark,' Nicholas replied, 'and it's better than nothing.'

'We can't go into the barn.'

'Why not?

'The princess came to see Bowman,' Richard said, 'we can't go in until she leaves.'

'Why would she do that?'

'Don't ask me,' Richard said, 'let's go into the castle and find a fire to borrow. Bowman can keep his barn.'

The Welsh archers let them cook the rabbit on their fire, and even shared some drink and bread with them. Richard couldn't speak to them, and thought they laughed at him too much, but was glad enough for the warmth and charity.

Nicholas nudged Richard once they'd finished eating the rabbit. 'There she is.'

'I've a mind to stay by this fire,' Richard said.

'Are you jealous?'

'Jealous?' Richard laughed, 'I've got a wife.'

'But she's not here, though,' Nicholas threw the last rabbit bone over to a large shaggy dog that scrounged around the archers. The dog crunched the bone until it was gone.

'What Bowman has done could get him killed,' Richard said, 'and there are enough things over the horizon waiting to try to kill me already. I don't need to find more.'

'These Welshmen are not so bad,' Nicholas said, 'I thought

they would be much less friendly.'

Richard agreed. He'd never heard a good thing about the Welsh, but they had been perfectly pleasant to him.

'Shall we go and see the new knight who would be a king?' Nicholas asked.

Richard took in a deep breath to smell the seasoned wood burning in the fire. It was the same wood as he burnt in his own hall. He sighed. 'When I'm at home, I want to be away, and when I'm away, I want to be at home,' he said.

Nicholas grunted. My father says that is the way of the warrior. I never understood what he meant but I think it means after too much war you don't feel right anywhere.'

Richard stared into the Welsh fire. 'I don't want to think about that, I'm going to see Bowman.'

They found Bowman asleep in the barn under his cloak.

'I'm happy to wake him up,' Nicholas looked down at him.'

'I really want to,' Richard said, 'but he looks so happy I actually am not going to.'

'You're growing soft on him.'

'Tomorrow he'll feel pain from this,' Richard said, 'and we might as well get some sleep while we've got the chance.'

The sun rose over the castle as Richard loaded Solis onto a ship yet again. The stallion lashed out with his teeth at Richard as he secured him into his sling for the journey. This time Richard left him as quickly as possible. The Welsh archers crowded onto the other cog and three cartloads of arrows were loaded on with them. Before dawn, Raymond had ordered them all to cut sharpened stakes to use when they landed, and the Welsh had already gathered them in a pile to load before Richard reached the waterside.

Bowman hadn't spoken much. He gazed off towards the trees as Richard and Nicholas loaded their saddles, shields and other gear, and Richard decided to leave him to it.

Strongbow watched them with his retinue close by. Raymond spoke with him at length, and when the last of the provisions had been loaded he left the Lord of Striguil and approached the ships.

'This is it,' Nicholas said.

A horseman cantered down the slope from the castle. His grey horse foamed with sweat around its red leather breastplate, and the rider's cheeks puffed as he slammed to a halt. He wore a bright red tunic without a cloak.

'He's got a messenger's bag,' Richard said.

The horse snorted and steam surged from its nostrils in the morning air. The rider dismounted and walked towards Strongbow without asking who he was.

Richard noticed sweat pool around the horse's hooves on the hardened earth around the water's edge.

A letter was handed to Strongbow, who took it slowly. He unrolled it and Raymond went back over to him as he read it.

Strongbow crushed the letter in his fist. 'He wants me to stop,' he shouted at Raymond.

'I thought he gave you his blessing?'

Strongbow's red face paused. 'I may have exaggerated that. King Henry did not forbid me from acting in Ireland.'

'I see,' Raymond said, 'but he never said yes, either?'

Strongbow swore. 'This is because I sided with King Stephen, isn't it. Henry is petty, he can't let it go.'

'We have the Papal banner,' Raymond pointed to the harbourside where one of his squires held a furled banner. It looked mostly white.

'I know we have the banner, and I know the Pope himself told us we can go, but he is not the King.'

Raymond frowned. 'You're right, we cannot go against the King.'

Strongbow put the parchment in his mouth and tore a chunk out of it. He spat some of the letter out into the wind. 'Does he know how much money I've borrowed to fund all of this? The Jews of London have all my family possessions as collateral, they might as well own my soul.' He ripped the rest of the letter into shreds and ran down to the water. He balled up the tattered letter and hurled it. The parchment scattered in the breeze and floated down to the water.

'If the King wants to get me he can follow me to Ireland. Who does he think he is?'

'He thinks he's your King,' Raymond said with a glint in his eye.

Strongbow whirled around and glared at him.

They both started to laugh, which made Richard wonder what sort of men he was following overseas into a foreign land.

'We're going to Ireland boys, damn the King,' Strongbow shouted.

All the Normans cheered, and after a translation, the Welsh joined in with a roar.

Richard exchanged looks with Bowman and Nicholas, who both stayed quiet. Then they boarded their ship with Raymond the Large, and disembarked for the unknown as enemies of the King of England.

FIRST CONTACT

As the ship bobbed on the sea, Richard decided that Ireland didn't look all that different to Cornwall or Wales. The two ships sailed at a snail's pace into a sweeping bay with a headland on its southern horn. The two cogs turned towards that headland which had a small but sheltered sandy beach.

'We have a welcome,' Bowman said before the ships dropped anchor just off the beach.

The sheer cliffs that hemmed the stretch of sand in were moderately tall, topped with long grasses and plants that flowered purple. A bunch of horses were being held on the clifftop, their riders presumably the men who stood below on the beach facing the two Norman ships.

'If they've left their horses up there,' Richard said, 'how are we getting ours up from the beach?'

Nicholas pointed to one end of the beach. 'There is a track there, it's steep but horses can do steeper.'

Richard hoped he was right. Solis had a tendency to get distracted and forget he had four feet.

Raymond stood at the prow of the cog with his hands on his hips. His great red cloak billowed in the sharp and strong coastal wind. 'That's why we've brought two horses each, master of Yvetot. This is a war, you should get attached to your riding horse, not your warhorse.'

'I have the same horse for both,' Richard considered asking a Welshman to lead his horse up the cliff so Solis wouldn't be angry with him about that, too.

'Horses are consumed by war,' Raymond said, 'no different to shields and lances.'

Richard thought that was all very well for knights who could afford to replace them, but kept that opinion to himself.

Their leader pointed to the cliff that curled around the southern tip of the bay, beyond the beach, and stretched back out into the sea. 'That is where we are going. Baginbun Head.'

'Bag in bun?' Bowman said, 'I could understand a bun in a bag, but these Irish are backwards.'

Raymond found that amusing but turned around to face everyone on deck. 'It will be a long task to ferry everything onto the beach, then up the cliffs. We will be working like common labourers for over a day, but I expect every man to do so willingly. We have to entrench before the hostile locals realise we're here.'

Alan of Auge stretched his arms out on the deck and burped.

Raymond turned his nose up. 'I'm going to meet our friends on the beach,' he looked at Richard, 'you and your knights come with me, you at least won't embarrass me by your appearance.'

The water was cold. Richard landed in it waist deep, wearing his two mail shirts and the Little Lord's old sword. The sword belt submerged straight away and Richard groaned loudly. He knew seawater rusted metal nearly as badly as horse sweat did.

Bowman splashed into the sea next to him and water sprayed up onto the rest of Richard's mail.

'Did you have to do that?' Richard asked.

Bowman held his very dry sword belt wrapped up over itself above his head and grinned. 'No.'

The four of them waded ashore, Nicholas having been given the white Papal banner to hold.

'Unfurl it,' Raymond said.

Nicholas did so as he pushed his legs through the swell. The banner unfurled with a snap and the wind blew it straight out of his hands. It landed next to him in the foaming waves and he had to jump to scoop it up. Nicholas raised the wet banner aloft and held it tightly. This time he was able to reached dry land without letting go.

'No one say a word,' Raymond said, 'that never happened.'

Seagulls fought each other loudly on the cliffs and the bushes all leant in the direction of the wind.

The handful of Irishmen on the beach looked like Eva's companions had in Normandy, except for one.

The monk stepped forwards and bowed to Raymond. 'I am Magnus, but you can call me Brian,' he held a brown cloak around himself that flapped in the wind. 'I am here to guide you.'

His accent was the same as Eva's.

'You're a Christian monk?' Raymond asked.

Brian nodded. 'Ireland is a pious land, but most follow the wrong Christian doctrine. I follow the Pope and it is my wish to replace the clergy, monks, and nuns we have here with correct ones from England.'

'Ah,' Raymond replied, 'so that's why you are helping us. Plant that banner in the sand, boy. Plant it deep.'

Nicholas jammed the banner into the sand as far as he could, then let it go.

'Our ancestors planted the Papal banner on the south coast of England a hundred years ago,' Raymond said, 'now we do the same here. This is the beginning of a new age for Ireland. A Norman age.'

Richard felt a shiver run down his spine, but that might just have been the wind on his his wet tunic and mail.

'A great day,' Brian said, 'the Lord blesses us. But we must not tarry here, the Irish in Waterford will hear of your landing before long. You must get off the beach.'

Raymond shrugged. 'I do not fear the local savages. No offence.'

Brian cocked his head. 'None taken.'

The monk was young, Richard's age, and unlike all the other Irishmen on the beach, had a shaved face.

Raymond bowed to the Irish men who Richard assumed were the local and loyal nobility. They bowed back and one offered bread, another salt. Raymond pretended to be impressed and then waved to the ships. The hard work was about to begin.

For the rest of the day they ferried men, horses, stakes, arrows, lances, shields, saddles, and food onto the beach. By the time night fell, Richard could hardly see the sand for everything they had unloaded. Welshmen climbed the cliffs in the dark with stakes over their shoulders, and Raymond led them to their new home. The promontory followed a short path that snaked along the top of the cliff to the left. The headland was already just several hundred paces wide, but they turned off it and into an ancient fort with an entrance only two hundred paces across. All around the promontory were jagged cliffs and the droning sea. When inside the fort, Richard had to raise his voice to he heard over the wind and the crashing waves below.

The horses were led up in the dark, and more than one man cried out when his foot was stamped under a hoof. Richard took Solis himself, and although the horse snorted the whole way up, he mercifully kept his footing. The horses were hobbled within the fort and trusted not to fall into the sea. Ancient earthworks lay around the mouth of the fort and the Welsh dug all night to refresh and deepen them. Richard and everyone else worked all night to carry every last item up from the beach. As the sun poked up over the sea to the east the next morning, he had never felt so tired. His eyes itched and whenever he wasn't moving he felt himself staring off into space. A noise hummed inside the back of his head.

Alan and his knights were the last men into the fort in the morning, and they looked too well rested for Richard's liking.

'Where have you been all night?' Richard asked as they walked through the Welsh digging party.

'Guarding the beach,' Alan said.

'From under a blanket?'

'Why not, it was a cold night.'

Richard scowled but was too exhausted to jam a pickaxe into his head.

Raymond worked non-stop. He moved from one place to another to check on progress and issue orders.

'He's inhuman,' Nicholas said as he stood next to Richard in the fort. Richard had taken his mail off and laid it on the ground to dry in the wind, then he'd wrapped himself in his cloak.

'If he works all night, then everyone else will, too,' Richard said, 'or nearly everyone else.'

Bowman dropped a pile of bow staves onto the ground. 'That is the beach clear,' he said, 'but I think I'm now too tired to sleep.'

Nicholas brought up the Papal banner, which he had furled

up again.

'Stick that in the ground by that old building,' Raymond pointed towards a square of stones as tall as Richard. The walls had stones missing and no roof, but it was the only structure on the site.

Raymond admired the banner. 'Glorious, isn't it? Get some sleep, take a few hours of rest until midday. The Welsh will dig us a deep ditch, and then pits beyond it.'

Richard lay down to sleep inside the shelter of the ancient building, its failing walls shielding him from the worst of the wind. He shut his eyes for a moment but then the sun was at its peak and Raymond stood over him nudging him with his mailed foot.

'You've had enough sleep to avoid madness, so now you're back to work.'

'What's the rush?' Richard asked.

Raymond pointed towards the rest of Ireland. 'Out there, the savages are gathering, arming, swelling their numbers. They are going to come here and try to push us off their cliffs. Until the mouth of the promontory is fully fortified, and food and water is safely stored behind it, we are dead men here.'

Richard got to his feet and stretched his neck.

'You and your knights will deal with the food. We need livestock inside this fort. Ireland is fat with cattle I'm told,' Raymond said, 'so it should be easy enough to bring some here.'

'You want us to steal cattle.'

'Yes, don't go so far you can't find your way back, mind,' Raymond said, 'but don't come back empty-handed.'

Richard poked Bowman with the scabbard of the Little Lord's sword until he woke up.

'Get that thing out of my face,' Bowman batted it away and yawned.

'Take the Irishmen with you, their horses shouldn't slow you down too much, but they know the land,' Raymond left them to finish waking up.

They mounted their horses with bleary eyes and rode out of the fort. The Welsh had left a channel of grass untouched by their renovations, and eight Irishmen on their small horses led Richard, Bowman and Nicholas out into the mainland of

Ireland.

They rode along the cliff above the beach and for a while could see the sea on either side of them. Soon enough though, they were inland, where Ireland didn't look all that different to England.

'It is green,' Nicholas said, 'and flat.'

'Do you trust these Irish?' Bowman looked ahead to the eight men who they followed.

'Not really,' Richard said, 'but they're here and what choice do we have? Do you know where to find cattle without them?'

'They don't look as high in status as the men who were with Eva in Normandy,' Bowman said.

Richard could see he was right. These riders wore just their tunics, no armour and carried only three shields between them. Richard had not thought twice about donning his double mail, slinging his shield and lacing his helmet onto his head. The lesson he'd learnt from Sir Wobble was to never forgo armour for comfort. Therefore, the three knights rode fully armed, including lances.

'Why do they keep looking back to us?' Nicholas said.

'Either they don't trust us either,' Bowman said, 'or we're slowing them down.'

'Or both,' Richard looked out over the meadows and land left to waste all around. They went by the occasional scatted roundhouse, but nothing that looked like a village. There weren't scattered houses like that in England, Normandy or even Brittany, for all were collected up into villages around manors or castles.

'This is a backwards place,' Richard mused to himself as the landscape opened out. Some of the bracken that had been common near the coast thinned out and was replaced by tall grasses and small woods.

'No cattle though,' Nicholas said glumly after a considerable time in the saddle.

'Where are cattle?' Richard shouted to the Irishmen, who had taken to riding even further out in front.

Two of them turned back, shouted something in reply, then laughed.

'Well, that helped,' Bowman spat onto the side of the track.

After a while the wind dropped and the roar of the sea faded away to silence. More land left as waste contained green grass and trees, and Richard could start to see raised ground in the distance. He wondered if it might be time to turn back when one of the Irishmen pointed off to their left. Richard craned his neck to see what he was pointing at, but could only see a long but low hillock. It looked black rather than green.

'Those are cattle,' Bowman said.

'Really?'

'Can't you see?' Nicholas said, 'they're moving. Not much, but that hill is crawling with them.'

An Irish rider said something that sounded like a command. When he got only blank faces in return, he gestured in a sweeping motion towards the hill and back towards Baginbun Head.

'They want us to go around the cows,' Richard said, 'then herd them back to the fort.'

'We should have brought that little monk to translate,' Bowman said.

'Maybe we don't need him, let's follow them,' Richard looked to the Irishmen who pushed their horses on to a gait that looked like a quicker amble. Richard had to trot to go the same speed, and the party took a wide curve around the herd on the hillock.

Once on the far side, everyone started to spread out in order to push the black cows back to where they wanted them.

Solis sniffed the air and coughed as they drew closer to the herd, and Bowman's horse arched its neck and snorted.

'They aren't sure,' Richard said.

'I don't blame them,' Bowman said, 'that's a lot of cows and they are the same size as those little Irish horses.'

'They have horns, too,' Nicholas shouted from further away.

The smell from the herd soaked into Richard's nose with an intensity that was overpowering. They mooed constantly and pulled grass up loudly. The first cows to notice them turned and regarded the horsemen. Most started to walk away, pushed into their fellows, and made them walk, too. The movement rippled along the herd and it started to slowly edge in the right direction. Some cows stood their ground against the smaller

Irish horses to start with, but all moved away from the knight's larger animals.

One cow pawed the ground and charged at one of the Irishmen. His little horse spun to escape and the man slid off its back. The cow ran him over in a flurry of small hooves and he yelped in pain.

Richard cantered Solis towards the cow to push it back towards its fellows. The animal had black eyes that blazed with anger, and Richard wondered if it was a bull. Solis pinned his ears back and lashed out with his teeth. The cow's bravado evaporated and it bounded back into the herd at full speed, crashed into it, and sent other cows barrelling into others.

A moment later and half the herd broke off and started a stampede.

The Irishman on the ground rubbed an ankle and shouted something rapidly at Richard.

'I think he wants us to get those back,' Bowman shouted from across the meadow.

Richard felt a pang of responsibility and pointed Solis in the same direction as the break-away cows. He held the reins out and kicked the stallion into a gallop. The horse put his head down and raced alongside the stampeding cattle. They jumped a dense hedge and thorns caught Richard's legs.

'Get in front of them,' Bowman shouted from behind, and Richard felt glad he wasn't alone.

The cows were fast, but their horses were much faster. Solis skidded on some shorter grass when Richard turned to cut the stampede off. The palomino, ear's still back, managed to keep his footing and flew in front of the cows. They turned away from him.

Bowman caught up and raced past. 'Hold them here and I'll guide them back,' he shouted.

Richard's breaths were short, and as soon as the cows were redirected by Bowman's black horse, they made their way happily back to the rest of the herd.

Once there, they settled back into a walk and Richard and Bowman exchanged a relieved look.

'You nearly lost them,' Bowman grinned.

The Irishman had remounted his horse, which hadn't gone

far, and nodded towards Richard slowly. The man had mud smeared across his tunic and looked like he was in pain but wanted to hide it.

'I'm not sure if you impressed him or not,' Bowman said.

'Who cares,' Richard said, 'we've got hundreds of cattle for Raymond.'

Nicholas rode over towards them, then pointed behind them. 'What's that?'

Richard turned but didn't see anything.

'That is sun reflecting on metal,' Bowman said.

'Where?'

Bowman pointed to the north. 'There. Open your eyes, young lord.'

Richard saw it. Then another flash further along the hill line. 'Someone's there,' he said.

'Obviously,' Bowman said, 'but the Irish cannot already know of our arrival, can they?'

Richard looked back at the cows who made steady progress in the direction of Baginbun Head. 'I think the cattle are under control, we need to find out if that is an army or just a farmer with a polished spade.'

Bowman pursed his lips. 'We should go back, I'd rather not run into an army with just the three of us,' he said.

Richard patted Solis on the neck, who stretched down and started to eat the long grass around them while they remained stationary.

'Raymond will want to know if that's an army, we do need to check. I know our horses want a rest, but we can outrun any Irish cavalry.'

Bowman pulled a face showing his disagreement.

'We could wait on the hillock and watch to see if they come, is that acceptable?' Richard asked.

'Fine, but we shouldn't go cantering right over to them if they're an army, we don't want to get too close.'

One of the Irish riders came back to see why the three of them had stopped. Bowman pointed him towards the reflecting metal, and the young native man with a respectable beard tugged on it. He said something.

Richard sighed. 'We can't understand you,' he pointed back to the hill, then to the three of them, and then to his eyes.

The Irishman laughed and nodded. He shouted something over to his comrades, one of whom rode over to join them. The rest continued driving the herd back to safety.

'I suppose they want to stay with us,' Bowman said.

'They're welcome too,' Richard pulled Solis's reluctant head up from the grass and walked him back to the crest of the hill where they'd found the cattle.

They watched and waited for long enough that their new herd disappeared over the horizon. The reflecting metal shone out in the distance here and there but didn't seem to be going anywhere.

'That's not just one farmer, or one wagon,' Nicholas said.

Richard thought he was probably right. 'As soon as you can make out spears or shields, we can go,' he said.

'I don't like it,' Bowman said, 'I feel like I'm being watched.'

The sun hovered not too far above the horizon to the west.

'We'll be riding back in the dark as it is already,' Nicholas said, 'should we go back now?'

Richard shook his head. 'Our horses can see in the dark. What will Raymond say if we return now, not knowing if we're about to be attacked by the natives or not?'

'If a horse breaks its leg on the way back, what will we do then?' Nicholas replied.

'Going back would be what fat-Alan would do,' Richard said, 'do you want to be like him?'

Nicholas let his horse's head down to eat and kept quiet.

Without the sun's power, and standing still, a coolness started to fall on them as they watched and waited.

'The reflections haven't moved for ages,' Bowman said, 'perhaps they're making camp.'

That was almost worse, Richard thought. Then they might have to ride closer to check.

'Don't even think about it,' Bowman watched Richard.

'Don't worry,' he replied, 'I'm not riding any closer. It's been a long time, maybe we should just go now.'

Richard pulled Solis's head up from the grass. A wedge of long green blades stuck out from either side of his mouth and he struggled to pull them past the bit and into his mouth to chew.

Richard turned him back towards Baginbun Head and froze.

'Look there,' he pointed, 'what's that?'

Something moved in the distance between them and Baginbun Head, but the sun was halfway gone and he couldn't make out what it was.

Bowman snapped his head around to see. 'Oh no.'

'What?'

Bowman pulled his own horse's head up. 'We may have underestimated the locals,' he said.

Nicholas swore. 'They must have seen us before we saw them, so they gave us something to look at.'

Richard's blood ran cold, how could he have been so stupid?

'Those are spear points bobbing above the ground, they've ridden around us in a depression in the ground,' Bowman said.

The two loyal Irishmen exchanged hurried words and started to ride off.

'We should follow them,' Bowman said.

'I hope they know what they're doing,' Richard clenched his lance and kicked his surprised stallion on.

As soon as they broke into a canter, Richard realised it was too dark to go that fast. He caught up with the Irishmen quickly but had to hold Solis back to stay with them. His horse stumbled on something and Richard had to fight to keep his balance. He felt real worry. How would they be able to avoid the enemy in the dark?

The answer when it came, was not very well. The track turned through a hedge and the five of them rode straight into three Irish cavalrymen. Unlike the two loyal Irishmen, these wore leather body armour and had round shields. The three newcomers held their spears aloft, cried out and charged. They thrust down with their spears at the two loyal Irishmen, and in a moment both had fallen from their horses.

Richard, Bowman and Nicholas all lowered their lances and crashed into them. Solis knocked one horse clean over and Bowman skewered one opponent through his chest, leather armour or not. The third kept going through and away from them, turning only to check he wasn't being pursued being fleeing into the night.

'Are you alright?' Richard asked the Irishman who'd earlier

been unhorsed by the angry cow.

The man had a gash across his forehead and blood poured into his eye. He looked dazed.

'We need to go,' Bowman shouted, 'I can hear hooves but I don't know where they are.'

Richard put his lance in his rein hand so he could offer a free hand to the man on the floor. 'Come on,' Richard shouted to snap him out of his malaise.

The Irishman looked up, his eyes flashed into life, and he clasped Richard's hand. Richard hauled him up behind his saddle.

The second unhorsed Irishman's horse had stayed around, and he remounted despite a bent looking arm.

'Move, follow me,' Bowman urged his horse on. He rode through some small bushes and Richard followed.

'I'm right behind you,' Nicholas shouted as they all cantered back towards Baginbun.

'No one was asking,' Bowman replied.

They charged across green meadows with no idea where the track was. More than once a horse jumped a small clump of earth because it couldn't tell how big an obstacle it was. Richard trusted Bowman to be going the right way, even though there was nothing but the stars to guide him. The moon was bright enough, but frequently hid behind clouds and darkened their path.

Richard realised they were going the right way only when Solis jumped over a huge cow-pat he'd nearly stepped in.

Bowman eased his horse down and stopped.

They all caught their breath and listened into the night. It was hard to hear anything over the breathing of their horses, and Richard could feel Solis's lungs expand and contract beneath him. When men and animals calmed, Richard could hear crickets chirp all around, but no hooves.

'I think we outran them,' Nicholas said.

'Charging around in the dark is just as dangerous for them as it is for us,' Bowman said, 'they probably gave up.'

'I think I can hear the sea,' Richard said.

Bowman nodded. 'I can hear the cattle, too.'

Richard couldn't, but he could tell which way led back to

safety so they started to ride slowly back.

They reached Baginbun Head just as the cattle finished making their way through the channel left in the defences. The entire promontory behind the Welsh ditches turned into a packed cattle paddock as they filled the fort, a sight which drew a cheer from the Welsh. Richard had to use Solis to clear a path through mooing cows to reach the old stone building where he offloaded his wounded Irishman. His companion with the bent arm was also taken there, and his countrymen started to treat their wounds.

Raymond arrived with his red cloak flapping in the breeze. 'I don't think we could fit even one more cow in here,' a wide grin spread across his face.

One cow tried to nibble his cloak and he had to shoo it away.

'We ran into the Irish,' Richard said.

'I gathered,' Raymond glanced over to what was now their hospital building, 'how many did you see?'

'Three?' Richard said.

'Three?' Raymond laughed, 'if only three come to fight us, all this digging will have been in vain. The Welsh will be furious.'

'There were more,' Bowman said, 'they let us see them in the distance, then rode around behind to cut us off. I'd wager a few hundred.'

Raymond scratched his cheek. 'A few hundred naked pagans won't make it through the arrows and the ditches,' he said.

Richard hoped he was right, and he did feel safer behind their fortifications.

'They have no knowledge of warfare,' Raymond continued, 'they have not read Vegetius. I say let them come, it shall give us something to do. I look forward to getting the measure of our opponents.'

'They laid a trap for us,' Richard said, 'so they must have known we were coming.'

'Nonsense,' Raymond flapped at a cow to make it go away, 'it was probably merely an accident that they got behind you. And how could they know we were coming, this expedition was planned with the utmost secrecy.'

Richard wrinkled his nose up at the smell of the cattle.

'You'll get used to them,' Bowman smiled, 'although I think

we should eat a few tonight. Might teach the rest some respect.'

Two young cows knocked over a pile of lances and the shafts spilled onto the grass.

'Do the Irish have archers?' Richard looked at the old stones that would provide cover behind their earthworks.

'Doubtful,' Raymond said, 'the Irish I'm told do not even take prisoners or ransom captives. They just kill them, imagine that. There's no profit in their wars, and that is why their armies are full of boys. You'll see, when they charge straight at us and we cut them down, you'll see.'

Raymond left them and started shouting in Welsh. Some of the archers selected a cow and went about slaughtering it for food.

'We'll eat well now, at least,' Nicholas said, 'I'm so hungry.'

They let their horses go and they stuck together as an equine herd in a sea of cattle.

'We need to put the lances and arrows in the hospital,' Richard said, 'before those cursed animals trample everything to pieces.'

They tidied up everything left vulnerable to inquisitive cattle as Alan and his knights watched from a ditch. Soon the Welsh had lit several fires and started to cook beef.

Richard felt his mouth water, his hunger the only thing keeping tiredness from him as he sat down for the first time since his short sleep that morning.

They ate the best beef they'd ever tasted as the sea crashed below them and cows mooed. The Welsh started to put a roof over the hospital made of lances in case it rained, and as soon as Richard's belly was full, he fell asleep, in the certain knowledge that the enemy was on the way.

THE BATTLE OF THE BAG

First light brought a change in the wind. The promontory fort pointed east out into the sea, with its new defensive ditch across its narrow neck to its west. The wind now blew from the east, bringing with it cool air.

Richard stood in the channel into the fort and admired the handiwork of the archers. A deep ditch provided the main defence, and directly behind that were the waist-high old stone walls of the ancient fort. Out in front of the ditch a myriad of knee-deep pits lay scattered to slow down infantry and discourage cavalry. The wooden stakes that had been imported from Wales had been jammed into the big ditch to make it harder for anyone to climb up and reach the archers. A row of dense stakes had been driven into the ground inside the fort and behind the channel that had been left open, just so there was something in the way, but also to help keep the cattle inside.

Richard kicked away a young cow that licked his cloak.

'They don't respect people,' Bowman said, 'and barely those small horses the locals have, either.'

'They respected our horses,' Richard grinned.

'Ours have more attitude. The cows do taste good, too,' Bowman patted his stomach, 'whatever happens, at least we'll fight with full stomachs.'

The wind blew the waves onto the bottom of the promontory harder than before and spray sometimes drifted up and over them.

'Everything is going to rust,' Richard looked down at his sword, the pommel of which had already gathered an orange tinge.

Bowman brushed some spray from his face. 'I hope the barrels of drink don't spoil, otherwise this place is a death-trap. What was it called again?'

'Bun-something,' Nicholas arrived and stretched out as the sun fully rose above the sea behind them.

'Bag-something, I thought,' Richard said.

'Feels like a bag,' Bowman said, 'and this neck is the drawstring.'

'That doesn't make me feel better,' Richard said.

Raymond pushed three cows out of the way to reach them. His hands looked big enough to pick up a cow in each. 'Are you ready for another ride, boys?'

Richard stared blankly back at him and Bowman shrugged.

'It has to be you, I'm afraid,' Raymond said, 'I can hardly send the other so-called knights out, can I?'

'You could,' Bowman said, 'then we wouldn't have to look at their ugly faces all day.'

'I need men who can ride fast to go and see if the natives are really marching to war already.'

'I see,' Richard said, 'I suppose we can go, they can't be far away.'

'Excellent,' Raymond replied.

'I don't think we need to bother,' Bowman said.

'Don't question me,' Raymond replied, 'I thought I could rely on you three.'

'No,' Bowman said, 'listen.'

'I can only hear the sea crashing and cows farting,' Raymond said.

A mist of sea-spray coated them again. It went in Richard's mouth and he tasted the salty water with disgust.

Bowman glanced over to the Welsh, some of whom had their ears pricked and looked out towards the mainland.

Raymond followed Bowman's gaze. He turned to the Welsh and shouted loudly. The less alert ones sprung up and suddenly men rushed everywhere, grabbing bows and sheaves of arrows.

The cows sensed activity and mooed even louder.

'Do we mount up or man the walls?' Richard asked.

'I need all knights to block the channel,' Raymond said, 'the nine of you should be able to keep their rabble out.'

'Time to get your mail shirts on,' Bowman said to Richard.

Richard agreed and they ran to their piles of belongings in the rustic hospital. Richard slipped on both mail shirts and slung his shield. He took two lances to use as spears and went with Bowman and Nicholas to the stakes that had been planted in the middle of the channel. The gap on either side of the stakes was three men wide, so Richard and his companions took up places in one of the gaps.

A while later Alan and his mercenary knights blocked the other gap. Alan's face twitched as he scanned the horizon, which was a low green hill several bowshots away.

The archers kept ferrying arrows to their positions, until every stone wall was covered in ammunition. Other arrows were stuck into the ground all around.

Richard heard voices drift over the hill in the distance, even though it was very much against the wind. The Welsh completed their preparations, now with lances lying to hand for all of them if their arrows failed to stop an attack.

Richard suddenly needed to pass water.

'Is that singing?' Nicholas asked.

Bowman nodded. 'The Welsh do this too.'

As if they had been listening, the Welsh archers started up a song of their own. As the wind blustered into their backs, they sung a low mournful tune that made the hair on Richard's neck stand up. He changed the grip on his spear.

Raymond walked up and down the fortification and spoke to men all along it.

He reached the stakes in the channel. 'If they charge here, the Welsh will shoot into their flanks, you only need to hold them back, don't take any risks to strike. Your job is to hold your ground and stay alive.'

Richard nodded.

Alan's red face paled.

'This is what you're getting paid for,' Raymond said to him, 'if you do your job you can eat a whole side of beef tonight if you want to.'

Alan didn't find that funny, and his companions didn't either.

'They're here,' Bowman said.

A line of men walked onto the crest of the small hill on the horizon. They stopped at the crest and stood motionless with their spears resting on the ground beside them.

'Less than a hundred,' Raymond spat salt water onto the grass.

'They're naked,' Richard said.

'They are showing their bravery by forgoing armour,' Raymond said, 'but I would use another word for it.'

'Stupid,' Nicholas said.

'Something like that,' Raymond grinned, 'a hundred naked men won't even reach you here, Sir Alan.'

Sir Alan turned and threw up. One of his companions followed suit.

Raymond sighed and turned to Richard. 'We Normans have a reputation to uphold, and Strongbow sends me men like that.'

Richard couldn't help sniggering.

'Here they come,' Nicholas said from beside him.

The naked natives marched down the hill and towards the neck of the promontory.

Archers nocked arrows ready to draw. Another second line of men appeared on the hill.

'There you go,' Bowman laughed, 'maybe there's enough of them for a real fight.'

'Don't get too excited,' Raymond left them and walked over to command the archers.

A group of horsemen appeared on the hill as the second wave of warriors started their approach.

'Those men have helmets,' Richard squinted to see them.

'And mail shirts,' Bowman said, 'but they're short-sleeved.'

'Old fashioned,' Nicholas said.

The sound of song still floated over from behind the hill, but the Welshed ceased their chorus as the first hundred natives approached.

The loyal Irishmen who hadn't been trampled by cows stood behind the Welsh, their short spears at the ready.

A third group of Irish walked over the hill, but they marched rank after rank deep.

'More than a few hundred, then,' Bowman muttered.

'You were right,' Richard said, 'I hope we have enough

arrows.'

'I doubt it,' Bowman replied and shifted his shield around.

Raymond shouted a command and the Welsh drew their bows. The naked Irish reached the pits and their line broke up as they picked their way through.

Raymond waited until they were nearly right up to the big ditch before he dropped his arm and shouted.

The enemy were so close that Richard could make out their bearded faces.

The first volley of arrows twanged as one, a loud noise that made the cattle nearest to Richard jump. The arrows flew dead straight, and at such short range few missed. Natives were knocked backwards or to the ground. Others sprinted on and started to descend into the earthen ditch.

Raymond shouted something else and the archers took their own shots. Arrows flew into the Irish and almost instantly they all lay dead or wounded, most with more than one arrow in them.

The second wave of Irish, who were at least clothed in earthy-coloured tunics, charged.

The twang of bowstrings hummed all around and arrows started to create gaps in the attackers. They bunched up to run around the pits, and attracted a storm of arrows as they did so. The attackers thinned out as they reached the ditch, and a handful of them sprinted down the channel and straight at Richard.

Two were struck by arrows from the side and fell onto the grass holdings thighs or chests.

Richard held his spear overhead and tensed his body.

Two Irishmen ran at their three-man shieldwall. They avoided the three spears and thudded into the knight's shields.

As an Irishman bounced off Richard's shield, he thrust down with his spear. The blade caught the native in the abdomen and he fell backwards onto the ground.

Bowman and Nicholas both stabbed the other attacker at the same time. When he hit the ground he was already dead.

Richard's victim stayed down and clutched his stomach as he screamed.

Alan and his knights had managed to kill the two men who

had reached them, too, but they fidgeted and looked down at the wounded man writhing before Richard.

'Put him out of his misery,' Bowman said.

Richard went to step forwards.

'Do not move out of line,' Raymond shouted.

Richard took the step back and watched as the man bled onto the flattened grass.

The third wave of Irish stopped flooding over the hill.

'A thousand?' Nicholas asked.

'I'm not counting,' Bowman said.

'That's not all of them,' Nicholas added as yet more infantry appeared on the brow of the hill around their horsemen.

'I think we're going to have a long day,' Richard said and looked up from the man who still cried in agony in front of them. Other wounded men littered the approach to the fort.

The mass of natives reached the pits, and those on the channel started to run along it towards them.

'This is going to hurt,' Bowman crouched slightly to brace for impact.

Arrows smacked into the sides of the howling natives who charged down the channel. Men fell and others tripped over their arrow-riddled bodies. Their casualties slowed them down, but they still shouted war cries as they reached the stakes and Richard.

Richard tensed as the bearded Irishmen raised their small round shields and smashed into their shieldwall. Richard knocked a spear aside with his and held his shield up to his eyes. A spear glanced off his own helmet. He thrust down into the face of an opponent who fell.

'They don't have helmets,' Bowman shouted as his spear cut into a face.

An Irishman grabbed Richard's spear with his hands and tried to tug it from his grip. Richard tried to pull it away, then gave up and thrust it forwards instead. The man's eyes looked up in horror as he pulled the iron blade into his own chest. Two others grabbed the spear and suddenly Richard had nothing in his hands. A spear point cut into the top of his shield and a splinter of wood came away.

He drew the Little Lord's sword and flashed it down. It cut

into a spear shaft but Nicholas speared its owner and the spear dropped. Richard's next cut cracked a jaw open and suddenly the enemy backed off.

Richard's lungs heaved and arrows hit the Irish from both sides. The warriors hesitated for a second as their numbers dwindled, then broke and ran.

The Welsh cheered and jeered once the enemy were back out of arrow range. Richard looked at Nicholas and Bowman, who watched the retreat in silence.

Alan waved his spear in the air. 'Run, you cowards,' he shouted.

Richard gave him a sideways glance as Alan's comrade joined in with his celebration.

Bodies lay on the ground up to the ditch, but none had made it up the final bank and to the archers.

'I think our only loss was your spear,' Bowman winked at him.

Richard wiped his sword clean on his cloak and put it away. He stepped forwards over dead bodies and retrieved his spear from the chest of the man who had died to take it.

Wounded attackers cried for help and some dragged themselves to each other. When one man sat up, a Welsh arrow found his neck.

The Irish horsemen up on the hill watched impassively, a great mass of their infantry still all around them.

'How many men do they have?' Nicholas asked.

'More than us,' Bowman replied.

Nicholas frowned.

Raymond shouted to the Welsh but they didn't do anything, so Richard assumed they were just words of encouragement. The cattle mooed behind him again as the wind blew their smell over the battlefield, which he knew later on would be truly foul when it mixed with the smell of death.

Some archers went back into the hospital and came out with extra sheaves of arrows.

Everyone waited in silence as both sides watched each other. Waves crashed below and spray started to eat their armour, but every man waited at his post.

Raymond made his way over to them. 'See, I told you this

would be easy,' he beamed.

Richard re-laced his loosened helmet under his chin. 'Only because we haven't run out of arrows yet.'

Raymond stayed silent longer than Richard would have liked. Then the big man strode off towards the hospital and uprooted the Papal banner. He carried the white flag to the fortifications and stabbed the shaft into the earth. Some men said prayers.

'While this banner stands,' he shouted in Richard's direction, 'we will hold.'

'Does the banner spit out arrows now?' Bowman asked.

Nicholas chuckled.

Richard groaned, for the Irish were on the move. The whole body of men walked towards the fort.

'Kerns,' Raymond shouted, 'keep your shields high.'

'Why?' Richard asked.

'Because they have bows,' Nicholas said.

He was right, for the men that approached, hundreds of them, had round shields and carried bows as well as short spears.

The Welsh nocked fresh arrows and waited. Richard rested his long shield on the ground and prepared to kneel behind it if he needed to.

The kerns halted just before the pits.

'If they can hit us from there, we are in trouble,' Bowman said.

The kerns drew their bows and unleashed a volley at the fort. Hundreds of shafts whistled through the air and Richard found himself marvelling at the sound. He thought it had its own beauty. The arrows didn't reach even reach the ditch, instead many fell on the bodies and wounded men who lay around the last of the pits.

The Welsh jeered, and a few spun around and showed the Irish their naked rears.

Bowman made the sign of the cross.

'I have never seen you do that before,' Richard said.

'I've never thought I was about to resemble a hedgehog before.'

'You still might.'

The kerns moved into the pits and the Welsh ceased their

taunts and prepared themselves. The Irish loosed a volley so quickly Richard never saw them nock. This time the arrows carpeted the main ditch and the stakes that dotted it.

The Welshmen's answering volley, backed by the brisk sea wind, did not fall short. The seventy arrows couldn't miss the kerns, and Irishmen screamed and died as their unprotected heads and chests took the brunt of the volley.

Sir Alan of Auge cheered and swore at the Irish.

Richard thought the kerns would back off now, but to his surprise they pushed on and deeper into the killing ground of the pits.

The second volley of Welsh arrows hit the kerns as they drew their bows. Irishmen dropped in droves even as their own arrows were launched up into the air. More than half fell short, but a few Welshmen reeled back from the wall with arrow wounds.

The archery duel continued for three more volleys before the kerns, at least those who survived, retreated. The Welsh shouted insults at them as they went, then tended to their dead and wounded. These may have been few in number, but there were precious few archers to start with.

'What now?' Richard asked.

'That depends on what else the natives have,' Bowman replied.

'They can't have much, they don't have knights,' Richard said.

Some of the archers left the fortification and started to harvest the arrows from the Irish volleys that had fallen short. Others drew long knives and roved amongst the Irish to finish off the wounded.

'Raymond might have complained about the Irish taking no prisoners,' Richard said, 'but it doesn't look like the Welsh do, either.'

'They do,' Bowman said, 'if you're wearing a mail shirt. They are making sure no one will crawl up on us during the night.'

'And clearing them out of anything valuable,' Nicholas said as one Welshman started to rifle through a dead man's bag. The Irish horsemen withdrew with their infantry, although a cluster of men stayed on the hill. Soon they lit a fire.

'They're deciding what to do next,' Richard said.

Bowman nodded. 'Go home, hopefully.'

Raymond walked over from the stone walls as the more seriously wounded Welshmen were carried into the hospital. Archers with bundles of arrows in their hands stored them safely behind the wall behind the ditch, some kept constantly re-checking them.

'I'd always heard the Welsh were lazy,' Richard said, 'but those ones are putting us to shame.'

Bowman looked at Alan, who had sat down on an old stone. 'Some more to shame than others,' he said.

'How long do we stand here?' Nicholas asked.

'We're going to have to take turns,' Bowman said to his half-brother, 'you're the youngest so you can stay here while we go and eat some more cows.'

'I'm not hungry.' Richard's eyes were drawn down to the red grass and the countless bodies strewn across the neck of Baginbun Head.

'Suit yourself,' Bowman had the sense to walk to Raymond to ask permission to leave the barricades. Bowman came back and nodded.

Richard followed him back into the fort despite his lack of hunger, and into the wind which threw yet more seawater into his face. He wrapped his cloak around his mail, although the cloak was now wet to the touch anyway.

Bowman and some of the archers saw to a cow and started to cook it. The sun reached its highpoint and hung in the sky as both sides took stock of the morning's attack. Richard ate a little, then tried to curl up in his cloak in a corner of the hospital. One of the archers in it had an arrow through his thigh. He argued with two others who clearly wanted to remove it, although Richard couldn't understand their words. The patient won the argument, and the arrow was snapped off and left in. Another Welshman lay on the grass moaning under a pile of cloaks. An arrow had nicked his throat and he'd lost a lot of blood. Richard tore his eyes away from the white face and tried to sleep, but the man moaned every time he dropped off. Richard hadn't slept properly since they'd landed and his head ached. He closed his eyes and tried not to think about battles, screaming or moaning men. He slept fitfully and dreamed of the devastated villages in Brittany where the Martels had piled up bodies and planted their banners in them.

Richard had to replace Nicholas on watch at the stakes before he'd wanted to, so he sat with the stakes behind him to keep the wind and the spray off his back. He watched the hill with the Irish sentries who watched him back. He tried to keep his eyes on them, and waited until the evening came and the light of a hundred fires lit the low clouds behind the hill.

Bowman arrived to take his place. 'That's a lot of fires,' he said.

'I hope it doesn't mean that more are arriving,' Richard said, 'or they'll push us off these cliffs tomorrow.'

Bowman sat down next to him, laid his spear on the ground, and pulled his cloak over himself.

Some Welshmen had built fires across the neck in between the pits. They lit up the killing ground as night fell.

Richard didn't get up to go back to the hospital.

'You want to sleep out here? Amongst the dead?' Bowman asked as crows landed on the battlefield and started to peck out eyes, ' what would a priest say?'

'Rather these silent dead men than the one in the hospital that moans,' Richard replied.

'Suit yourself,' Bowman settled into his place.

Brian the monk wandered over with a bucket of cold water. He squatted down beside them, poured a cup and held it out.

Bowman ignored it.

Richard reached over and took it. The water was cold and he realised he hadn't drunk all day. That was probably why his head ached.

'I always forget to drink, too,' Brian said. His face with its flat nose reflected the light of a fire behind them.

'In all those battles you've fought,' Bowman laughed.

Richard smiled faintly.

Brian refilled Richard's cup. 'Are the priests and monks in England from the warrior class?'

'They are noble-born,' Richard said.

'It is the same here,' Brian passed the cup back, 'I've always wanted to visit England.'

'Don't,' Bowman said.

'And why not?'

'The land is less green than here,' Bowman said, 'and the people are at least as ugly.'

Richard almost found it within himself to laugh, but a flying crow dropped an eyeball and it landed in a red puddle of blood with a horrible splash.

'The cathedrals are said to be a wonder of God,' Brian said, 'and that a man can lose himself in prayer in one for days.'

Bowman snorted. 'Only if one enjoys incense and boredom.'

Brian frowned. 'A man in the situation you are in should look to his soul. This is not the time for blasphemy.'

'I think it is exactly the time for blasphemy,' Bowman ripped up a blade of grass and let the wind take it out into the cold field of corpses.

'I shall pray for you,' Brian said.

'Don't bother,' Bowman said, 'praying never works. I've tried it before and it always makes things worse.'

'Then you have been doing it wrong.'

Richard looked at the young man and saw sincerity. 'I wear a cross on my tunic. I will pay for all my sins in the Holy Land, so there is no need to pray here. Bowman will be coming with me so he can leave the praying until then, too.'

'You might have to drag me there,' Bowman grinned.

'There are many of my countrymen over that hill,' the monk said, 'I would not be so sure either of you will ever reach the Holy Land.'

'And it is that sort of attitude that explains why you are a monk and not a knight,' Bowman said.

'We don't have knights in Ireland.'

'Whatever,' Bowman folded his arms and pulled the hood of his cloak down over his eyes.

'We are all knights of Christ here,' Brian said.

Bowman gently shook his head and groaned under his hood.

'Maybe you should pick up a spear and help us when the time comes,' Richard said.

Brian looked at the two spears that lay on the grass. 'My weapon is the Papal banner, not the blade.'

'I suppose you can still hurt someone with that,' Richard replied.

'This is a serious matter.'

'And I'm sure you can seriously hurt someone with it.'

Brian regarded Richard's face, saw a faint twinkle, then his face cracked and he laughed. 'I heard the English like to drink and laugh.'

'I heard the Irish are pagans, but here you are speaking of the Papal banner.'

Brian sucked in some air. 'The English like to think everyone other than themselves are uncultured oafs,' he said.

'Many of the Irish have come to this battle undressed,' Richard said, 'which seems uncultured to me.'

The Irish firelight shone a dark orange up onto the clouds beyond the hill, and song still beat the wind to drift into Richard's ears.

'My people have a way to go, for sure,' Brian rubbed his chin, 'but the Lord will guide them. Through the Papal church.'

'And Norman iron,' Richard cast his eyes over the battlefield, 'do you not regret the deaths of your countrymen?'

A shadow cast over Brian's face. 'As David had to kill the Philistines to leave Christianity in his wake, so shall we leave a trail of blood.'

Richard chewed his tongue before realising he was doing it. 'I'll leave the bible talk to those who understand it,' he said.

Brian's eyes softened. 'You shouldn't,' he stood up, 'it is your soul, do not trust it to others.'

Richard watched the monk leave and saw the white Papal banner as he looked. A stain from the sea covered it, a yellowish corruption that leaked across the pure fabric.

Bowman pushed his hood back. 'You know that banner isn't from Rome?'

Richard furrowed his brow. 'But it's the Papal banner?'

'That's what Raymond says it is,' Bowman said, 'but have you looked at it up close?'

Richard shook his head. 'Why would I?'

'Exactly. The sewing looks like I did it after too much wine.'

'So?'

'A true Papal banner should be a thing of beauty, I would think,' Bowman said, 'this one is thin, you can almost see through it. It only has two colours. It looks to me as if someone threw it together at the last moment.'

'You don't know it's a fake, then, you just think it might be?'

Bowman shrugged under his cloak as a thin cloud of spray drifted over the cliffs, landed on some fires and made them sizzle.

'I don't really care,' Richard said, 'I just want those natives to leave.'

'They aren't done yet.'

The wounded man groaned in the hospital loud enough to hear and Richard shivered.

'Don't mind him,' Bowman said.

'I can't not. Did I ever tell you about the crippled veterans I saw in Lillebonne?'

'No.'

'I see them when I think of battle. Missing eyes and limbs,' Richard said, 'it's going to happen to me. It already has, I'm missing a finger and I think it might happen again here.'

'You already danced with a missing eye,' Bowman said, 'and you won that one. Worry not.'

Richard couldn't help it, and he also knew he wouldn't sleep well that night. He touched the scar that cut down his face and shuddered.

'Find some ale, young lord,' Bowman said, 'the Welsh will see your eyes and take pity on you.'

Richard didn't want pity. He wanted to be back home. He remembered his yearning for travel and felt guilt. Guilt for his wife and his children. 'I should never have left them,' he mumbled.

Bowman pretended not to hear and pushed himself to his feet. 'I'm going to test the Welsh hospitality,' he said.

Richard was left alone with his back leaning on the stakes defending the grass channel. Although since the attacks the grass had been overtaken by drying mud.

He felt the weight of his two mail shirts on his shoulders but if he didn't move he could forget about them. His eyes stuck on the Irish watch fire in the distance, and his mind disengaged. Numb, Richard tried not to think as the waves crashed into the rocks below and cattle moved restlessly behind him.

Bowman sat by Richard as much later the darkness softened. Seagulls whirled overhead and the Welsh prepared another cow for eating.

'I don't think I'm going to eat beef after this,' Richard licked his cracked lips, 'or wish to add salt to my food.'

Nicholas had returned at some point while Richard had drifted off to sleep. The young man now stood next to him, armed and ready.

Welshmen stirred and a few had gone out to drag Irish bodies into heaps. Richard assumed that was to make the neck of Baginbun even harder to traverse.

The moaning man in the hospital hadn't made a noise for hours, and Richard wondered if he still lived. He caught himself almost hoping not, so he said a prayer for his recovery instead.

Raymond walked from man to man and woke all those who still slept. He reached the channel and looked down at Richard, who was almost entirely covered by his cloak.

'Today will be a day for heroes, boys,' Raymond said.

Richard looked up at him, then had to look up even more due to his height. The look on Raymond's face made Richard think the big man was enjoying himself.

No one answered their leader so Raymond went round to Alan and his knights and kicked them all awake. They cried in annoyance but none dared complain. Alan's face was puffed up from sleep and his eyes blinked as he returned to the world.

Bowman's head turned towards the Irish hill. 'They are not wasting time today,' he said, 'stand up, young lord.'

Richard pushed back his cloak and stood up. He yawned.

The Irish horsemen returned to the top of the hill and were followed by several ranks of infantry who stretched from cliff edge to cliff edge. They stood on top of the hill and banged their spear shafts into their shields. The sound of wood on leather thudded and thumped in a steady rhythm.

The sound fought against that of the waves below, and largely lost.

'They're trying to intimidate us, aren't they,' Richard said.

'Aye,' Bowman said, 'but I don't think they realise our cattle are farting louder than them.'

Nicholas laughed.

'They can waste their time making music as long as they want,' Bowman said.

The Welsh lined their wall and arranged their supply of arrows around themselves. Richard saw four of the loyal Irishmen take up bows and join them.

Richard closed his eyes and found the Irish taunt soothing.

He was woken by Raymond's laugh. 'Look at this one, he's so relaxed he's fallen asleep.'

The large man's laugh echoed around the promontory and Richard realised all of Alan's knights were staring at him. He didn't even remember sitting down, let alone drifting off to sleep, but he got up again and yawned back at his leader.

'All they're doing,' Richard said to him, 'is tiring out their spear-arms.'

Raymond studied Richard. Then he started to laugh.

'The balls on you,' he glanced over towards Alan, 'and unlike those overweight braggarts, you don't feel the need to shout about it.'

Alan pulled a face, and even though he could hear, he turned away and pretended he couldn't.

'They are the weak link,' Raymond said, 'if the fort falls, it will start with them.'

The Irish on the hill beat their shields. Others now descended and approached the promontory.

'The kerns have come back for more,' Nicholas said.

The kerns advanced up to the pits, and to the edge of where the bodies lay. They opened their order and spread out to make harder targets.

'They've learnt, then,' Bowman said grimly.

Richard stood next to the stakes and watched as the Irish archers picked their way into the killing ground in pairs. One man in each pair drew his bow, while the other held both of their shields up to cover the two of them.

'They really have learnt,' Richard felt his mouth go dry.

The Welsh knew their task, and as pairs of kerns fell into range, they were met by flurries of arrows. Shafts buried into the leather covered shields, which were too small, and kerns started to get hit.

The rest continued their advance, stepping over their wounded comrades. Still more men marched over the hill behind them.

'There's thousands of them,' Nicholas whispered.

'Don't get overexcited, it's hundreds,' Bowman said, 'and they'll all die.'

Die they did, but by sheer force of numbers they pushed closer and closer to the fort. Welsh arrows sprung from the fortification like the angry bees of a threatened nest. Arrows started to fly in the other direction and clattered into and over the small stone wall.

A Welshman cried out in pain and another cried out for more arrows.

'They'll die all right,' Richard said, 'but how many of our arrows will it take?'

The pairs of kerns started to reach the big ditch, but that meant the Welsh could shoot along their line and shoot around the shields of the Irish. They fell quickly.

More Welsh archers cried out and fell backwards from their posts as more arrows started to fly into the fort than out of it.

One arrow cleared the Welsh entirely and landed amongst the cattle. It hit a young cow in the flank and the surprised animal crashed into two others. The young cow rebounded into its fellows and suddenly there was a stampede. Richard looked for Solis in case he needed to go and herd them, but he saw his yellow-coated horse canter towards the commotion on his own. The stallion pushed cattle out of the way with his chest, and bit others who moved too slowly. The horse made straight for the startled cattle and slammed to a stop in front of them. The panicked cows lost their panic at the sight of Solis pawing the ground. The cows backed off and immediately lost interest in their stampede.

Raymond laughed from his place in the middle of the archers. 'I'll pay you a knight's fee for his work,' he shouted.

Raymond stood tall behind the short wooden wall, his mailed torso fully exposed to arrows. He turned back to the kerns, many of whom aimed for him, as the Welsh reduced their number. An arrow caught in his cloak and ripped it. Raymond swore at the Irish.

'I can see why Strongbow sent him,' Bowman said.

Hundreds of newly dead kerns littered the neck, and the rest started to pull back out of range.

The Welsh jeered them as they went, but not with the same energy that they had the day before. Many of the archers jumped into the ditch to retrieve unbroken arrows.

Spear-armed Irish infantry poured over the hill like ants fleeing a nest.

'They keep coming. How many of them are left?' Nicholas asked.

'Enough for you to earn your fee,' Bowman picked his shield up and took his position.

The archers, arms filled with bundles of arrows, bounded back behind the wall as the Irish closed in on the pits. One of Alan's knights ran back from the channel and squatted down between two sleeping cows.

More native warriors flooded over the hill. Richard couldn't see the grass at all anymore for their numbers. These warriors were not naked, they wore tunics and most wielded spears with two hands.

'They might as well be farmers,' Bowman said.

'They probably are,' Richard replied as they reached the pits and started to run. Welsh arrows smashed into them and sunk into unarmoured flesh. Men tripped over fallen bodies and trampled them into the ground that grew muddier and muddier. Some of the advancing Irishmen slipped over and were unable to get back up. The torrent of warriors charged on and over them despite withering arrow fire.

'Get ready,' Bowman crouched behind his shield and lifted his spear.

Richard did the same as a mass of Irishmen charged along the channel. Just as during the previous day, arrows started to slam into their flanks.

The Irish shouted war cries and Richard braced. The block of warriors collided into the three of them and sent them two paces backwards. For a terrifying moment Richard was lifted off his feet. When he landed, he stabbed down with his spear and a man fell. Then another. A spear glanced off his helmet and his left ear rang loudly. The lightly armed warriors fell easily and Richard and his friends killed them as they came. Soon their bodies started to block the gap between the stakes, and Richard could use them as a palisade. The Irish facing them hesitated. They saw the death visited upon their fellows, and untouched Norman devils still standing in their path.

'They're scared of us,' Alan cried and giggled.

'I really hate him,' Bowman said through gritted teeth, although his eyes never left the Irish dithering in the channel before them.

Richard recovered his breath as the Irish decided what to do. Along the rest of the line, warriors climbed the upwards slope of the main ditch. The Welsh dropped their bows and started to fight them off with spears. Raymond jumped off the wall and stood halfway down the ditch, pushing past spear points and flashing his sword as if his opponents were mere playthings.

'Should we attack?' Richard said.

Bowman grinned. 'If those fat dogs of war will join us.'

'Alan,' Richard shouted, 'if we charge will you follow?'

The knight in his yellow surcoat with the two red balls on it didn't answer.

Richard turned his head to look at him and shouted again. 'If we attack, they'll run,' Richard said, 'this is the moment.'

Irish warriors started to breach the ditch and jump up to the wall, fencing with the spears of the Welshmen, who started to take casualties.

'God's teeth,' Richard shouted, 'Alan, we're attacking, and if you don't follow, we're all dead.'

Alan's face shone white, even though his spear point shone red.

'If I go, will you go?' Richard asked Bowman and Nicholas.

The younger man looked jittery but nodded. Richard knew Bowman would be beside him.

'Ready,' Richard tested his footing on the corpse wall they needed to climb.

'Go,' he shouted. Richard's feet climbed the soft mountain and he and his comrades reached the mud on the other side. The Irish ahead of them took a step back.

'Charge,' Richard shouted and ran.

Bowman and Nicholas on each side howled and the Irish

backed up more. Richard pushed himself into the dense ranks who stood shaking right in his path, and his shield cracked a nose open. Richard's spear cracked another man's skull, and the rest of the warriors started to flee. Richard caught one last man in the hip and he tripped and fell as his fellows left him alone in front of the stakes in the channel. Richard looked down at the wounded man, who clutched his hip and screamed. Richard thrust down his spear and the man fell silent. He looked back and Alan and his knights started to run over.

The warriors fighting the Welsh heard the rout and backed off. They quickly ran back through the ditch and around the pits.

Bowman whirled to Alan and pointed his spear at his face. 'We aren't robbing nuns now, this is a real fight. Your cowardice could have got us killed.'

'It wasn't cowardice,' Alan backed away from Bowman, 'I just took longer to climb the bodies than you did.'

'There are barely any bodies on your side,' Bowman growled, 'you're just too unfit to lift your legs high enough.'

Raymond appeared, blood dripped from his sword. 'Enough.'

Bowman seethed but Raymond's sudden presence was enough for him to back away.

The Irish went beyond arrow range and regrouped.

'We don't have time for squabbles,' Raymond said, 'we've lost too many of the Welsh. Richard, your charge saved them, and you Sir Alan of Wherever, if you show cowardice again, I'll make your real balls blood-red. Do you understand?'

Alan nodded quickly and retreated back to the stakes.

Raymond looked at Richard with a hard expression. 'They can break through the archers,' he said, 'and now they know it.'

Richard sensed worry in his commander's voice for the first time, and that made Richard nervous.

'Look at them,' Raymond surveyed the mass of warriors in front of the hill, 'there must be two thousand there.'

And less than seventy Welshmen, now, Richard thought.

'I need you and your men to hold the ditch with me,' Raymond said, 'we'll have to leave the stakes to those pigs of war. Hopefully the Irish won't bother to attack here again.'

Richard swallowed, but his throat was so dry it hurt. He

could taste blood on his lips, which he realised he'd done himself by biting them.

'Follow me,' Raymond led them to the stone wall where the Welsh readied the last of their arrows. Archers lay dead with arrows in them or spear wounds that gushed blood. Some went about their work with arrows snapped off and the heads still in them.

The ditch was less than two hundred feet long, and Richard wasn't sure how four men were going to hold it.

Raymond put a giant hand on his shoulder. 'Don't worry, son, you don't need to kill them all, just give the Welsh longer to shoot at them.'

Richard sat down on the wall next to a dead Welshman and glanced down into the ditch. It was steep and deep. The dark brown soil was littered with a hundred corpses and broken arrows.

Richard, Bowman, and Nicholas spread out along the ditch with Raymond and waited for the Irish to try again.

The cattle in the fort had run out of water, and by this time grass to eat, and complained loudly, their cries drowning out the waves below.

Richard felt alone with only archers around him, their faces all set and serious now. There was no singing, no taunting. They had collected all the used arrows and now could only wait.

They didn't have to wait long, for the next assault was made by the entire Irish army. Waves of men crested the hill and approached the killing field. This single unbroken mass of the enemy reached the pits and started to run. They immediately slowed down and broke up into groups to navigate the piles of dead and the pits.

Richard put his spear down on the wall and drew his sword, for the enemy were going to get close to him very quickly.

The Welsh loosed a volley and lightly-armed attackers fell. A second volley caused carnage amongst their ranks but they kept running. Some reached the ditch and jumped across it. One man landed just below Richard so he cut down hard into his shoulder and he fell to the bottom of the earthwork. Arrows flew by his ears and Richard hacked another opponent's arm almost in two.

The noise of battle enveloped him, but this was the loneliest fight Richard had ever fought. A spear stabbed him in the stomach but he only felt a push. The owner of the spear felt his sword. Two others attacked him at once, but a Welshman intercepted one with a spear and Richard cut the other in the face. An Irish arrow sunk into his shield. Some of the attackers jumped the ditch too far away from him, and ran at the wall to fight the archers there.

Richard broke a man's nose with his shield. A spear's blade ran across his arm but his mail deflected it. An arrow hit his shoulder painfully. Richard didn't have time to glance down, but it hadn't penetrated his skin, instead it hung limply from the inner layer of his mail.

Irish kerns scrambled up the ditch around him, and Richard swung his sword without pause at those within range. His arm soon started to feel heavy. His lungs worked hard and he kicked a kern down into the ditch. The Irish attackers started to go around him, leaving Richard as an island in the chaos.

He looked to his left and saw his friends fighting. To his right Alan and his knights held the channel against only a few of the enemy. That was when Richard saw the armoured Irish. A dozen mail-covered men with iron helmets walked calmly down the channel and towards the stakes that Alan defended.

An arrow whizzed past Richard's head.

The well armed Irishmen pushed their way through their unarmoured compatriots and charged at the Normans. The song of metal on metal rang out, a rare song so far in the battle. Alan may have been fat, but he had strength and some of the Irish fell to him. Their swords flashed back, and one of Alan's knights reeled away with a face wound.

Alan took a step away from the enemy. His knights took a step back with him, and the Irish sensed their chance and pushed.

Richard ran across the ditch towards them, the steep slope and loose earth causing his feet to slide and sink as he went. He killed a man fighting with an archer and pushed on. The Norman knights backed up more. They were but a step from conceding the stakes and therefore the fort.

Richard sliced a man's hamstring from behind and jumped up out of the ditch and onto the channel behind the enemy. Richard charged at the Irishmen, who he assumed were their noblemen, from their rear. He cut one's neck and shoved his shield into another. Through their heads he saw Alan run.

Richard was too late.

Alan's Normans backed up as their leader fled into the cattle.

Some of the nobles realised Richard was behind them and turned to face him.

Richard severed the hand of one, but another cut into the mail coif around Richard's neck and he gasped as pain shot down his arm and across his shoulders.

Over the top of the Irish, the Papal banner appeared, and then dropped. Richard saw the white fabric swing back and forth out of the corner of his eye as he smashed the pommel of his sword into a man's bloody face. A sword bounced off the rim of Richard's shield and nicked his cheek. The Irish started to push back towards him, as if fleeing from the banner.

Their mass pushed Richard over backwards and he fell into the mud. His elbow landed hard, and his sword fell from his hand. He grabbed the leg of an Irish noble and the man fell next to him with a spray of mud. Richard drew Sir John's dagger and stabbed through the Irishman's mail coat. The mail slowed his blade but a final push sent it between two ribs. The nobles fled. One kicked Richard in the face as he went, leaving mud in his mouth. The fleeing nobles ran beyond Richard, and beyond him, in front of the stakes, stood Brian the monk, the Papal banner in his hands. The shaft had blood on it's end and Brian looked down at Richard.

'You may have been correct about the banner,' he said, 'you can indeed hurt people with it.'

Richard sheathed his dagger and collected his sword. 'I think you saved my life,' he said.

'You probably saved mine,' Brian looked up at the banner, 'although I had expected the banner to be more impressive.'

Alan's knights reappeared at the stakes and reformed their shieldwall. Alan joined a moment later.

Richard checked where the Irish had gone. Their mailed opponents had stopped their retreat out of arrow range, but the rest of the army still poured across and into the ditch. Raymond and Bowman still fought furiously, although Richard couldn't see Nicholas.

'They're being pushed back,' Richard said, 'I need to help them.'

He pushed through the mercenaries, who avoided eye contact, and ran back along the inside of the wall.

Arrows flew overhead into the fort and Bowman backed up the ditch and hopped over the wall. Even Raymond, his sword arcing left and right, was pressed up the ditch one hard-fought step at a time.

Flames in the corner of Richard's eye caught his attention. The Welsh had laid some lances over the top of the hospital to act as a roof, but this now burned.

'They've broken through,' Richard shouted mostly to himself. A handful of Irish were trying to fight their way in to the hospital. The wounded Welsh inside thrust spears out through the gaps in the walls to keep them at bay.

Richard sprinted. He had to dodge a roaming cow but crashed into the first Irish kern he found. The man bounced off Richard and smashed his face on the hospital stones.

Another Irishman climbed onto the roof and thrust his spear down between the lances.

Nicholas loosed an arrow from the ground and the man twisted as it pierced his throat.

Two of the kerns rushed Nicholas. A third ran into the hospital, but the fourth and fifth attacked Richard.

He let one spear hit his shield and flicked the second away with his sword. Richard rammed himself into that kern and jammed his crossguard into his face. As that opponent staggered away, the other stabbed at Richard's foot under his shield. The spear point hit his little toe and Richard heard mail rings crunch. He screamed. His foot exploded in agonising pain and red anger coursed through his veins. He thrashed his sword down and the kern blocked it with his spear shaft. Richard, unusually, was bigger than his opposition, so he battered down with his sword again and gouged wood out of the spear shaft.

The kern dropped to a knee under the blow.

Richard's next strike, rage-fuelled, cut through the spear and left the Irishman staring at his snapped weapon. He never looked at anything else again, as Richard dealt him his death blow. Without pause, Richard ran into the hospital and collided with the kern who had entered it.

Richard dropped his sword as the Irishman bounced off him. The Kern had a long knife in his hand and he lunged. Richard didn't move out of the way quick enough and it sheared one layer of mail open down his side. The arrow that had caught in his shoulder flapped up and hit him in the nose. Still angry, Richard grabbed the arrow, pulled it free, and stuck in straight in the Irishman's eye. His opponent howled, then his chest exploded as the wounded Welshman who had moaned all night drove the spear that had fallen through the roof into him. The victim's look of surprise as he sunk to the grass broke Richard's rage. He nodded at the stricken Welshman, who coughed in the smoke, and Richard felt very bad for nearly wishing him dead.

To help to sooth his guilt, Richard dragged him out of the smoky space by his shoulders, then looked for Nicholas. Two kerns lay dead where he'd last seen him, so Richard ran back to the wall and the ditch.

There the battle raged. Brian the monk stood on the wall swinging his bloodied banner back and forth, the Irish seemingly happy to avoid him and fight someone else.

A horn blew in the distance. Its long note droned and tailed off. The attackers who heard it disengaged and ran back over the ditch and pits. Those that were lost in the fighting didn't hear the call and were cut down by the surviving Welsh. Half of the archers now lay dead, their bodies littering the fortification they had fought so hard to keep.

Bowman picked up a bow from one of them and shot arrows into the Irish as they fled. Some of the archers did the same. The Irish ran the last part of their retreat, and looked as confused as Richard was.

'Have they given up?' Richard said to himself, 'why would they retreat now?'

Raymond saw him. 'They are not done,' he spat blood from his mouth, 'they have only committed one half of their number, look.'

Richard followed his gaze. Up on the hill, hundreds of Irishmen stood and watched their fellows fall back.

'We can't fight them,' Richard's body grew heavy, 'we're out of arrows and half-dead.'

'I'll admit, but only between you and me,' Raymond said, 'I might have slightly underestimated them. Strongbow told me only a few hundred of the enemy could possibly be mustered here.'

'Someone told him wrong,' Richard started to feel the pain from his little toe. He looked down and a haggard flap of mail told him rings had been split. The toe stung worse than a horse stomp and it hurt to put weight on.

The unused Irish warriors left the hill and began to march towards the promontory.

Raymond sighed. 'I regret that I am going to die on a sea-swept rock for land I don't care for,' he said, 'although their beef is the finest beef I have ever tasted.'

Richard nodded because it was.

Brian stood up on his wall with the Papal banner held proudly aloft. The monk had a spatter of blood across his face.

'Tell me one thing,' Richard said quietly to his leader, 'is that banner real?'

'Of course it's real. You can see it and touch it can't you?'

'No, I mean is it from Rome?'

Raymond smiled a red smile for between his teeth his gums ran with his own blood.

'I knew it,' Richard said and sat down on the wall, 'so if I die here, I'm not even dying for the church.'

'You sound like a whining monk,' Raymond said.

Brian turned around and glared at him.

'No offence,' Raymond said.

'Some taken,' the monk turned away.

Welsh archers nocked the handful of arrows they had left.

Irish warriors filled the neck of the promontory, and the Welsh held their few remaining missiles for point-blank range.

'Don't worry about God and heaven,' Raymond said, 'you are a knight, worry about your sword and your life.'

The cows mooed and Richard cursed them for their stench.

That was the last thing he was going to smell, he thought. Once he was dead, an Irishman would take Solis and probably use him to herd the cattle back to wherever his home was.

Richard swallowed, blinked and a thought crept into his mind. That was it. That's what they could do.

He jumped off the wall and ran to Raymond who had gone back to his post. 'The cows, the damned cows,' Richard cried.

'What about them?' Raymond asked, 'we don't have time to roast one.'

'No,' Richard waved his arm towards the herd, 'there are barely forty of us left, but we have another army.'

Raymond looked at the cows, one of which was only a few feet away, a year old cow that looked up at him with black eyes. 'They are not an army, Richard, they are cattle. Have your senses taken their leave?'

'No,' Richard said, 'they're armed too, their horns, don't you see?'

Raymond saw. His eyes widened. 'God's legs, boy, you're as mad as a walled-up-nun but it might just work.'

'We need to hurry, we need to be on horses for the cattle to listen to us,' Richard said.

Raymond turned towards the stakes in the channel, 'Sir Alan, get on your fat horse and herd those cattle out through the channel.'

Alan happily left the front line and he and his knights went to round up their mounts.

Richard ran back into the hospital where his saddle and bridle were. A burnt through lance had fallen from the roof and scratched the wooden saddle, but not broken it. Richard ran out of the building, which was still on fire, as Bowman scrambled in to do the same.

'Was this your idea?' Bowman bent down and scooped up his saddle.

'You know it was,' Richard left and pushed through ignorant cows until he reached his horse. Solis snorted at the smoke in the air as Richard threw his saddle over his back. He buckled the girth strap, flung his bridle on with less care then he ought to, and put his foot into the stirrup to jump on.

His little toe split open, or at least that's what it felt like.

Richard cried out but grabbed his saddle and pushed himself up anyway. He took hold of the spear he'd leant against Solis and made his way back through the cattle to the very far back end of the fort.

Nicholas jumped onto his horse nearby, and two of the loyal Irishmen were still alive to vault onto their horses.

'To me,' Richard shouted.

Bowman and Nicholas arrived first. Richard could see Alan carefully strapping on his horse's breastplate.

'Leave that off,' Richard shouted.

Alan carried on buckling it but some of his knights joined the horsemen at the back of the promontory. Richard looked behind him and the edge of the cliff was closer than he liked. He could see the sea foam below and crash and break on the dark jagged rocks.

'Let the fat knight rot,' Bowman said, 'drive the cows over him, if we wait for him, a dozen more Welshmen will be dead. And I'm starting to like them.'

'The Devil take him,' Richard muttered, then shouted, 'spread out and push the cattle through the channel.'

Bowman and Nicholas started to fan out, and between them they rode towards the herd. Solis pinned his ears back and bit a cow above its tail. The startled animal pushed into its neighbour and the cattle started to move. The other horses pushed on and the herd picked up speed.

The cows didn't want to go near the burning hospital, or into the the fighting along the ditch. Instead they headed for the closest thing to open space that they could see, which was the channel. The foremost cows were young and they jumped or clambered over the bodies piled up around the stakes. Richard pushed them on, aware that the Welsh were being overrun and Raymond and Brian were both now fighting behind the wall. The cattle sensed their chance for freedom. Chased by the knights and their horses, the cows bolted out of the fort and towards the Irish army.

'Faster, faster,' Richard cried and Solis snapped at the tails of the cows that lagged behind.

The herd accelerated and it became a stampede.

The majority of the Irish still hadn't crossed into the

slaughterhouse of the pits yet, and they stopped at the noise of several hundred cattle moving at full speed.

The warriors who stood in the way of the cows turned to run, but it was too late. The herd fanned out from the channel and widened their front. Their hooves slipped on the grass that was wet with blood and crushed the bodies of the slain, but it didn't slow them down.

'It's going to work,' Bowman reached Richard at the end of the channel as Richard stopped his horse.

They watched the cows begin to gore the unarmoured Irishmen. Cows mooed and men died. A few fell beneath their horns, but hundreds more died under their hooves. The Irish horsemen on the hill turned and fled before the bovine tide.

'I could kiss you,' Bowman said.

'It's not over yet, look,' Richard pointed his spear over to the ditch where the Welsh were locked in mortal struggle with those Irish who'd reached them before the stampede.

Alan rode up behind them. His face was covered in cow manure and he'd lost his spear.

'What happened to you?' Bowman asked, 'tried to make love to a cow?'

'You tried to kill me,' Alan replied.

'There's no time for this,' Richard said, 'charge the Irish from behind, but watch the pits and the bodies.'

Richard pointed Solis towards the line of combat where he saw the Papal banner whirling through the air. The stallion bounded over pits, slipped on spilled guts, and finally jumped the entire ditch between two stakes. He almost tripped himself up on the wall, and jumped that too because he had no other choice. As they did so, Richard skewed a kern in the back. His leaping horse nearly knocked Brian over, and Solis skidded round on the mud.

Bowman's horse followed. The now cut-off Irish clustered together and backed off, their situation suddenly horribly apparent to them. Richard and the other riders pushed them towards the cliff.

The herd of cattle disappeared up and over the hill, a trail of broken bodies left in their wake. With them gone, all Richard could hear was the hospital burning and waves crashing below the cliffs.

'Surround them,' Raymond ordered from on top of the wall in both languages. The Welsh stalked their prey, eager for revenge.

'Monk,' Raymond said, 'order their surrender, I don't want to lose any more men.'

Brian marched forwards with his banner, now torn clean in two, and spoke to the enemy.

After barely any discussion at all, they threw their weapons down into the ditch and walked over with bowed heads.

'They yield,' Brian replied.

Raymond barked commands and the Welsh lined up the captives in front of the ditch.

Richard didn't want to dismount because it would mean his damaged foot would have to land on the ground, so he counted the captives instead. Seventy. Then he counted the surviving Welsh. Twenty.

Two of Alan's mercenaries lay dead on the field, but he appeared in time to point his sword at the defenceless prisoners.

'Why don't they just run?' Richard asked.

Bowman had also stayed on his horse. 'They fear us. They've seen Raymond fight. They can see us on horses with long lances and they know they can't outrun us.'

'They still outnumber us,' Richard said, 'if they ran we couldn't kill them all.'

Bowman shrugged. 'Maybe they're tired. It's easier to give up than it is to push through a difficulty and fight.'

Raymond spoke to Brian and the monk relayed words to the Irishmen. Some fell to their knees and others dropped their heads. Brian said something else and turned. He thrust the banner into the earth of the ditch and walked away, his eyes down.

'What's he doing?' Richard asked.

Bowman rested his lance on his foot. 'No idea, but I can't believe we're still alive.'

Raymond retrieved one of the pickaxes scattered along the wall and walked slowly over to the captives.

'I don't want to watch,' Richard said.

'Don't, then,' Bowman said, 'if you want an excuse, someone should probably put out the fire over the hospital. It will have already torched most of our lances.'

Raymond approached the first kneeling Irishman. The big Norman brought the pickaxe down onto the man's skull, his eyes rolled up into his head and he sunk to the ground. The Norman moved to the next man and shouted at some of the Welsh archers. Four ran over and held the kern down, who struggled. Raymond drove the axe down onto the man's hands, then used the flat side of the tool to crush both feet. The prisoner howled.

Raymond and his team moved on. They repeated the treatment on the rest of the prisoners until he reached the end of the line.

Richard's stomach churned as over sixty men screamed and cried at their battered limbs. It took so long the fire in the hospital burned itself out.

Richard caught Bowman looking away.

'This is not right,' Richard said.

'The Irish kill all prisoners, that's what he told us.'

'They might,' Richard said, 'but it isn't our way. We need to spread the word of God, not the way of those who crucified his son.'

'I'm not going to tell him that,' Bowman's eyes moved up towards Raymond as he picked a mutilated prisoner up by his tunic. 'Are you going to tell him that?'

'There's no point,' Richard said, 'those men are already dead.'

Raymond dragged the mangled man towards the cliff with only one hand. The hulking Norman hurled his tortured captive from the promontory and he fell out of sight.

Richard blinked. 'I cannot believe he just did that.'

'Me neither, I thought he was a good one,' Bowman said.

Raymond picked up the next Irishman and dragged him over to the cliff. The man flew from the promontory just as his comrade had, and disappeared below.

The big Norman worked down the line, ejecting man after man off the cliff. The final Irishman still knelt, his hands and feet unharmed, his eyes full of terror.

Brian returned and his eyes met Richard's. 'I've brought the devil to my country,' the tearful monk said.

'I'm sorry,' Richard said, 'so sorry.'

'Monk,' Raymond shouted once he was down to the final captive.

'The devil awaits,' Bowman said to Brian.

The monk pressed his lips together and went over to his new master.

'He's sparing one of the Irish so he can tell all his friends what happened here,' Bowman said.

'He's the savage,' Richard said.

'They would have done the same to you,' Bowman said, 'had they captured you.'

Richard knew he was right. 'I want to go home.'

'We've just got here, and we've got a whole kingdom to conquer.'

Richard looked over at his shoulder and inspected the hole in the top layer of his mail. He wondered if anyone in Ireland even knew how to mend mail.

Raymond pushed the lucky Irishmen on his way. The released man jumped the ditch and ran for his life.

Richard half expected an order to run him down but it didn't come.

Raymond spoke to the Welsh and they cheered. Then they fell to their knees and prayed. The tall Norman pointed over to Richard. 'This is your victory,' he said.

Richard didn't much want it.

'You saved all of us,' Raymond said, 'this victory will be known for a thousand years. Our song will be sung across the world, and everyone will know our names and what we did here.'

Richard definitely didn't want that.

RED EVA

The ships took an age to anchor off Baginbun Head. The wind had disappeared the day after the Irish had been driven away, so the ships without oars could only drift towards shore.

Richard walked along the channel through the promontory fort's earthworks. The Welsh had been joined by a few dozen loyal Irish from the surrounding area, and had already built up a chest-high wooden rampart on top of the old stone walls. The dead bodies had been rolled off the clifftop, and seagulls cawed and fought over the broken corpses draped on the rocks below.

Bowman and Nicholas followed Richard, who walked slowly because of his damaged toe.

'That needs seeing to,' Bowman said.

'Why?' Richard asked, 'we have no healers or wise old women here, who can help me?'

'If it goes a funny colour, tell me,' Bowman said.

Richard narrowed his eyes at his friend, unsure of the seriousness of the comment.

'If it goes green,' Bowman said with a grin, 'we need to cut it off.'

'You're not cutting my toe off,' Richard walked down towards the cliff overlooking the beach. The trampled grass had started to straighten itself in places, but blood still pooled and the green blades needed a good rain to wash the battle away.

The cliffs that overlooked the beach grew warm in the August sun. Raymond stood next to the Papal banner, visibly relieved now reinforcements had arrived. Holding his banner, Brian the monk gazed out to sea with unreadable eyes. Most of the ships were of the old type, long and shallow with a single square sail. Those at least had oars, and it was these smaller vessels that rowed directly up onto the beach.

Alan beamed a smile out to sea. He had attempted to wash the manure from this yellow surcoat, but still brown stains covered it.

'What's he so happy about?' Bowman mumbled.

'Now he can hide behind all the new soldiers when the Irish come again,' Richard said.

'I can't believe he's getting paid the same as us,' Nicholas put his hands on his hips and admired the fleet.

'None of us have been paid anything yet,' Richard replied.

'With all of these new arrivals,' Bowman said, 'perhaps we can capture a fair chunk of Ireland. Maybe even enough to pay us. Then we can go home.'

'Unfortunately, I think it's a bit early to think of home,' Richard said.

'You were thinking of home yourself not that long ago,' Bowman replied as men started to jump from the ships and unload their cargo.

A thousand men landed that day. A hundred knights came first, then their horses. Richard counted at least two hundred good riding animals, before packhorses too reached the beach.

Strongbow was the first up onto the cliff, where he spoke to Raymond in private.

Bowman edged closer to eavesdrop, got bored, and returned.

'And?' Richard asked.

'Nothing interesting,' Bowman said, 'a thousand more Welshmen and a hundred knights.'

The hundred knights had got as far as Alan, who regaled them with stories of the battle.

'They really believe him,' Richard said. Then he remembered that his uncle was somewhere in the crowd and he tensed. He could keep hiding, but it was only a matter of time before Luke spotted him.

Alan was tall and his voice loud, and the knights didn't take their eyes off him. The mercenary swung an imaginary sword and mimicked arrows flying through the air.

'You'd think he was Raymond,' Nicholas said, 'and that he won the battle on his own.'

Alan mimed himself throwing water into the hospital to put

the fire out.

'You're too lazy to lift a bucket,' Bowman shouted, 'and where did the water come from? We'd run out by then.'

Alan paused and indecision flashed across his face.

Bowman chuckled to himself.

'Don't bother,' Richard said, 'if you argue with him it just looks like we have no courtesy.'

'King Dermot is lapping it up,' Nicholas said as Alan continued his story with a little less certainty than before.

Dermot stroked his beard and nodded along to Alan's tall tale. He cheered when Alan rode his horse up behind the cattle and drove them into the Irish ranks.

A knight with white chevrons on a red surcoat shook his head and left the large group of listeners. He had dark sunken eyes and and a round head with black hair.

Richard caught his eye and the knight came over.

'Is he telling the truth?' The knight asked.

Richard grinned but stuck to his own advice and kept quiet.

'Richard here might be sticking to the moral high ground,' Bowman said, 'but seeing as I've never been up there, I will tell you.'

The knight regarded Bowman with penetrating eyes. 'You do not look any more trustworthy than the loud one,' he said.

'Well,' Bowman said, 'believe what you want to believe, but when we herded those cattle out of the fort, that loudmouth there was under their hooves and being covered by their droppings.'

The corners of the knight's mouth imperceptibly curled up. 'I think I believe you,' he said, 'although I see little to convince me that you deserve the spurs you wear. You do not carry yourself as a knight should.'

Bowman paused and looked over to Richard.

'I agree that he does not have the dignity of a nobleman,' Richard said, 'but he does fight like one. And in this instance he does tell the truth. Who are you that questions my man?'

The knight frowned. 'Such rudeness, but I will forgive it if my cousin speaks well of you.'

'Who is your cousin?' Richard asked.

Raymond and Strongbow walked back and stopped by

Richard.

'Him?' Strongbow asked.

'I know,' Raymond replied, 'not much to look at.'

Strongbow sniffed. 'Sometimes the best ones aren't. Not everyone can be a mountain like you.'

Raymond grinned and looked at the new knight. 'Milo, I see you've met our heroes.'

Milo adjusted his red surcoat and bowed to Strongbow. 'My lord,' he said.

'What about me?' Raymond's grin widened, 'no words for your cousin?'

'You are not the king of Leinster,' Milo's dark eyes never left Strongbow.

Strongbow snorted. 'I'm not the King of Leinster until he dies,' he glanced back to the storytelling where Dermot hung on Alan's every word.

'And once I've married that Irishwoman,' Strongbow finished.

Bowman's face hardened. He left them and walked over to the crowd.

'What is his problem?' Raymond asked.

'He is unpredictable,' Richard said, 'but mostly he's tired.'

'We are all tired,' Raymond said, 'although you did more than most. Do you know my cousin?'

Richard shook his head.

'This is Milo de Cogan,' Raymond said, 'he has the good fortune to be related to me.'

Milo's eyes searched Richard's face.

'This one can ride as well as you,' Raymond said, 'you'll like his horse.'

'Will I,' Milo replied flatly.

'Enough of this back-slapping,' Strongbow said, 'we have an army crawling around a clifftop in a hostile land, as open to attack as a woman's legs on her wedding night.'

'That hill,' Raymond pointed to the hill the Irish had flooded over during the fighting, 'reaches across the promontory. Use it as a base for our fortifications.'

Strongbow studied the hill and nodded. 'Very well, the Welshmen will make short work of that. I want a wooden palisade up before midday tomorrow. We shall garrison this fort while we push inland. It may be that we build something permanent here.'

'At least until we capture Waterford,' Raymond said.

'Yes,' Strongbow said, 'but today is Saint Bartholemew's day eve, so tomorrow we shall celebrate his feast and give thanks for our victory here.'

Raymond nodded.

'Come,' Strongbow walked towards the fort, 'show me the place where we won Ireland.'

Milo followed closely on their heels.

Nicholas watched them go. 'I don't know if I like him.'

'Who cares,' Richard said, 'we need to worry about your brother.'

'Half-brother.'

Bowman stood at the front of the crowd and heckled Alan.

The mercenary's face grew brighter each time, and some of the new knights started to laugh at him.

'Should we stop him?' Nicholas asked.

Richard shrugged. 'We should.'

'But?'

'I'm not going to,' Richard replied, 'I'm going to see if those ships have brought any horsebread, because my horse is going to start eating people soon.'

The real reason Richard didn't want to be closer to the knights was his uncle, but he didn't want to talk about that.

The newly arrived Welsh archers made short work of ferrying supplies up from the beach. Before the sun set late in the evening, a wooden wall stretched across half of the hill. Over a thousand men finished setting up a camp on what had so recently been a field of death. Strongbow sent out the fresh knights on their horses to find the battle-winning cattle, which they drove back into the promontory in the late afternoon. The feast of Saint Bartholemew was celebrated with much beef that night, and the camp rung with song and laughter.

'How come he gets a tent?' Bowman crossed his arms sitting by their fire.

Due to the warm evening, they all sat back from the heat it

put out.

'He's got a king with him,' Richard said, 'and he's paying for everything, so if he wants a tent he can have one.'

The large A frame tent was the only one on site, and had been erected in the centre of the camp. The Papal banner had been planted in the ground one side of the door, Strongbow's personal banner on the other.

Bowman's eyes lit up. 'She's here,' he said.

Eva walked slowly out of the tent and around the cooking fires that dotted the landscape. The smell of cooking meat clogged the air.

'You should probably make it less obvious,' Richard said.

Bowman peeled his gaze away. 'I don't know what you mean.'

'Stop staring,' Richard said, 'there are hundreds of men who can see you.'

Eva stopped by their fire. She had braided her brown hair and wore a long dress instead of wargear.

'How was the crossing?' Richard asked.

'Slow,' Eva replied, 'but I'm surprisingly glad to be home.'

'How are you?' Bowman asked.

Eva kept her eyes on Richard. 'Quite well once the sickness of the sea passed. Probably not so well once I've had to spend the night in that tent with all the farting old men.'

Nicholas laughed. 'It's going to get hot in there.'

Eva frowned at him and he shut up.

'One thing I wanted to ask you,' Richard said, 'your father's messenger. Is he a trusted man to your family?'

Eva tilted her head. 'Why do you ask me that?'

Richard looked her in the eyes. 'Because in Pembroke Castle I got the impression that he was keeping an eye on you.'

'Really?'

'A close eye,' Richard said, 'if you know what I mean.'

Eva almost looked at Bowman. 'Cormac is my father's man, not mine. That is why he went ahead with your advanced party.'

'He did not,' Richard said.

Eva paused. 'He was not with you?'

Richard shook his head and looked at Bowman who met his gaze.

'He did not sail with us,' she said, 'but he was gone the morning you set sail.'

'That explains a few things,' Richard said, 'but you shouldn't be seen with us. Or at least him.'

Bowman's cheeks turned the faintest shade of pink.

'I shall take my leave,' Eva said, 'I was merely curious to know if you had survived what I'm told was an epic battle. All three of you, that is.'

'Of course,' Richard smiled, 'all three of us.'

'But you are right, lord of Yvetot, I must go. Strongbow is over the moon and wants me by his side for all to see. Strongbow is such a stupid name, don't you think?'

Bowman choked and had to cough.

Richard laughed. 'You can thank him for that.'

Eva didn't understand. 'He thinks we've broken the back of Leinster's resistance and that Waterford will fall easily now. They're calling it the Battle of the Bag. You should rest tonight, for he will march us all off tomorrow.'

Eva never looked away from Richard, even as she turned and left. She picked her way back indirectly to the great tent.

Bowman twirled a cow's leg bone in his hand.

'You should get a dog,' Richard said.

Bowman looked up and threw the bone in the fire.

'Don't do that, we could have kept that for flavour,' Nicholas said.

'I would like a dog,' Bowman said, 'a good scent hound.'

Richard thought Yvetot would be better with some dogs running around. He just couldn't afford any.

'Speaking of dogs,' Bowman said, 'wasn't your uncle with the invasion fleet?'

Richard had just about forgotten about him. 'Yes, but I haven't seen him yet.'

'Don't worry, you're famous now, and surrounded by men who know it. He won't harm you in camp.'

Richard wasn't sure he quite believed that, but maybe Bowman was right. It would be in battle where Richard would have to watch his back.

The balmy night rolled on as the stars came out in the still sky. Excited talk floated up from the campfires, but around

Richard's it was quiet. His bones felt weary and his right arm ached around the elbow. His toe hurt to flex so he lay on his cloak, looked up at the stars and let sleep take him.

As the sun started to shine the next morning, the Irish started to arrive. This time they came in small groups, and this time to join the army rather than oppose it.

The Welsh restarted their work on the palisade as soon as it was light enough. By midday a wooden wall blocked off the whole of the promontory to create a bailey in front of the fort itself.

Some of the newcomers were not Irish.

'They look like us,' Nicholas said as he lay stretched out on his bedding.

Richard agreed. Men in mail shirts and mail leggings rode under iron helmets. Some had surcoats and colours painted on their shields. Their horses were not Irish-sized, and their supporters rode well equipped.

'So we were not even the first Normans in Ireland,' Richard said.

'Does that make you feel less special?' Bowman stood up and stretched.

Truthfully it did, but Richard didn't want to show it.

'Don't complain,' Nicholas said, 'the larger our army the better.'

'Where were they when we were under attack?' Richard put his hands on his hips.

Bowman laughed. 'That de Clare thinks he's so big and brave, but he didn't even lead our small force. And he waited to launch his invasion until these other Normans proved it was possible. He's not so courageous.'

'Jealousy looks bad on you,' Richard said.

Bowman pulled a face and wondered off.

More Norman lords arrived as the army assembled to move on. Richard found his horse and tied all his belongings to the back of his saddle. The army rode out of the newly expanded fort, Raymond in the vanguard and Milo de Cogan leading the rearguard.

Richard rode behind Raymond and the Papal banner. Solis was glad to be moving again, and for the first part of the march he had to hold his horse back to stop him getting in front of Raymond.

They rode north and by the hill where they had found the cattle herd. Richard enjoyed the slow riding. He could watch the hills start to grow and roll as birds flew overhead. They reached a river, which Richard was told was called the Suir, and rode along it.

The city of Waterford lay on the south bank of the river, and being no bridge, they rode west along the north bank looking for a way across. Waterford had walls along the river and a decent harbour. A tall tower protected the waterside and he could see the spire of a cathedral beyond. Men, woman and children came out to watch the long army snake by, and Richard wondered if Strongbow was doing it deliberately as a show of force.

The army left the city behind it and carried on for some time before they found a ford low enough to allow the Welsh to get across on foot.

Raymond ordered Nicholas to test the ford first. He rode his grey horse gingerly across the river, still as wide as two good spear throws, but he safely reached the other side with water having reached only his horse's chest.

Crossing the river took the rest of the day, and Richard's already rusted leg mail was thoroughly soaked at the end of it. The rings on the inside of his legs had already gone bright orange, but he knew the whole thing would now be covered in rust by the morning.

That night was a tenser one, everyone slept in their armour and with their weapons beside them. Horses were kept saddled and with bits in their mouths in case of a surprise attack. None came, but in the morning Solis was angry at Richard for what he'd endured and pulled his head away whenever Richard tried to touch him.

Strongbow left five knights and a hundred archers to guard the ford, and everyone else pushed on towards Waterford.

The city had better walls than Richard had hoped. The scattered roundhouses that dotted the countryside so far had all been wooden, and Richard hadn't yet seen anything that resembled a castle. Therefore, the stone walls of Waterford, as high as his own at Yvetot, made his heart sink. The walls stretched from the Suir to the north to a tributary of it to the south, and made the city look very easy to defend.

The plain to the west of the city was the site of their new camp, and again the Welsh worked tirelessly to ring it with a ditch. The earth from the ditch was thrown up to form a rampart on the inside, and Strongbow's tent was again pitched in the middle of everything.

At first light the next morning, Brian the monk rode out of the camp with Strongbow and Raymond. Brian sat unsteadily on the horse he'd been given, but stayed in the saddle and didn't drop his bloodied banner.

Raymond ordered the few knights who'd been in the advanced party to ride out with them, but to stay just behind Strongbow.

'It's a great honour to ride out with us,' Raymond said to them as they left their camp.

Milo rode with them and his dark eyes looked at Richard. 'Don't be so sure of that,' he said, 'your job is to sacrifice yourself if a host of enemy horsemen sally out and try to kill Strongbow.'

'They can try,' Richard replied, for the small native horses held little fear for him.

They rode towards the main gate of Waterford and waited for someone to come and parley with them. Scattered housing filled the plain, a few clusters of houses even being built right up against the walls.

Some time later the gate swung open and a dozen mailed warriors walked out on foot. They had their own banners too, and one was a giant wooden cross.

'So much for the pagans of Ireland,' Nicholas said.

'I don't think their Christianity is going to save them,' Bowman replied, 'if it isn't just an act.'

Two men stepped out of the mailed group. The man in front was tall, broad and blonde.

'He looks like you,' Richard said to Bowman.

'He's older,' Bowman replied, 'and I'm better looking.'

Strongbow spoke to Brian and the monk questioned the man in Irish.

To everyone's surprise, the reply came back in Norman French.

'I am Ragnall, son of Ragnall and I rule here,' he said with a strong, sure voice.

'I am Richard de Clare,' Strongbow rode a step towards him so he could look down on him from his horse, 'and I am here on behalf of King Dermot of Leinster.'

'Where is he?' Ragnall asked.

Strongbow gestured towards the camp. 'Back there, but you are dealing with me. Kneel and submit to your rightful king. Let us into the city and there will be no need for bloodshed.'

Ragnall looked at the host of armed Normans. 'You look intent on bloodshed. But there is no need for violence, you and we are kin.'

'Kin?' Strongbow asked.

'You are descended from the northmen,' Ragnall said, 'and you are still called the Normans after them. We too are from across the north. Waterford is our trading centre and our home. We will defend it with our lives, for we are not inclined to be ruled by an Irish king.'

'This is awkward,' Bowman said as Strongbow spoke quietly to Raymond and Milo.

'I thought Waterford would be Irish,' Richard said.

'I think we're learning not to assume anything about Ireland,' Bowman said.

Strongbow pointed to the Papal banner. 'We have a Papal Bull. The Luadabiliter Bull gives King Henry of England the right to act in Ireland.'

'Is the King of England hiding in your camp, too?' Ragnall asked.

His companions laughed.

One stepped forwards, he had raven-black hair and a protruding nose. 'Do not think your victory over the natives at the old fort means you will find victory easy here,' he said.

Strongbow pushed his horse forwards. The big white stallion snorted at the mailed man and looked like he wanted to take him on.

'You must yield to the Papacy,' Strongbow said, 'for the salvation of your souls.'

'Does that ever work?' Ragnall turned to his companion, 'they think we are weak children, Sigurd.'

Sigurd chuckled.

Strongbow clenched his reins and put a hand on his sword.

'You are quick to anger,' Ragnall said, 'will you really break a parley?'

'You disrespect both the Pope and the representative of the King of England,' Strongbow shouted.

'I thought the King of England didn't want us to sail,' Bowman whispered.

'Quiet,' Richard hissed back.

'Your banner,' Ragnall continued, 'is torn, covered in blood, and looks like my child made it. Your Bull gives King Henry the right to interfere here, not you. Show me King Henry and I shall open my gates to him.'

Strongbow bristled.

'Looks like we'll be fighting our way in,' Bowman said.

'There is no point resisting us, your city will surely fall,' Strongbow said.

'We Norse will no more give in than you Normans would, should our positions be reversed,' Ragnall said.

'Think of your womenfolk,' Strongbow said, 'think of the lives that will be lost for no reason.'

'Do not pin their blood on me,' Ragnall snarled, 'it is your army that circles us like a pack of wolves. Do not blame the deer for the predator's bloodletting. We have heard what you did when you landed in England a century ago, and we know what you Normans have done further afield. If we open the gates we shall die anyway, so instead we shall fight and at least die with honour.'

Strongbow pursed his lips and stared back at the men on foot. He shook his head and backed his horse up.

'Have you ever felt like you're on the wrong side?' Richard asked quietly.

'Who knows what the right side is,' Bowman thought for a moment, 'although I doubt we're on it today.'

'If you close your gates to us, all who live inside will forfeit their lives,' Strongbow said.

'We know,' the dark-haired Sigurd rested his hand on his

sword pommel, 'we know the rules of war.'

'Your men lie at Baginbun Head,' Strongbow said, 'you only have boys and old men with no teeth left to man your walls.'

'Enough,' Ragnall said, 'if I have precious little breath left in this life, I do not wish to spend it arguing with you.'

'You can't keep us out,' Strongbow turned his horse away.

'No, perhaps not, but we can die with our swords in our hands,' Ragnall turned his back on the Normans and walked back into Waterford.

Bowman sniffed as Strongbow watched them go. 'That went well,' the blonde man said.

'Someone else can be first up the ladder this time,' Richard felt his missing finger even though it wasn't there, 'and neither of you two go volunteering, either.'

Bowman laughed. 'No need to worry about that.'

'I'm keeping as far away as I can,' Nicholas said, 'don't worry about me, either.'

In the end the three of them had very little choice. Ladders were built in far off woods and hauled before the city walls. Then bundles of arrows that had got to Waterford strapped to pack animals were brought up. Finally, they were laid behind wooden screens for the archers to hide behind. The Welsh started to dig trenches opposite the walls, all the time under sporadic, but optimistic, arrow attack from the defenders.

The knightly class were able to watch this work from safety and in comfort, but once Strongbow ordered the assault, there was no hiding from Raymond.

The large Norman grinned towards the fire where Richard and his companions sat, Richard sighed and reached for his second coat of mail without arguing.

Once armed, Richard limped on foot towards the siege line with Bowman and Nicholas under a sun they all wished could shine a little fainter. Alan and his four surviving knights had been rounded up too, and Raymond pointed at the ladder that was to be theirs.

'You, fatty. You're first up,' Raymond said.

Alan's eyes bulged. 'I'm not so quick up ladders,' the mercenary said, 'someone younger should go first.'

'Are you frightened?' Raymond laughed at him as an arrow from the wall nearly reached his foot.

Alan's shoulders dropped and he walked to the ladder. More heads appeared up on the walls.

'I think they know we're here,' Richard said.

Bowman shot him a look under his helmet, which he adjusted. 'You think, do you?'

Richard and Nicholas picked up the rear of the ladder and Alan and his knights lifted it at the front.

Welsh archers filled the trenches and they started to lay down suppressing volleys of arrows. Other knights picked up their ladders and the attack began.

As they went, Richard's shield banged into the ladder and made gripping it difficult.

'Hurry up Alan,' Bowman shouted, 'if you haven't noticed, they're shooting at us.'

Alan didn't reply but Richard could hear him panting as he tried to run.

They covered the grass quickly, but the closer to the wall they went, the more arrows flew down from it. An arrow hit one of Alan's knights but he seemed to shrug it off.

Raymond was behind them urging them on, he waved his sword and pointed it at the wall. 'If you want to get paid, you'll need to get onto that,' he shouted.

Their ladder reached the shallow ditch in front of the stonework and they slowed down to get over it. The ditch was full of rubbish which Richard could stand on, so the ladder's progress was only held up for a moment.

Arrows thudded into the ground around them and one of Alan's knights was hit in the shoulder. He fell away from the ladder, his hands clawing at the shaft.

'Get back to the ladder,' Raymond ordered.

Richard let go of the ladder as it started to rise towards the battlements, Alan at the base of it guiding it up.

'Now Richard,' Raymond shouted, 'let Red Balls go first.'

Bowman started to laugh.

A rock fell from the battlements and the man who threw it was hit in the chest by a Welsh arrow. The rock landed a finger's width from Bowman's foot and he stopped laughing. 'Get up the damned ladder, Red Balls' he cried.

Raymond walked up to the weighty mercenary and picked him up by his sword belt.

Alan flailed his arms. 'Put me down.'

Raymond lifted him up onto the first rung and dropped him there.

'You've got a bear's strength,' Richard said.

Raymond shook his arm. 'It almost wasn't enough,' he said.

Alan started to climb the ladder one rung at a time. Once he was a few steps up he started to wobble.

His knights followed behind him, then Bowman went up. A jagged rock was hurled from the battlement and crunched into the helmet of one of the mercenaries. The man dropped off the ladder and kicked Bowman in the face as he went.

Bowman shook it off. 'Hurry up or I'll feed your red balls to a mangy dog,' he shouted up the ladder.

Richard climbed up beneath Bowman with his shield held over his head.

A stone hit it and the force compacted Richard's neck and jarred him. Alan wasn't moving up and Richard looked over across the wall. The next ladder along was pushed off the wall and collapsed to the ground. The ladder snapped, men fell and broke limbs in a pile of screams and twisted bodies.

Richard couldn't put his toe on the rungs, it stung when he tried. He looked to his other side and the nearest ladder there was pushed from the wall by a pole with an iron claw on its end.

The sound of cracking wood tore through the air above Richard.

Alan screamed and one of his knights fell off the ladder and hit the ground with a crunching sound as an ankle gave way.

Richard moved his shield so he could see what was happening above, just as Bowman's foot slipped off the ladder and and landed on Richard's nose.

A rung snapped and Alan dropped. Richard, only two rungs off the ground, threw himself backwards out of his way.

Alan hit his last remaining knight and they dropped together onto Bowman.

Richard hit the ground flat on his back and felt the air get knocked out of him.

Bowman tumbled down awkwardly as Alan smacked into the ground at the foot of the ladder. Norman knights lay everywhere and the defenders on the wall cheered.

Then they started shooting arrows down at the disorganised attackers.

An arrow glanced off Bowman's helmet and he swore as he tried to get back to his feet.

Richard stood up, cursed at his toe, and held his shield back up over his head. He ran to Bowman and held the shield above the two of them.

Bowman looked down. 'He broke my scabbard, the red one from Castle Tancarville,' he said.

'Never mind that,' Richard said, 'we need to get out of range. An arrow thudded into his shield as if to make his point.

One of Alan's knights fumbled at his leg where an arrow had pierced between the lacing of his leg armour. His howls of pain stuck in Richard's ears.

Nicholas appeared with his shield up and used his free hand to haul Bowman up onto his feet.

'I don't need your help,' Bowman said as they all started to run.

'You could help me,' Alan cried behind them.

Richard kept going until they reached the Welsh trenches and crossed them with a leap.

Sweat dripped from under his helmet, and Richard's eyes stung as beads ran down his forehead and into them.

Bowman sat down on the grass and unlaced his helmet.

'Bet that second mail shirt is making you hot,' Nicholas said.

Richard looked down and saw an arrow tangled in the first layer. 'I think I'm quite happy to be a little warm,' he picked the arrow up and inspected its sleek tip.

The Welsh still loosed arrows into the city, and two ladders were still up against the walls.

Bowman held the snapped scabbard.

'The leather looks alright,' Richard said.

'But the wooden core is broken,' Bowman threw it down, 'I've had enough.'

Nicholas looked down at the red scabbard. 'My brother had

one just like that.'

Richard glanced at Bowman, who swallowed.

'I'm sure many scabbards look like that one,' Richard said.

Nicholas frowned. 'I know when you're lying, and you're both lying now. This was Simon's, wasn't it?'

Bowman pushed himself back to his feet. 'What if it was?'

'Simon was murdered in Normandy,' Nicholas replied, 'and now I know by who.'

Richard stepped between them. 'Fine, he did take the scabbard and sword, but only after Simon had died. A boar got him.'

Nicholas's eyes burned bright. 'I knew you were a thief,' he said to Bowman, 'everyone at home always said you were the bad one, the foul one, the outlaw.'

Raymond stomped over, his torn red cloak fluttering behind him. 'Get back to the assault, you can't just stand around arguing like children halfway through a battle.'

Richard pointed at the walls. 'It's over, look.'

The poles with iron hooks reached the remaining ladders and the defenders tried to push them away. A Norman knight reached the top of one ladder and speared a man on the wall. Archers started to shoot along the wall into the men on the ladders, and they started to drop.

'They look like hedgehogs,' Bowman said, 'they have no chance.'

Alan limped back over the trench with all three of his knights helping each other.

Raymond groaned. 'Strongbow hoped the Irish would break before we reached the walls,' he said.

Richard felt his back ache and knew it was going to hurt the next day. 'Now what?' He asked.

Raymond watched as the Norman knights started to fall back, arrows in their shields and bodies. 'We'll try going around the wall instead,' he said.

Around the wall meant getting wet feet. Two days were spent building rafts, half of which were sent to the river Suir to the left of the wall, and half to the unnamed river to the right of it.

More ladders were built in an attempt to stretch the

defenders, but Richard was sent to the rafts on the Suir.

They left their leg armour in the camp, and Richard took off one of his mail shirts. Everyone knew the weight of armour would be bad if they fell off the rafts.

'Do you remember when we spoke of swimming?' Richard said as they stood on the bank of the river watching the chilly water rush by.

Bowman nodded. 'Don't fall in,' he said, 'but if you do, keep hold of some wood and kick your legs.'

Richard's lips were cracked. The water looked too fast moving to swim against, and he wasn't sure they could even paddle against the current if they needed to.

'The current will take you round the walls,' Raymond said, 'just paddle towards the bank and fight your way into the town.'

'Why aren't you coming with us?' Bowman asked.

Richard went to kick him, but his toe caught on a clump of mud and he winced.

'I'm going up a ladder,' the big Norman replied, 'which is more dangerous.'

Bowman accepted his answer, which was when Richard noticed that Raymond had acquired a second mail coat of his own.

A trio of salmon swam up the river, their bodies pushing up above the surface. The Welsh had laid nets by the camp for them upstream, and they had eaten well on salmon for the past few days.

Those Welshmen now clambered onto the rickety looking rafts and prepared their bows and oars.

Nicholas looked unimpressed. 'I can't swim either, I'd rather climb a ladder.'

'Are you sure,' Richard said, 'that didn't end so well last time.'

Raymond left to rally some Normans to join him so Richard sat down on the bank and prodded the raft with his foot. It bobbed up and down rather more quickly than he would have liked.

'There is no way that can take our weight,' he said.

Bowman went to take off his mail shirt. He bent double and shook it slowly off his body until it hit the grass in a heap. 'I think you're right,' he said, 'and I think we'll more than likely be going for a swim.'

Bowman, now lighter, stepped onto the raft. The collection of small trees lashed together ducked under water before it righted itself.

Other rafts with archers pushed off from the bank and paddled out into the river. Over twenty rafts cast off, with Richard one of the last to clamber aboard his sorry excuse for a vessel.

Bowman held it to the shore as Nicholas climbed onboard and pulled his shield on with him. The raft nearly unbalanced and Richard had to throw himself around to avoid falling off.

Richard lifted his eyes from the brown water which splashed up onto his face. The far bank had rocky cliffs that were topped by trees. It looked quite uninviting.

Rafts with three archers on each now drifted past the walls, and those who had gone further out in the river frantically tried to paddle towards Waterford. To Richard it looked like those rafts would be swept out beyond the town before they made it back to the bank. Those who stayed nearer the shore started to take arrows from the walls. Most splashed into the water.

Bowman pushed their raft off and stuck his paddle into the murky river.

'Should we stick close to the shore?' Nicholas asked, 'some of those Welsh look like they're struggling to get back to it.'

'Probably,' Bowman used his paddle to keep them close to the shore. It took his strength and he strained against the current.

One raft drifted around the bend in the river and out of sight.

'Although,' Bowman noticed them, 'at least they won't be getting killed today.'

'Not by arrows anyway,' Nicholas remarked.

The first raft to float underneath the wall was spotted by the defenders on the tower at the end of the city walls. They lifted up a rock the size of a man's head and carefully dropped it from the battlements. The stone fell and hit the middle of the raft. Wood snapped and splintered even as a splash of water soaked the archers. The lashing that kept the raft together slipped off one length of wood and the raft disintegrated.

The defenders cheered and the Welshmen tried to swim back to shore. One sank down into the river after splashing his arms around in panic.

'Actually, I think we should take a wider berth,' Richard said.

Bowman nodded grimly as the man's screams were swallowed by the depths, and pushed them further into the river.

The second raft to be hit by a stone lost a corner, and the mail-clad Norman on it sank as fast as the stone itself.

Richard's raft started to pick up speed.

'Steer us back in, we're nearly past the tower,' Richard said.

Bowman paddled furiously as arrows started to pepper the rafts. A dozen of them still floated towards the city, but the ones without knights and shields had no cover. The Welsh started to take wounds from arrows. They returned volleys, but the defenders had stone to shelter behind.

'I told you this was a bad idea,' Bowman said as they bumped into another raft, and the occupants swore at them. The other raft started to spin out to the centre of the river.

'Sorry,' Richard shrugged at the two Welshmen on it. Their third companion floated down the river with two arrows in his chest.

'We need to get closer or we'll drift by,' Nicholas said as an arrow buried itself in his shield.

Richard looked up at the stone walls that, as they had seen when they marched by a few days ago, also followed the river. There was a small bank below them, and some wooden gates, but no obvious way into the city.

'I don't think we can even get in,' Richard said.

An arrow stuck in their raft and Richard and Nicholas's eyes met over it.

Richard looked up to the wall and saw a man in a mustard-coloured tunic lift a rock above his head.

'Look out,' Richard shouted.

The rock hurtled through the air and struck the edge of their raft. It skidded off and caught Bowman, who knelt to paddle, in the thigh. It knocked his body off the raft and he dropped the oar.

Nicholas grabbed his ankle.

Bowman's head fell into the water and Richard reached out to grab his other foot.

An arrow hit Nicholas in the forearm but he pulled Bowman out of the water anyway.

Bowman, his blonde hair matted his to his face, swore.

An arrow landed between his legs. 'We need to get out of here,' he said.

Nicholas cried in frustration at the pain from his arm. 'We don't have a paddle because you lost it.'

'It's not my fault,' Bowman said.

Two arrows thumped into Richard's shield. Their force pushed it roughly into him and it grazed his face.

'Paddle with the shields,' he cried.

Richard jammed the large, slightly curved shield into the water and started to paddle.

Nicholas did the same on the other side of the stricken raft, despite the arrow that still stuck out of his arm.

'Back the way we came,' Richard said, 'or they'll shoot at us as we drift all along their waterside wall.'

An arrow hit Nicholas in his backside and he dropped his shield.

Bowman lunged and caught the shield just before it floated away.

Nicholas cried out and rolled over to grab the arrow. 'Not there,' he moaned.

Bowman started to paddle, and while he did so, he laughed. 'That's what you get for blaming me for dropping the oar,' he said.

The corner hit by the stone broke off and drifted away. The raft floated, but water washed over it by an finger's width. The water was icy cold on Richard's legs.

'How is it not sinking?' He asked.

'Worry about that later, young lord,' Bowman said, 'just paddle.'

The assault went no better for the other rafts. Bodies floated in the river and bumped into bits of wood from destroyed rafts. Some rafts reached the bank, but with nowhere to go they were easy targets for the archers on the walls.

Richard paddled until his arms ached, then had to paddle

some more. His back, painful before their voyage, felt as if aflame, but he had to keep going to fight against the strong current.

Once back alongside the grassy plain, they steered the raft towards shore, muscles burning and lungs stinging.

Strongbow stood, hands on hips, watching. 'I don't pay men who run away,' he said.

'We aren't running,' Richard replied and stopped paddling. He stood up and balanced awkwardly on their precarious craft.

Strongbow nodded. 'Good answer. How is that still floating? I can't even see it under the river. It looks like you're walking on water.'

Richard looked down at the water that covered both his feet. At least his toe didn't hurt.

Bowman threw a hand out and grabbed a tuft of long grass.

Richard looked at Nicholas. 'Do you need help?'

'Leave me alone,' he pushed Richard's hand away and leapt onto the shore. The leap pushed the boat away and Richard fell forwards, landing face first in the water that covered the raft.

Bowman fell down between the bank and the craft, and that tipped the raft up into the air.

It fell back to the water and sank.

Strongbow's arm appeared in front of Richard and he clung onto it with both hands. The Norman lord hauled him out of the river.

Bowman lay next to him, dripping wet as Nicholas inspected the arrow in his buttocks.

Richard spat out some water and wiped more from his face. It tasted like cold dirt. The Little Lord's sword remained in its scabbard, as did Sir John's dagger.

Strongbow straightened up. 'You were looking biblical until you went for a bath,' he looked over to the ladders, which had already been repelled. 'Capturing this city may take longer than I'd thought.'

Richard unbuckled his weapons and took his tunic off. He wrung it out and water pooled on the earth below. His ribs hurt when he took a deep breath, but at least the sun would burn off the water quickly.

Nicholas looked at him. 'Do I take this out? I've never been shot before.' The arrow in his arm had snapped off and both halves had fallen out.

'Stop your whining,' Bowman said.

'I'm not whining, we only ended up in the river because of you. I pulled you out,' Nicholas said.

A raft full of archers paddled up to the bank and jumped off their vessel. They left it to float away down the river.

Strongbow frowned at the scene of failure and walked away.

Nicholas hobbled off to find someone to pull the arrow out of him while Richard and Bowman laid their tunics out to dry. As his feet dried, the pain in Richard's toe returned, so he lay down on his back and thought of home.

Wounded men from the assault were taken in to the camp in ones and twos, and Raymond walked back into the tent with a dark expression. His red cloak was torn even more than it had been at Baginbun Head.

Bowman made Richard wrap his toes tightly with a strip of linen, and they waited for the day's serving of salmon to appear. Richard could smell the mouth-watering taste of it drift over the camp, and noted the contrast to the downcast expressions on the faces all around.

'What else can we try?' Richard asked when Bowman returned to their place with a jug of water, 'and no one likes drinking water, is there anything else?'

'Dig under the walls,' Bowman said, 'or find someone inside who wants to open the gate. And if you don't want water, go and find drink yourself.'

Richard didn't much like the idea of any of those options.

Brian found their place and slumped down with his banner in his hands. His eyes fell to the floor and he didn't speak.

'What's wrong with you?' Bowman asked.

The monk looked up, his eyes red. 'You are not the only man around who is allowed to be unhappy,' he said.

'Who said I'm unhappy?'

'We're all unhappy,' Richard said, 'none of us want to sit here in the sun for a few weeks while the Welsh dig under the wall. We'll wilt in the heat, get shot at in the town, then have to march somewhere else and do it all again. So let us at least be unhappy together and not snap at each other.'

Bowman sighed, laid back down and closed his eyes.

The Papal banner's blue had been bleached by the sun so much that Richard couldn't make it out anymore. Now it was only white with red on it, and most of that red was blood.

Nicholas returned with the arrow out of him some time later. He lay down on his side and refused to talk about his wound.

The rest of the day was quiet, no one knew what to do and everyone was exhausted from the attack. Richard started to wonder where Alan of Auge had been when he noticed Eva heading their way through the camp.

She stopped next to Richard and her shadow fell over Bowman.

He awoke and sat up quickly.

'I see you all got through that debacle,' Eva said.

Nicholas grunted. 'Mostly,' he mumbled and flexed his pierced forearm.

'Has he been keeping you in his tent?' Bowman asked.

'He has,' she replied, 'which gets very warm in this sun. Insects collect in the top of it, along with all the bad smells from the men.'

'It sounds more like he's holding you as a prisoner in there,' Richard said.

'Why did he let you out?' Bowman asked.

'The grown-ups are having a war council,' Eva said, 'so they threw me out. Which suits me very much.'

'It's terrible that he keeps you locked up,' Bowman said.

Eva glanced at him. 'There are no locks, and there is little you can do about it. I shall marry him and that cannot change.'

'There is little any of us can do,' Brian mumbled without looking up, 'about anything.'

'Maybe you can cheer him up,' Richard said to Eva.

The princess squatted down by the monk. 'What is wrong with you?'

'I think that you,' Brian looked her in the eyes, 'are the only one here who knows what I am struggling with. You are Irish, and yet you've brought these dogs of war to tear our land apart like a lamb's carcass. These Normans will fight over our remains even as we pay them to do so. What have you done?

What have we done?'

'I have done nothing,' Eva said, 'and my father only does what is needed to find justice and restore order.'

'That does not justify the bloodshed.'

Eva sighed. 'Men are not perfect and we are where we find ourselves. What can we do to change our fate?'

'I will stop aiding our oppressors, for that is what they will become,' the monk said.

'I think we will do just fine without that rag on a stick,' Bowman grinned at him.

'Be nice,' Eva frowned at Bowman.

'Waterford may have kept us out so far,' Richard said, 'but Strongbow's victory feels inevitable. However gloomy everyone seems today.'

'Everyone is gloomy because they are so stupid,' Brian pushed his banner over so it fell onto the ground.

'Why are they stupid?' Eva asked.

Brian let out a deep breath. 'The Normans are all supposed to be experts in the science of warfare, that's what everyone in the cathedral told me. But you sit on this plain and do the obvious, ignoring the answer to your question that is staring you in the face.'

'Can you stop calling us the Normans,' Richard said, 'I don't really feel like I'm one of them.'

'I'm English,' Bowman said.

'You aren't,' Nicholas said.

The monk groaned. 'We could be in the city already.'

'Fine then,' Richard said, 'if you're so clever, what has everyone else missed?'

Brian turned his head towards the city which they could see clearly enough. 'Tell me what you see.'

'Monks and their games,' Bowman sat back down.

'The wall, a gate, some towers and a river,' Richard said. 'And?'

Richard looked harder. 'A cathedral spire, a lot of grass.' 'And?'

'The houses outside the town, I suppose,' Richard said.

'Finally,' Brian said, 'and where are they.'

'Right up against the wall,' Richard's face lit up, 'we can climb up the houses. You're a genius.'

'You are not quite there yet,' Brian rubbed his eyes and sighed, 'look at the houses.'

Richard squinted but it was still a bright day. 'They are wooden, do we burn them?'

'No.'

'Just tell me,' Richard said, 'you are clearly much smarter than every Norman here.'

Brian pointed at a single house between the two clusters of buildings up against the wall. 'That one, you see it? It is raised up because this plain can flood. Can you see what it sits on. What the whole house rests on?'

'I understand,' Richard said, 'we don't need to undermine a tower, we can just undermine that one house because it rests on a single wooden post.'

Bowman sat up and took a look. 'That's just a tree trunk,' he said.

'If we get there with some axes,' Richard said.

'We'll cut it down,' Bowman said.

'And the whole house will tumble over,' Brian said sadly, 'and give you a staircase of rubble right up to the top of the wall. No doubt you'll cut a bloody path through the defenders and sack the city.'

'We need to tell Strongbow,' Richard said.

Bowman folded his arms. 'I'm not going in there.'

'I'll go,' Eva nodded and walked back towards the tent and its council of war.

'Why didn't you mention that before?' Richard asked, 'did you spot that before or after I nearly drowned?'

Brian shrugged. 'What would another death have been? The crows will soon feed on my countrymen regardless.'

'Someone get him a strong drink,' Bowman said, 'or I'll have to crumple up that old flag and shove it down his throat.'

'Don't take it out on him,' Richard said.

'Answer the question, monk,' Nicholas said, 'did you spot the post before or after I got shot?'

Brian pushed the banner pole away with his foot. 'Maybe I only just saw it now,' he said.

Maybe I should ram that flag pole where my arrow nearly

went,' Nicholas scowled.

'That is the Norman solution to everything, isn't it? More violence.'

'War runs through the veins of this world, not just us,' Richard said.

'I don't want the blood of the inhabitants of Waterford on my soul,' Brian said, 'it is already stained enough with Baginbun. Had I kept the banner down during that battle, you'd all be dead and no one in Waterford would have to suffer at all.'

'I'm quite glad you kept swinging that banner,' Richard said.

'Strongbow isn't going to raise the city to the ground and wipe it out,' Bowman said, 'he's here because he wants a port. A working port.'

'What about the captives Raymond threw off the cliff at Baginbun, what is he going to do here?'

Bowman chuckled. 'Don't worry about your soul, monk. Richard here is responsible for the blood of hundreds at this point, and he is fine.'

Richard let a breath out as a hiss. 'Thanks,' he said.

Brian put his head in his hands.

Nicholas rubbed his rear but saw movement at the tent. 'The Butcher of Baginbun is on his way,' he said.

Raymond wore a great smile. 'Everything seems to revolve around you three since we landed,' he said.

Raymond clapped his great hands on Brian's shoulders and shook him vigorously. 'My boy, Strongbow is pleased with your eyes. He says you will have the honour of blessing his marriage bed.'

Richard looked for Bowman's reaction, but the man just pressed his lips together.

'A senior position in the Norman church of Ireland awaits you,' Raymond continued, 'this invasion will succeed only because of your efforts.'

Brian groaned.

'Oh,' Raymond said, 'and sort that banner out. We can't have the Papal banner going around soaked in blood can we, what sort of message does that send to the locals? Do it quickly, we have a city to sack.'

Raymond went around the camp telling the army to prepare

for action. Arrows were collected and Normans started to put mail and surcoats back on. Richard wanted a surcoat, he knew he looked like a poor country-knight without one.

Brian hadn't moved.

Bowman sat up and put an arm round the monk. 'Don't take it onto yourself, someone would have spotted the post eventually,' he said.

Brian pulled the banner over with his foot and picked it up.

'Go and wash it,' Richard said, 'it might make you feel a bit better.'

The monk did, slowly.

Richard glanced over at the house that stood on a post. 'Who do you think they're going to send to cut that down?'

Bowman snorted. 'Is that a question or a complaint?'

Richard re-armed himself, which hurt. By the time he was done he already sweated, so he sat down and waited for the army to assemble.

Raymond appeared again once he had made his rounds of the encampment.

'We know,' Richard said when he arrived.

The big Norman raised his eyebrows.

'You want us to cut down the post,' Bowman said, 'because we haven't yet cheated death enough for you.'

Raymond laughed. 'I cannot rightly send the fat mercenary and his broken knights, can I? How long would it take them? I need younger and fitter men for this job.'

'You're rewarding Alan for being fat,' Richard pushed himself to his feet and picked his shield up. The shield retained water from their river-excursion and was nearly twice as heavy as it should have been.

Raymond grinned. 'The Welsh have two saws for you. The big saws, the kind it takes two men to use.'

'Why can't the Welsh come and use their saws?' Bowman wondered.

'Because the Welsh don't have mail, and we're going to get shot at a lot,' Raymond said.

'We?'

The big Norman walked up to Richard and held him by the shoulders. 'I'm not asking you to do anything I wouldn't do myself, and there's only three of you, so you need a fourth man to do the sawing.'

Richard didn't know how he felt about Raymond, except that he'd much rather be on his side than against him.

'I'll fetch the saws,' Raymond let him go, 'then we'll bring this bloody wall down.'

Bowman put his cloak on over his armour and tied some of his blankets around himself.

Nicholas looked at him questioningly.

'For the arrows,' Bowman said, 'you heard the butcher, every man in that city is going to be shooting at us.'

Nicholas thought for a moment, then started to put his own cloak on.

Richard was happy enough with his two mail shirts, but after watching his companions, slid his cloak on over his head anyway. He laced on his helmet as Eva joined them.

In her hands was a crossbow.

Bowman turned to her. 'What do you think you're doing?'

'Fighting for my land,' she patted the bag of bolts that hung at her waist. She wore a mail shirt and a leather cap.

'Does Strongbow know you're here?' Richard asked.

Eva flicked her braided hair onto her back. 'I'm not married to him yet,' she said.

Bowman put a hand on her arm. 'Please don't.'

Eva walked away from him. 'I'm here to shoot anyone who tries to shoot you. No one will be aiming at me.'

'It would be much safer in the tent,' Bowman said.

'Strongbow and his pretentious priests and lawyers fill that tent. You can barely move in it, and they smell too much. I need to take Waterford so that I can sleep in peace in a proper house,' Eva said.

'You aren't going to talk her out of it,' Richard said, 'let's just make sure we cut this post down quickly.'

Raymond brought the two long saws over. They had a wooden handle at each end and sharp iron teeth.

Eva turned her back to him and walked away.

'Here we are,' Raymond said, 'let's go cut down a city.'

Brian sighed.

Brian didn't get time to wash his banner because Raymond dragged him along as they made their way towards the Welsh trenches. Bowman and Raymond carried the saws as hundreds of Welsh archers and one crossbow-woman readied their weapons in support.

Strongbow himself marshalled another ladder attack, a diversion designed to keep attention away from the sawing party for as long as possible. Richard noticed his uncle holding a ladder some distance away, and suddenly felt ill.

Bowman looked at the post, which was now just a bowshot away. 'If we take this city, today could be the last time I'll ever see her.'

'Probably,' Nicholas said, 'which is for the best. She'll get you hung.'

'So you don't want me hung?'

'I didn't say that,' Nicholas grinned.

Heads appeared on the walls and a horn sounded from inside Waterford.

'Why didn't we do this at night?' Richard asked.

Raymond stopped still. 'That is a very good point,' he started to laugh, 'I think Strongbow wants everyone to see his great plan.'

'His plan is it?' Nicholas glanced at Brian, who was too melancholy to be listening, or to care.

Raymond shifted both of his mail shirts around under his surcoat. 'Ready boys?'

Bowman moved his shield round to cover his front, but the saw was big and awkward and got in the way.

'That's a lot of blankets,' Raymond said.

'I don't want to get shot,' Bowman replied.

Raymond laughed. 'There, they're starting, off we go.'

The knights carrying ladders left the trenches and stormed towards the walls. Nearly a thousand arrows flew from the Welsh, and everyone on the wall ducked.

Richard followed Bowman out of their shallow trench and they ran towards their target.

The house stood at only a single storey tall, its thatched roof level with the top of the wall. It had a wooden frame that rested on the single post that bore the full weight of the building. The closer they got, the bigger that post started to look.

'Is that an ancient ok?' Bowman asked.

Arrows whistled down from the walls. Richard held his shield up and an arrow glanced off it in two broken pieces. An arrow pinged off Nicholas's shield, the head snapped off and spun through the air towards Richard. It hit his helmet on the side and Richard's nearest ear exploded in noise.

They all sprinted. In their armour though, the distance was far enough for that to be a bad idea. When they reached the relative safety of the wall, all four of them were covered in sweat and gasped for air.

Richard leant against the wall with the bottom of the house over his head. It blocked the sun and the space was cool and shaded.

Raymond caught his breath first. 'No time to waste, lads, everyone else is getting shot at so we can do this,' he held up the saw to Nicholas, 'take the other end.'

Richard took the other handle of Bowman's saw, and they started to saw at the tree trunk from both sides.

Their saw bit into the tree, which had been stripped of its bark, and dragged the teeth across it. The first time the blade bounced off and Bowman swore. The next time it dug in, and they started pulling the toothed tool back and forth.

Both saws cut into the trunk and sawdust started to fall around its base. The rasping noise drowned out the sounds of battle from further away.

An arrow skidded along the grass near Richard's already damaged foot.

'They've spotted us,' Raymond said.

Richard was already sawing as fast as he could, and he and Bowman had picked up a working rhythm.

Sweat dripped down his face and his biceps and forearms ached. They were only part way through the post when Richard heard sound above him.

'They've got into the house,' Raymond said, 'hurry up.'

Welsh arrows started to twang into the the side of the building, one flew too low and tangled in Bowman's blankets and pushed him a step away.

'See,' he said as he re-caught his balance.

Richard was too out of breath to reply. The sawing made his hands feel numb and he really wanted to stop.

Richard heard what had to have been the crossbow, and a scream rang out from the house above.

Raymond's saw made better progress than theirs, and had reached the half-way point. The post started to creak.

'When do we stop?' Richard asked.

'When it falls,' Raymond said.

'We'll be under it,' Bowman replied.

'It won't fall unless we're here to make it,' Raymond said, 'you'll have a chance to run for it.'

Richard saw the fire in Raymond's eyes. He was enjoying himself.

The whole house cracked and dust fell down from above. It landed in Richard's eyes and he had to saw blind while he tried to blink the scratching particles away.

He could be back home, Richard thought, arguing about something trivial with his wife, then forgetting about it. But no, he had to be under a house that was about to fall on top of him, with dust in his eyes, a broken toe and sore ribs. Another arrow sailed in from along the wall and hit Bowman's blankets. The blow unbalanced him and he fell over. The saw sprung from the post and the serrated edge tried to bite Richard's arm. The two layers of mail stopped a cut, but it still knocked down Richard's arm.

The top half of the post disconnected from the bottom and slid down a hand's width onto the lower half. The whole house dropped the same distance and the timber groaned above them. Another cloud of dust shook free and hung in the air, which made Richard cough.

Richard looked up and a splinter hit his chin.

Raymond dropped his saw. 'Don't look at it, get out,' he shouted.

The house teetered on the two halves of the post. Yet more dust fell from above. Richard snapped back into life and ran out from under the house. Bowman scrambled his way out behind him. The structure slid as the post started to buckle. Then the house collapsed. The whole building fell to the ground in a torrent of beams, planks, chairs, defenders, reeds and dust. The force of the debris hitting the ground pushed Richard off his feet. He rolled over as the dust settled on his face. Bowman lay next to him groaning and swearing. The swearing meant he was fine, so Richard sat up and ignored him.

The house lay in a pile of rubble from the ground half way up to the top of the wall. Except it had torn the top half of the wall down with it, leaving a house-sized breach in the city's defences. Raymond picked himself up from the edge of the rubble, but his red cloak was stuck under a stack of twisted beams. He ripped the cloak out, tearing it and leaving the bottom half under the building.

Raymond coughed and spat out dust. 'I told you you'd get out,' he beamed.

Richard couldn't see Nicholas. Everyone on both sides had paused when the building came down, but now everything increased in pace.

Strongbow yelled across the plain so loudly Richard could hear him, and every knight and half the Welshmen rushed towards the breach. Arrows flew towards the battlements and again the stunned defenders kept their heads down.

Richard picked a long splinter out of his forehead, just under his helmet and above his eye.

'Where's my brother?' Bowman stood up and dusted his blankets down.

Richard looked at the rubble. 'He was right behind us.'

Bowman ran up to the wall to see if there was a pocket of air behind the rubble.

A man in mail and with an old fashioned shield appeared on the top of the breach. An archer joined him and drew his bow at Richard.

Richard ran to join Bowman which got him out of the arrow's path as it whistled by.

Raymond started to climb up the rubble on his own, sword drawn.

'He's mad,' Richard said when he reached Bowman.

'So are we, just find my brother.'

'So it's brother now is it?' Richard asked.

Bowman shot him a look that made Richard back off.

Instead, they started to move beams out of the way to get under the smashed house.

Knights charged up the rubble, which made it shift and threw yet more dust up into the air.

A log rolled down and fell to the ground next to Richard.

Bowman started digging his way in as the sounds of battle erupted above them. He pulled a plank out and threw it behind him.

'There's a cavity,' he said and crawled on his hands and knees into the mound of debris.

'Hurry up,' Richard said, 'it's going to collapse on you as well soon.' He looked up and defenders on the walls shot arrows into the those charging up the breach. Welshmen shot back but some in turn were struck and fell.

Bowman's head popped out of the hole he'd dug. 'I've found him, help me pull him out.'

Bowman disappeared and pushed Nicholas's arm out towards Richard. He grabbed it and pulled. Bowman pushed his half-brother out and his unconscious body flopped onto the earth.

Milo de Cogan started to run up the rubble and saw them. 'Forget about him, storm the city, do your duty,' he ran off into Waterford.

'We better go,' Richard looked down at the the pale face of the man on the ground, 'we'll have to come back for him.'

'I'm not leaving him,' Bowman crawled out, 'I'll throw water on him. You can go and fight.'

Richard thought for a moment. 'I'll go, you stay and help him.'

Bowman nodded and ran back towards the trenches.

Missile fire along the wall had ceased as the defenders abandoned it and tried to plug the rupture in their fortification.

Richard drew his sword and started to climb. The footing was loose and bodies of archers lay all around. He reached the top of the wall and looked into Waterford for the first time. Buildings lined narrow streets, and the Normans pushed down the one that led deeper into the city. Other groups pushed left and right along the inside of the wall.

He heard Alan's wheezing before he saw him. The large knight clambered to where Richard stood and gasped for air.

'Are you out of breath just climbing that?' Richard asked.

The mercenary couldn't speak, his bright cheeks pulsed.

The last group of Norman knights rushed in and pushed by Richard. He felt a heavy push in his back. Richard spun around and as the knights ran down into the city, he thought he recognised one. He looked around at his cloak and a gash ran across the wool. He pushed it aside and felt the mail below. Sure enough, a few rings were split in his back.

'I'll kill him,' Richard mumbled, but he wasn't surprised. He'd forgotten about Luke and it had nearly killed him.

The knights with his uncle turned right, so Richard thought it best if he followed Raymond instead.

Richard went down the street that headed into the city. A shieldwall of locals blocked the way. Behind them he recognised Sigurd, Ragnall's companion, and he seemed to be directing the defence. Richard climbed down the wall and into the city. His feet hit the beaten earth that was the ground and his toe sent pain up his leg. He made his way to the back of the press of Normans pushing into the enemy shieldwall.

He heard the twang of the crossbow and turned to see Eva standing on the breach, shooting her weapon along the street. A great cry went up and the Normans surged forwards. Richard went with them, all he could see were the mailed necks and helmets of the men in front of him. He nearly tripped on a body as they moved along the street's houses.

'They're running,' someone shouted.

The knights kept going, deeper and deeper into the city. The buildings didn't look like those in England or Normandy, most had walls of planks driven into the ground, with roofs supported by these planks.

Knights and some lesser armed squires broke off and started entering the buildings. Screams rang out from inside, some of terror, some of death. Brian was not going to be happy, he thought.

The knights ground to a halt and Richard bumped into the back of one. He turned around to look back along the street, Alan and two of his knights still stood at the top of the breach.

'What's happening up ahead?' He shouted.

'No idea,' the nearest Norman replied in a Welsh accent.

Richard stepped in the channel of filth that ran down the side of the street and swore. The heat of the summer had baked the street hard, but wet and semi-dry waste still ran down its edge.

Richard started to push through the crowd, sick of not knowing what was happening. Normans let him through, but more and more started to leave to sack the vulnerable houses.

Richard could hear iron on iron and before he knew it he'd pushed through to the second rank of the attacking force.

A rearguard of mailed defenders blocked the street that led into the square in front of the cathedral Richard could see rise up in the distance. There were only just enough defenders to bar the way, and weight of numbers pushed them back step by step. They hacked at the Normans who hacked back. One defender fell and Raymond and Milo pushed into his place. In the time it took to take two breaths, they turned and rolled up the shieldwall, killing men who couldn't defend themselves.

A moment later and the mailed men all lay dead.

'Secure the cathedral,' Raymond bellowed, 'take the tower.'

The Normans cried in victory and cheered as they swarmed into the centre of the city. Some spear armed Irish levymen fled. Sigurd, limping with a bolt in his shoulder, made for the tower.

Alan walked along the street and made for the large cathedral. Screeches and cries filled the air from all around Waterford as the invaders spread out and took their vengeance for the stubbornness of its defence. Richard had little appetite for that, so he went to the tower which looked to be where the last stand of Ragnall and Sigurd would take place.

Arrows occasionally whistled out from arrow slits in the small round tower. It only had one door, which was shut, and Raymond banged on it. 'There's no point,' he shouted, 'you might as well yield. Our lord is known to be merciful.'

Unlike you, Richard thought.

Ragnall leant over the battlements that crowned the tower. 'I know what you did, you set a man free to tell us, remember. This is what your brutality will earn you.'

A crossbow bolt launched up at him but hit the stone and

split into pieces. The remnants of it landed around Raymond. 'Stop that,' he ordered, 'get out of the way of the arrows and don't bother shooting at them. We'll wait for Strongbow.'

Richard found the corner of a house to stand behind and waited for something to happen.

While he waited, the city was sacked. A few small plumes of smoke started to rise into the blue sky and Richard hoped that things wouldn't get too out of hand.

A group of archers approached the tower with axes, and someone in the tower shot an arrow at them. It missed and hit the house Richard hid behind just as he looked around the corner.

Strongbow walked down the street, his retinue of knights in yellow surcoats with red chevrons arrayed around him.

'Richard,' he stopped, 'having a rest?'

'Yes,' Richard nodded.

The lord looked him up and down. 'You're covered in dust,' he started walking again, 'follow me.'

Richard peeled himself off the wall and followed Strongbow's guards.

The Welsh with the axes went to the door and started to heave away at it. Splinters of wood flew off, but it wasn't going to give way quickly.

Strongbow stood halfway to the tower, stopped and put his hands on his hips. 'Ragnall,' he shouted.

The only response he got was an arrow, which embedded itself in the earth in front of his foot.

'If anyone else shoots at me, everyone in there will die,' he shouted up.

Ragnall's head popped up from the battlements.

Another arrow whizzed past Strongbow's face and hit one of his guards in the shin. The knight hopped on one leg and swore loudly. He pulled the arrow out and threw it to the ground.

Strongbow sighed. 'That was already your third chance, Ragnall, I'm trying to be merciful.'

'I didn't order them to shoot,' Ragnall replied, 'but you're going to kill us all anyway.'

'Then you've got nothing to lose by yielding and trying your luck,' Strongbow said. 'If you walk out of that door,' he continued, 'I'll let you govern Waterford for me.'

Ragnall paused, then his head bobbed back up. 'That's too good an offer to be true,' he dropped out of view.

A flurry of arrows flew out of the arrow slits, and one only went a fraction above Richard's head.

'Chop that door in,' Strongbow walked towards the tower.

Richard followed his retinue, happy to get so close to the tower that no one could aim arrows at him.

The axes hit the door at regular intervals, and it was loud enough that it almost sent Richard to sleep. The vibration of the blows went up through his feet and through the stone wall he leant on, and he realised how tired he was. He tried to pick grit out of his eyes.

Dermot arrived from along the street, dressed in a green linen tunic and with a red cloak. He looked up at the tower. 'Good work, de Clare,' he said, 'Waterford is a fitting city for me to recapture.'

Some of Strongbow's knights laughed quietly.

Alan, along with his knights and half a dozen others walked out of the cathedral, their arms brimming with golden cups, crosses and trinkets. They all looked very pleased with themselves.

Dermot watched them walk past him airily and paid them no mind.

Strongbow's voice, however, boomed across the square. 'Those had better not have come from the cathedral. Who do you think we are, common pirates? Turn around right now and put them back, or you'll all swing from this tower once we've taken it.'

The robbers froze. Alan was, surprisingly, the first to react. He turned and jogged back the way he'd come, his mail rings clinking as he moved. A golden cross fell from his arms and fell into the dirt, but he didn't look back.

Dermot went and picked it up, just as an arrow narrowly missed him.

'Get over here,' Strongbow shouted at Dermot.

The hopeful king obeyed. 'Would you mind killing everyone in here so we can get on with ruling this city?' He asked.

Strongbow pointed at the axes that bit chunks out of the

172

door. 'We are working on it.'

An axe went through the door. A moment later an arrow flew out of the jagged hole and hit the Welshman in his throat. He fell away and Milo ran forwards with his sword. He plunged it into the hole in the door. Nothing happened.

'Keep going,' Strongbow said, 'we can't fit through that hole, can we.'

Milo picked up the axe himself and started to enlarge the hole.

Another arrow zipped out but Milo dodged it and it lodged itself in the roof of a building across the square.

Milo hacked down with the axe and a whole plank came away and fell inwards into the tower.

'Get a spear,' he shouted, 'lever it open.'

Raymond appeared, the Papal banner in his hands, and jammed it into the damaged door. He leant back and more planks of wood pinged and fell away from the iron hinges.

The banner pole snapped and Raymond fell backwards onto the ground.

Strongbow laughed at him, then waved his sword at the door. 'Come on, get in there and kill everyone. If you can take Ragnall alive, do so, but I won't cry if you can't.'

Richard had no wish to be involved, but felt he had to follow Strongbow's men into the tower.

Milo went first and Richard heard him kill the archer who had so nearly struck him through the door.

Richard stepped through the remnants of the door and into the dark tower. Some men went down a level, while Milo led two knights up the spiralling staircase. Richard followed them. His toe, despite being bound, hurt when he pushed off on the hard stone.

Milo reached the next level and clashed swords with a man.

The Normans in front of him joined in and soon two mailed defenders lay dead.

One knight started to loot their bodies.

'Keep going up,' Milo pointed his red sword to the stairs. Richard, realising he was now closest, groaned inwardly.

'Go, now,' Milo ran behind him and pushed Richard up the stairs.

Richard gave in and ran up himself. The stairs opened straight up to the tower's roof, which meant the defenders on it could stab down with spears as they climbed.

Richard raised his shield and pushed his way up against their blows. Spear points jammed into the shield as he went. Richard's head reached floor level and he could see the feet of all who stood on the tower.

A spear flashed by his eyes, but Milo pushed him yet further up.

A man ran at him from behind and cut at Richard's exposed back. The blade connected with the leather strap of his shield and almost managed to slice through it.

Milo cut at the man, and Richard kept pushing forwards.

Now standing on the roof, Richard swung his sword at a man in a mail shirt and a bushy red beard. Richard's cut hit only his raised shield.

Milo swung under the shield and sliced the man's thigh open.

As he fell in agony, Richard pushed the remaining spears aside with his shield and jumped at the two men who wielded them. Except they were only boys, younger than himself and wearing only tunics. Richard felt pity but their eyes were harsh, and they would show no pity back.

Richard used his body as a ram to thump into them, then brought his sword around at their faces. With no helmets to save them both boys fell to the ground.

Richard turned and saw Milo fighting Sigurd.

Ragnall was the last defender, and he held his sword high and attacked Richard.

The crossbow bolt still in his shoulder, Sigurd couldn't raise his sword arm high enough to parry, and Milo's first strike cleaved a gash in his neck. Milo left him to die and pointed his sword at Ragnall.

'It is over,' he said.

Richard stayed his sword to see what their opponent would do.

Ragnall glanced between the two of them. Then his body sunk and he lowered his sword.

'Drop it,' Milo said.

Ragnall dropped his sword.

Milo punched him in the face. 'That's for being stupid enough to try to resist us,' he said.

Ragnall clenched his bleeding nose and looked up at Milo with hatred in his eyes.

Richard could think of at least three reasons why he could punch Ragnall too, but held himself back as Raymond ascended the stairs.

'I missed the fun,' the big Norman said.

Raymond walked over to the stone crenelations and gazed out of Waterford. 'This is a good view,' he said.

Richard lowered his sword. One of the plumes of smoke over the city had grown and blackened, and he could still hear shouts and screams in the air.

'I suppose we should take him to see Lord Strongbow,' Raymond said, 'Richard, would you be so good as to drag Sigurd down, too?'

Richard almost dared complain, but instead wiped his sword on his ripped cloak and put it away. He picked up Sigurd by his legs and dragged him down the spiral stairs. The dead man's iron helmet bounced on each step, and the cut in his neck left a trail of blood the whole way down. Once he got back to ground level, and having nearly tripped on his own spurs, Richard again was blanketed in sweat.

Strongbow stood shouting at Ragnall. 'I don't want to see you again, someone lock him somewhere in this tower while I decide what to do with him.'

Milo spun the captive around and pushed him back into the tower.

Richard dropped Sigurd's foot once he was through the doorway and caught his breath.

Strongbow walked over and peered down. 'He's not got such a big mouth, now, has he?' The Norman squatted down and tugged at the bolt buried in the dead man's shoulder. It didn't come out. Strongbow stood up. 'Who here has a crossbow?' He asked.

'We didn't bring any,' Raymond shrugged, 'I didn't think the Irish had them, either.'

Eva stepped forwards from the hundreds of men who gathered in the square. She held her crossbow in one hand. The bag of bolts was empty.

'You?' Strongbow said, 'what are you doing with that, those are not for women.'

Raymond laughed. 'They aren't, but you cannot argue with results,' he pointed at Sigurd, 'that bolt is what made them lose their resolve.'

Blood had splashed across Eva's mail at some point, and it dropped down slowly from ring to ring.

Richard noticed she wore a new sword belt too, bright red leather and engraved.

Strongbow stroked his chin. 'I never said you could fight.'

'You never said I couldn't.'

Raymond laughed hard behind his leader. 'You can't argue with that, that's the same argument you've got against King Henry.'

Eva smiled for the briefest moment.

'A princess cannot risk herself in combat,' Strongbow said, 'and besides, it is an affront to God. What will the common people think of you when they hear of this? They will not want you as their queen.'

Eva's face remained as stone.

'No one wants a bloodied queen,' Strongbow complained, 'I don't want to give the people a reason to revolt.'

'Then call her the red queen,' Raymond said, 'scare them into submission.'

'Ha,' Strongbow turned to his friend, 'she can be Red Eva. The bloody princess who strikes fear into the hearts of those who oppose us.'

Eva frowned.

'Well,' Strongbow said, 'I don't know if I should be impressed or terrified, but tomorrow I shall marry her in this city.'

His army cheered. Richard noticed that Eva did not.

FRACTURES

In the end, Strongbow had to wait. A Bishop who had crossed the sea with him intervened and insisted the proper process was followed. The couple instead had to fast for a day before they were deemed pure enough to marry. Richard spent that day quartered in a newly abandoned house in Waterford. The rumour going around was that over seven hundred of the inhabitants had been put to the sword, which handily meant that there was room in the city for the army to billet itself.

Nicholas spent the day on a merchant's low wooden bed, a bed that was actually raised off the ground. He regained consciousness, drank some water, then fell asleep.

Brian sat in the corner of the single room that made up the house, which was dark due to a lack of windows. No straw or reeds covered the hard earthen floor, but it was cooler than outside so Richard was glad of it.

Bowman examined a decent blue tunic that hung from a peg in the wall, rolled it up and put it by his bedding.

Richard walked to the door so he wouldn't have to think about the previous owner of that tunic too much.

Horse's hooves sounded from the direction of the gate.

Their house was on the main street where the heaviest fighting had taken place, and Richard watched as the gate was opened by some of the Welsh. A procession of horsemen paraded slowly in.

'More Irish are coming,' Richard said.

Bowman wandered out to watch.

'Brian, who are they?' Richard asked.

'Who cares,' the monk replied from his corner.

'You can't hide from the world for the rest of your life,'

Bowman said, 'get your sorry bones out here and tell us who these people are?'

'Why bother?'

'Because I'm bored,' Bowman replied, 'and if you don't, I'll just drag you out here anyway.'

In the face of such a compelling argument, the monk got to his feet and went out into the light of the day. Brian blinked and rubbed his eyes.

'Monks spend too much time indoors,' Bowman laughed.

'They are natives from Dublin,' Brian said.

'Are the friendly?' Richard asked.

The monk nodded. 'We wouldn't have opened the gate to them otherwise, would we.'

Richard frowned, the monk's mood had been foul since the assault.

The first of the nobles from the northerly city rode by their doorway. They were mounted on native horses without saddles, but their clothing was strongly coloured and each noble came with a small retinue of followers. Brian named them all, but most of the names were too foreign for Richard's ears.

'They have all been in exile,' Brian said, 'I suppose they return to King Dermot's side.'

The followers included men with shields, bows and spears, and Richard counted over a hundred of them before he lost interest.

The final nobleman was no nobleman at all. She held herself as tall on her horse as the men had, but she was unmistakably a she. She wore a bright green dress with golden trim and a cloak of fine brown fur. Her hair was a mix of blonde and brown streaks.

Richard's eyes followed her.

Brian tapped his foot on the ground. 'You need to master your base impulses,' he said, 'especially with that one.'

'Can women rule here?' Richard asked.

Brian shook his head. 'Every woman of standing needs a male guardian by law. She is the only one in Ireland who scorns that law.'

'Who is she?' Richard asked.

Bowman started to laugh, which ended in a coughing fit. 'Young lord, if you're upset with me, then maybe you should forget about her.'

'You won't be able to pronounce her name,' Brian said, 'but she calls herself the Countess. Even though that rank does not exist here.'

'How do you know I can't pronounce her name?'

'Because for all of the other names I have just spoken,' the monk said, 'you and your friend pulled childish faces and made babbling noises.'

Richard looked away from the monk as the last of the Countess's retinue filed by.

'She's considered a witch, Richard,' Brian said.

'I'm married, anyway,' Richard looked away from her and to her men.

'She is a relative of the High King of Ireland,' Brian continued, 'and I doubt he is taking kindly to a Norman army on the soil that he surely considers his.'

'I thought Dermot was the king?' Bowman asked.

'Of Leinster,' the monk answered, 'Rory is the king above the other kings.'

Bowman nodded, but Richard hadn't been listening because one of the riders niggled his memory.

He nudged Bowman. 'Do you recognise him, or am I going mad?' He asked.

Bowman's eyes followed the rider, a man with black hair and a woollen hood over his head. 'The hood hangs closer to his head on his left side,' Bowman said.

Richard stood straighter with a start. 'What's he doing here?'

'Who?' Brian asked.

'King Dermot's messenger,' Bowman said, 'Cormac. He bought me these golden spurs.'

'Why does he ride with the Countess?' Richard wondered out-loud.

Brian frowned but he looked more alive that he had for a while. 'Most inappropriate of him to ride with someone aligned to the High King.'

Bowman yawned. 'I don't care,' and walked back into the house.

Brian's gaze followed the last of the newcomers as they rode towards the cathedral and central square.

'Do you want to see what they do?' Richard asked.

Brian thought about it.

'I do want to,' Richard said, 'so you're coming with me.'

Richard walked off down the road, leaving Brian to sigh and follow.

The sun had dried the pools of blood out, but the red stains still darkened the street. Richard looked up from them as they reached the square between the cathedral and the tower.

The Dubliners filled the area and most dismounted. Some locals and a few of the Norman army came out to see what the noise was as chatter bubbled up all around.

Strongbow left the tower with Raymond and Milo behind him.

The new lord of Waterford still wore his mail and his chevron-covered yellow surcoat. 'Where's that monk who speaks Irish?' He looked around.

Dermot appeared from the crowd. 'As the King of Leinster, I can translate between all,' he said, 'we need no monk.'

Brian folded his arms.

Richard looked at him, his annoyance unhidden.

Dermot pointed at various of the Dubliners and told Strongbow who they were. They came to greet him one by one. The men held themselves highly, but their eyes darted from Dermot to Strongbow as they spoke.

'They do not know which is the real king,' Brian said.

'They'll work it out soon enough,' Richard said.

'Follow the blood and follow the money,' the monk mumbled.

'Can you see Cormac? I've lost him,' Richard asked.

Brian shook his head. 'There's too many people here.'

The whole square was covered in Irish retainers and increasing numbers of the Norman army.

The countess stayed in the middle of the square and never approach Strongbow.

The Norman lord turned to the assembled crowd. 'I have fasted for a night and a day. Tomorrow I shall wed the princess of Leinster and become the tanist of Leinster.'

'What does that mean?' Richard asked.

'That he is the elected heir, so when King Dermot dies, Strongbow will succeed him,' Brian said.

'I can see why the Irish are unsure,' Richard said. He noticed that Dermot had not translated that part for the Dubliners. Instead he toed the ground and looked down.

'What's the matter?' Strongbow asked him loudly, 'are you ashamed of the deal you struck with me?'

Dermot looked up, his eyes a mixture of shame and anger.

Strongbow laughed and waved him away. 'I don't need to tell them anything anyway,' he said. The Norman walked back into his tower without giving the Dubliners a second thought.

Dermot's eyes flashed around the crowd before he stalked off through the square back to wherever he was staying.

The Norman crowd started to disperse, but the Irish were unsure of where they would be lodging.

Dermot walked past the Countess and she grabbed his arm.

Richard walked closer and pulled Brian with him because he wanted to hear what she said.

Dermot replied to her and she snapped at him. The current King of Leinster nodded and walked away.

'Did you hear any of that?' Richard asked Brian.

'She told him: not here.'

'Anything else?'

'No, it's too loud here,' the monk replied.

Richard watched the Countess give orders to her followers, who rushed to obey.

'Let's go back,' Richard said, 'I think we should find somewhere for Bowman to have a drink. If he's drunk right through this wedding, he might not do anything stupid about it. We can worry about messengers and Countesses later.'

Later that day Richard and Bowman found a house with a sign up to indicate ale had been made and served there. Someone had hung up a Norman shield next to it to signify that the army was welcome, so they went in.

Brian had sunk back down into the corner of their lodgings, his eyes on the broken banner across the room, and refused to leave, which Richard wasn't overly upset about.

The ale house was a normal town house, one floor and a

hearth in the centre of it. The brewed ale was dispensed in one corner by a woman in a faded old dress, and overseen by a Norman knight who leant against the wall with his eyes half shut.

The house was full of Welshmen, who had taken all the benches, so Bowman stood by the fire and drank ale until he really needed a bench to sit on.

He tried to stagger over to get more drink but nearly fell over instead. The Welsh laughed at him.

One Welshman picked Bowman up and patted him on the back as he said something. His friends laughed. The Welshman took a second look at Bowman and his mocking ceased. He said something in a low tone, then pushed a space free on the benches.

Bowman swayed and regarded them in confusion.

The Welshman patted the seat. 'Bag in bun,' he said.

Richard breathed easily again.

Bowman flopped onto the bench and cast his bleary eyes around for a drink.

One was given over and Richard wondered if it would work for him, too.

A man burst into the doorway, a squire to a knight judging by the sword at his waist. He wore a passable yellow tunic but his face was red from running.

'The city's weapon store is on fire, everyone is to come to its aid,' he said before rushing off out of the house.

Someone translated it to the Welsh who spoke hurriedly between themselves, but went to the aid of no one. Bowman laid his head down sideways on the table and started to fall asleep.

Richard left him and went outside. From the street he could see a stack of black smoke rise from another quarter of the city.

The knight who had been guarding the ale distribution came to watch beside Richard.

'That will be the locals,' he said in an accent that sounded like it was from the English west.

Richard nodded. It wasn't going to be the Normans or the Welsh.

'That's the garrison's arrows, spears and those bastard wall hooks all gone, then,' the knight said.

'Hopefully it doesn't cause any trouble for the wedding,' Richard said.

'Who cares about that?' The knight asked, 'all we should care about it getting out of here alive. Kill the locals, and burn the place, it's the only way to be sure.'

'We can't kill all of them,' Richard said, 'they are Christian here.'

'All the men then, crush this resistance before it's too late.'

Richard hadn't seen a single local man since the city fell, only women and children. 'If we start killing here, the sabotage in the next town we take will only be worse.'

'You sound like a priest,' the knight said, 'I can see why you want to go to the wedding.'

'I'm not invited,' Richard replied.

'Of course not, he doesn't want any of us there. It is a show for the natives.'

'There will be a feast afterwards,' Richard said, 'I don't think we should miss that.'

'Indeed, at Ragnall's hall, though I don't suppose it's his anymore,' the knight said.

Richard doubted it was, and while they spoke of the wedding Richard could just imagine Bowman's teeth grinding at the very thought of it. He knew he really had to make sure Bowman was drunk for as long as possible.

Which was an objective Bowman was fully aligned with. They toured seven houses that brewed ale the next day, as the wedding happened elsewhere. Strongbow sent knights around with money to buy all the drink Waterford could produce, but no effort was made to ensure riot-free drinking. This tentative state of order lasted until the evening of the next day, when wedding completed and the feasting began.

Richard overheard one story that two hundred cattle had been slaughtered for the occasion. To the story's credit, there was beef on every corner of the square, free for anyone who wanted it.

Richard and Bowman obliged, the blonde man finding his appetite after a day and two night's drinking.

183

They slept for a few hours in the deadest part of the night, but had gone out again as soon as Bowman had been able to string a sentence together.

That ability, Richard thought, was now on the wane again.

Bowman swayed to the music being played on a small platform near the cathedral door, six musicians played the loudest and fasted music Richard had ever heard. His head ached and his lips were dry despite the cups he'd been emptying.

Bowman looked worse.

'Do you need to go to the house and sleep?' Richard asked.

'Sleep is for the weak,' Bowman pointed at the men who danced in the square, 'I should go there.'

'You don't look that strong to me,' Richard said.

'Tell me, young lord, do you miss your mother?'

Richard blinked slowly and looked at his friend. 'That's the drink talking.'

Bowman took a step to the side that ended up being three. 'That may be, but you never speak of her.'

'I lost her a long time ago,' Richard said, 'and thinking about her won't bring her back.'

'Was she good to you?'

Richard nodded.

The musicians started a song that everyone else seemed to know and a round of violent singing began.

'What about yours?' Richard asked, 'you only mentioned her when you thought you were going to die.'

'Yes, that coward of a half-brother nearly did for me,' Bowman waved a hand around, 'a special place in hell is reserved for those who kill their kin, you know.'

Richard did know, and was happy to pay that price if his uncle tried to kill him again. 'It must be hard knowing she is with the man responsible for your family's tragedy.'

Bowman burped, which seemed to surprise him. 'Hard? I am not sure it is even true,' he said.

'You told me it was.'

'Did I? Doesn't sound like something I would say,' Bowman said.

'Can you just hurry up and drink more,' Richard said.

'Are you trying to get me drunk?' Bowman said too loudly.

'Yes,' Richard replied, 'that's the whole point of this.'

'Ah, yes,' Bowman finished whatever had been in the wooden cup.

'I need you as drunk as possible that you can still walk back to your bed.'

'Don't talk about it,' Bowman dropped the cup, 'it reminds me why I'm letting you do this to me.'

'Sorry.'

'We had a deal,' Bowman forgot about the cup, 'if it's a boy, she'll name it Robert, and if it's a girl, she'll call it Isabel.'

Richard frowned. 'What are you talking about?'

A fight started in the square amongst the dancers and Bowman surged off to join in.

Richard caught him by the arm, which was enough to make Bowman nearly fall over.

'No fighting,' Richard said.

Bowman steadied himself. 'Where was I?'

'Drinking one more then going to bed,' Richard said.

'You know what you're problem is?'

Richard sighed. 'You're going to tell me, aren't you?'

'You're boring,' Bowman pointed to the square where two knights dragged the fighters apart, 'everyone else is having fun, and you're not.'

'I'm looking after you,' Richard said.

'That's just your excuse because you're boring.'

'I'm bored of you telling me I'm boring.'

Bowman held a finger up to quieten him.

'What?'

The blonde man turned away and threw up violently into the gutter around the square. Some splashed up against the wall of the cathedral, but some landed on the cloak of a Norman knight.

'That fur is ruined,' the knight looked down at the wet stain.

'I'm sorry,' Richard said, 'he didn't mean it.'

The knight looked up and his face curled into a snarl. 'You?'

Richard's heart sank. It was one of Alan's knights. He was without his surcoat or mail, but his face was unmistakeable.

Alan stood next to him, a wooden plate piled high with

roasted meat in his hands. His mouth was full. 'Your drunk friend hates me,' Alan said, 'this was deliberate.' Food fell from his mouth as he spoke.

'Have some courtesy,' Richard grimaced at him, 'come on Bowman, let's go.'

Bowman leant on the wall and groaned.

'The fur is spoilt now,' the knight held it up, 'look. You need to pay for that.'

'We have no coin between us,' Richard said, 'that's why we're in Ireland in the first place.'

Bowman rebalanced himself, looked at Alan and the knight, then ran. 'Run, Richard,' he shouted as he pushed through two Welshmen and started down the street.

Richard sighed. 'He really didn't mean it, he's just drunk,' he said.

'Then why is he running?' The knight asked, 'running means guilt, everyone knows that.'

'You tried to rob a nunnery, what do you know of guilt?' Richard said.

The knight's face steeled and Richard regretted it. Part of him wished Bowman had been there to see how not-boring he could be.

'You'll pay, coin or not,' the knight said, 'I know you have weapons and mail.'

Richard looked down the dark street but Bowman was out of sight. The knight threw down his cup and walked towards Richard.

Richard ran after his friend. He pushed through the Welshman Bowman had nearly knocked to the ground and they cursed him.

'Get him,' Alan shouted, meat flying from his mouth.

The knight was behind him, Richard knew it without turning around. He scrambled on the dry earth of the street and dodged some singing Irishmen. This was not the street to their lodging, which Richard thought was probably for the best.

He thought about fighting, but only had Sir John's dagger on him, and wasn't sure if he was more sober than the knight.

'Come back,' the knight cried behind, his voice strained but not yet out of breath.

Richard looked for Bowman ahead as he sprinted between rows of houses. He caught a glimpse of Bowman leaning on a wall.

The big man saw him, then ran down a smaller street.

Richard followed and that street opened out into a small, unlit square up against the inside of the city wall. The buildings that lined it showed no sign of life and no fires shone through the gaps around their doors.

Bowman rested against one of the buildings, holding his stomach. 'I'm going to be sick,' he said.

Richard caught his breath. 'Again?'

'Again? When was I sick?'

Richard groaned. 'Why do you think we're running?'

Bowman shrugged. 'Sir Wobble used to run to stay strong, are we not doing that?'

'No,' Richard pointed back the way they'd come, just as the knight burst into the square.

'Give me that dagger,' he pointed to Richard's waist.

'That's mine, I didn't throw up on you,' Richard said.

'Someone threw up on you?' Bowman asked very loudly, 'how rude. You should teach them a lesson for that.'

Richard stepped backwards. 'You know what, if you'll be content with giving him a beating,' he said to the knight, 'I'll walk away and you can have him.'

'That was my best cloak, and my only cloak,' the knight drew a short knife Richard hadn't noticed before.

'Young lord,' Bowman said, 'if you soiled his cloak, the least you can do is apologise.'

Richard backed up to the wall Bowman leant on.

The knife pointed at him drew nearer.

'This isn't an argument that warrants a death,' Richard held both his hands up, 'we can settle this without bloodshed.'

'Drop the dagger on the floor and I'll happily agree with you,' the knight replied.

Bowman burped, stepped forwards and threw up on the knight's leather shoes.

The man looked down with his mouth open.

Bowman stepped back and wiped his mouth. 'I feel a lot

better now,' he nodded.

'His head,' the knight muttered, 'I'll have his head.'

'We'll pay,' Richard said, 'we'll find some coin and replace the cloak.'

He looked down at the mess on the ground. 'And some shoes, I suppose.'

The knight's face, even in the darkness of the square, was red. He slashed at Bowman with the knife, who half-stepped, half-fell onto Richard, then bumped onto the wall.

Richard stepped forwards but the knight swung the knife around to him. Richard held his hands back up. 'No one needs to die.'

'Who said anything about dying,' the knight said, 'I'll just take a finger from each of you for theft.'

'Theft?' Richard said, 'we haven't stolen anything.'

The knight lunged. The knife tore a hole in Richard's cloak as he jumped back, and his aching ribcage jarred against the wooden planks of a house.

The knight snarled and attacked again.

Bowman pushed off from the wall and threw himself at the knight's arm. The knife fell to the earth and the two men tumbled.

Richard rushed forwards and reached for his dagger but it wasn't there.

The knight screamed and Bowmen stilled.

Richard froze as the mercenary's legs kicked out violently. 'What did you do'? He asked.

The knight coughed blood. Bowman pushed Sir John's dagger up his throat and into the base of his skull with a crunch. The knight went limp.

Bowman got to his feet and held the dagger out to Richard.

Richard couldn't help the urge to look down, but obviously the dagger's sheath lay empty on its belt.

'How did you do that?'

Bowman smiled. 'When he attacked me I fell back by you because he'd attack you next. And you're too self righteous to draw the dagger.'

'You pick-pocketed me,' Richard put his hands on his hips.

Bowman gestured with the knife. 'Or saved you. Take it, we

should probably go.'

Richard snatched the knife and wiped the blood off on the knight's cloak. 'You didn't have to kill him,' he said.

Bowman turned away. 'He was going to kill you, then me.'

A shadow moved in the street they'd entered along.

'Who's there,' Richard shouted.

Footsteps echoed away.

'You need to find out who that is,' Bowman said.

'Why me?'

'Because I'm too drunk to run.'

Richard groaned and started off, dagger in hand. He turned out of the square.

'You're still boring,' Bowman shouted behind him and the words echoed off the houses.

Richard ran and his lungs gasped for air. The shadow ahead was clearly a man, and Richard tried to keep up but his prey was fast.

A crow flew overhead, Richard heard its wings flap as he turned down a street and saw no one, the man had disappeared. He stopped and tried to breathe quietly. He could hear the party far away across the city, and two dogs barked at each other. The street was too long for the man to have left it, so he must have entered one of the houses.

A door flew open and cast a yellow glow across the road. Three men filed out, followed by the sound of voices from inside. They turned Richard's way, laughing and joking. Their words were Irish, Richard knew that much, but he couldn't hide anywhere so, his chase unsuccessful, he left and went back to Bowman.

Bowman had already stripped the cloak from the knight and left. Finding the square empty of life, and eerily so, Richard made his way back to their lodgings. There he found his friend snoring, the stolen cloak in a pile on the floor.

Richard burnt the cloak before he went to bed. The smouldering wool smelt horrible and it made getting to sleep unpleasant.

In the morning as birds sung from the rooftops, Richard awoke to find Bowman hadn't moved. His snoring sounded like the sawing of the post that had brought down Waterford's walls.

Brian opened his eyes in his corner. 'Why did you burn a cloak last night?'

Richard looked at him and contemplated how much of the truth was a good idea. 'Bowman did something stupid,' he said.

Brian rolled his eyes and closed them again.

Richard thought through the events of the night. He needed to know who had witnessed something they shouldn't have. If the fleeting shadow had been an Irishman, then they probably wouldn't be able to pick Richard or Bowman out from a crowd of Normans. But he wasn't sure, and Richard wanted to be sure.

His stomach felt uncertain from the night's drinking, so Richard left the house without eating, not that they had any food. The air was chilled and fresh, so as he walked he wrapped his now tattered cloak around him. Despite the holes and rips in it, it kept him warm.

Richard found retracing his steps was much harder in the daylight. A few carts rumbled into the city, and groups of Welshmen staggered about as if they were only now on their way to bed.

When Richard couldn't find the road where the shadow had vanished, he instead walked to the walls to find the quiet square where the death had occurred. That proved to be a better strategy, but when he found it, the square was far from quiet.

The buildings that lined three sides had removed their shutters and opened for business. An old man laid out eating knives onto a wooden board under one window. In the back of his house there were horns and a lathe, both of which were used to put handles onto blades.

Another shopfront was already festooned with leather pouches and belts. A cart with a sleepy looking mule waited in the very centre of the square. There was no one investigating a body, and indeed Richard realised, no body.

Richard walked over to the house selling leather goods because that's where he thought he'd been when their attacker was stabbed. He tried not to look too closely at the beaten earth ground, but his eyes searched for traces of blood.

The leather vendor, an old Irish woman, said something to

him and pointed to one of her belts.

Richard shook his head and looked back to the ground. His eye caught a small patch of darkened earth. He felt the gaze of the woman on him and looked up.

She had her hands on her hips, and the look she gave him told Richard that she knew what had drawn his eye. He walked by the cart and patted the mule gently on its neck. He noticed that amongst the piles of wicker baskets on the cart lay one rolled up length of material. It could have been canvas or linen, Richard wasn't sure, but it was the exact size he'd expect a rolled up Norman knight to be. He glanced back to the leather-seller without thinking.

Her eyes were still on him and he cursed himself. Richard tucked his head down and walked out of the square quicker than he should have done.

Out of the square, he tried to remember which way he'd chased the witness. Luckily he had sobered up by that point of the night, and he found his way to the road he had been searching for.

The doors of many of the houses were now open, and the sounds of morning life drifted out into the air. Men and the odd woman walked from house to house, and Richard felt very out of place. His short hair and beardless face marked him out as Norman in a street of long hair and beards.

Richard decided by these hairstyles that the witness probably wouldn't recognise him. And also that he also should not stand around looking suspicious any longer.

He turned away as a trio of men walked down the middle of the street and they stuck in Richard's mind as he started to walk. They stuck in his mind because the man in the middle of the group had an uneven silhouette. Which probably meant, knowing Richard's luck, that the man was Cormac with his missing ear.

Richard walked quicker and round the next corner. The next street was long and Richard didn't want to give Cormac time to recognise him, so he dove into the first open door he came across.

Richard shut the door behind him. The house was a single story one with a hearth in the middle and only a single bench by it. A man's tunic and pair of shoes hung on one wall, but huddled by the fire was a young woman clutching two small children.

The woman had long brown hair and stirred a pot, but she froze solid on seeing the intruder.

Richard looked at the faces of the children and immediately felt homesick for his own. He then felt a pang of guilt that he hadn't thought about them for two whole days. The woman grabbed hers tighter and shuffled backwards.

Richard held up his hands and shook his head. 'I mean you no harm,' he said.

The woman threw a blanket over the children and looked like she was going to cry.

'I have children that look just like yours,' Richard said, 'if I had anything to give you, I surely would.'

The woman held the wooden spoon out like a weapon. Liquid from it dropped onto the blanket.

Richard realised the terror that he'd unwittingly unleashed on her, and backed towards the door. 'I'm sorry, sorry,' he said gently and pulled it open.

Richard stepped outside and closed the door again. His embarrassment had warmed him up, and he hoped to forget the episode quickly.

Luckily for Richard, Cormac and his two companions had already walked on beyond the doorway. Richard watched their backs get further away and decided to follow them.

Richard kept his distance as Cormac entered a square with a well at its centre. The men with him lowered down the bucket as Cormac looked slowly around the area.

Richard flattened himself against a wall around the corner. He reached down to check his dagger was at his side, and it still was.

Richard rested his hand on the handle of Sir John's old blade and peered around the corner.

The bucket had been retrieved and one of the Irishmen drank from the communal cup.

Cormac held the bucket. His cloak rippled as his arms moved beneath it, and for a moment Richard couldn't see the bucket. Then Cormac put his cloak aside and gently held the bucket out over the well. He nodded and his other comrade started to lower it.

Richard frowned. He always let the bucket drop when it was empty.

Cormac turned away from the well and his eyes moved from person to person in the square.

Richard had seen all he needed to and ran off down the street.

A voice inside his head told him that if he wanted to keep that head, he needed to keep it down. Return to their lodgings and go to sleep. Another other voice told him if he atoned for the killing of the previous night by reporting what looked a lot like a poisoning, his guilt might vanish.

Richard ran back to their house and threw open the door.

Bowman rolled over. 'That thunder is close,' he mumbled.

'It's not thunder,' Richard rushed over and started to pick the big man up, 'Cormac has poisoned a well and we need to tell Strongbow.'

Bowman shook him off. 'We? We need to sleep until my head doesn't feel like it's on an anvil and a smith is trying to flatten it.'

'Do you remember what you did last night?"

Bowman rubbed his forehead. 'I think I threw up.'

Brian's small eyes opened from the bundle of blankets in the corner. 'He killed someone, didn't he?' The monk said, 'that's why you burnt the cloak.'

Bowman scrunched up his face. 'I thought it smelt bad in here, but I'd assumed that was just me.'

Richard grabbed his arm and dragged him half out of bed. 'Come on, we need to deal with the well.'

'It's nothing to do with us,' Bowman got up anyway. He had to hold a hand out to the wall to steady himself.

'I was right,' Brian mumbled, 'the only thing that you Norman's are good for is killing.'

'If you want to help save people,' Richard threw Bowman's shoes at him, 'then come with us.'

Brian shrugged.

'Hurry up,' Richard said and made for the door.

Bowman had to sit down to lace his shoes on, his fingers clumsy with the leather thonging.

'Come on,' Richard waved his hand out of the door, 'I need you to go to the well and stop people drinking from it while I go to Strongbow.'

Bowman used the wall to get to his feet and staggered out of the house. He raised his hand to shield his eyes from the sun, which was not even in his eyes.

'It's too early for this,' he muttered.

'Follow me,' Richard walked off.

Bowman walked a lot slower, so Richard went back to physically pull him towards the square with the well.

When they reached it, Richard pushed Bowman towards the water source. 'This one, don't let anyone drink from it.'

Bowman clutched his stomach and went and leant on the stone structure of the well.

Richard wondered if this was really a good idea, but decided it was too late now either way. He rushed off towards the tower Strongbow would hopefully be in, using the spire of the cathedral to guide him.

The wooden door leading into the tower had not yet been mended, but two men with spears and shields stood on guard outside it.

A wave of apprehension flowed over Richard and suddenly he felt his toe and ribs hurt again. He approached the guards and asked if Strongbow was inside.

'He is,' one with a very young face replied, 'but I don't think you'd want to wake him after his wedding night.'

Richard had almost forgotten about that. He chuckled to himself because that meant the plan for the previous night had worked. Well, apart from the murder.

'I need to speak to Strongbow, someone has poisoned one of the wells,' Richard said.

The young guard looked at the other one, who shrugged back. 'Wake Sir Milo and ask him,' he suggested.

The young guard disappeared into the tower.

Richard started to tap his foot but he picked the one with the broken toe and had to swap.

Some time later Milo walked out of the door with Strongbow behind him.

Milo looked coolly at Richard. 'This guard described you as:

That man who took the city.'

Strongbow, dark bags under his eyes, chuckled. 'I wouldn't get out of my marriage bed for many, this had better be good.'

Richard grimaced and told him everything. Except, of course, for the murky night time killing.

Strongbow sighed. 'First they set fire to the weapons, and now they start killing the people. When will this end?' He asked.

When the Normans leave Ireland, Richard thought, but kept that to himself.

'Milo,' Strongbow said, 'go and see to the well. If it has been poisoned then we'll speak about this Cormac character.'

Milo nodded. 'If we can trust this one,' he looked into Richard's eyes.

'We can,' Strongbow said, 'Raymond tells quite a tale about Baginbun. I should really reward you for that.'

'All I need is my pay,' Richard said.

Strongbow laughed, but not as loudly as usual. 'Ask me again when we're inside Dublin's walls,' he yawned and went back to bed.

The yawn spread to Milo. 'You dogs of war only ever care about money,' he said.

Richard suppressed an urge to argue. 'We should go now,' he said.

'Very well. Show me which well it is,' Milo pointed at the guards, 'and one of you come with me.'

The younger guard fell in behind Milo as Richard took them to the well. Richard walked quicker and kept having to wait for Milo and the guard to catch up.

When they reached the square, Richard's eyes widened. 'We're too late,' he said.

Bowman was pinned down on the ground by two Welshmen. He struggled and shouted. By the well, a woman, her belly carrying one child, held another in her arms. It was limp and she cried.

A Norman knight vomited nearby and two Welshmen lay on the floor in spasms.

'God's legs,' Milo stopped dead.

The young guard paled and his mouth dropped open.

An old Irishman woman lowered the bucket into the well.

'Stop her,' Richard shouted, 'can't she see what's happening?'

'Go and stop her,' Milo gestured to the guard.

The young man ran over and grabbed the bucket. The woman pushed him away and he responded by pushing her over with his spear shaft. She clattered to the ground and her head hit it with a thud. She groaned but didn't really move.

'Why do I bother?' Richard sighed.

Milo pointed to Bowman. 'Is that your rude friend?'

Richard nodded. 'He was trying to stop them drinking, but I suppose no one understood him. I should probably have thought of that.'

Milo barked an order at the Welsh, in Welsh. They let Bowman go and spoke back to Milo.

'They said he stinks of drink, his eyes are red and that he was babbling like a madman.'

'They aren't too far wrong,' Richard said grimly, 'how do we help them?'

The Welshmen who'd drunk from the well stopped moving.

'By finding them a priest,' Milo said.

The Norman knight who'd drunk from the well sat down on the ground and held his stomach as it cramped. 'The Irish,' he shouted, 'this was the Irish.'

'Of course it was,' Milo replied, 'and they will be punished.'

Richard had less sympathy for the knight, because he alone would have understood Bowman's warning.

The young guard looked down at the woman he'd knocked over and water billowed from his eyes.

The voice in Richard's head that had told him to stay in bed now laughed at him.

People of all types converged on the square, drawn by the screams. Townspeople clustered and shouted at Milo and a company of Welsh archers arrived and tried to revive their fellows. They raged at Milo when they couldn't.

Milo spoke to the Welsh but they shouted and spat back at him.

But no one at all understood the locals as their numbers grew. Richard noticed a few knives being waved around.

Bowman was released and made his way over. 'I tried,' he

said, 'those animals treated me like I was a native.'

'The Welsh are just scared of you,' Richard said.

'They will be once I'm done with them,' Bowman burped.

Richard waved the foul air away. 'You really do stink.'

Behind the Irish mob, Richard saw Cormac and his friends leaning on the wall.

'He's come back to see the fruits of his work,' Richard said, 'he's a monster.'

'Who?' Milo shouted above the clamour.

'Cormac,' Richard said, 'he's over there.' Richard pointed to him and Milo nodded. He ordered the young guard to level his spear in his direction, and shouted something to the Welsh.

The Irish mob saw the spear lower. That was the moment everything changed, and in an instant their protest became a riot.

Four Irishmen ran at the guard, who wavered and stepped backwards. He pointed his spear at one of them, but the skinny blonde man he targetted had hatred in his eyes and he pushed the spear aside. His knife plunged into the young guard's neck and his eyes bulged in surprise.

The Welsh roared.

'No, no,' Richard shouted, but no one was listening.

Milo drew his sword and ordered the Welsh to stand down.

The Welsh, their blood up, charged the locals.

This is your fault, the voice in Richard's head mocked. He reached down for his dagger, then realised he didn't know which side to pick.

'We need men,' Milo shouted.

Local men stabbed the Welsh, and the Welsh stabbed the local men. The women in the Irish mob joined in, too, and their knives were just as sharp.

Bowman howled and Richard could see a vein pulsing on his forehead.

'Don't do anything stupid,' Richard said.

Bowman ran at the Welsh.

Richard's shoulders slumped.

'What's he doing?' Milo asked.

'I think he blames them for ignoring him,' Richard said and ran after his friend.

197

Bowman punched a Welshman so hard that he dropped to the ground and stayed there.

Richard jumped on him from behind and tried to pin his arms back.

Bowman threw himself around, and his balance already impaired, the two of them fell over.

Richard landed on his back and was winded, but Bowman landed on him, and Richard's ribs burst with pain.

Bowman rolled off him and Richard moved to get up. He saw Raymond and a dozen squires charge into the square.

Milo joined them and they drove an armoured wedge between the two sides. Raymond swung a mace through the air and everyone jumped clear of him. The big Norman shouted at the Welsh. They backed off and some cast their eyes down. Many had ribbons of red on their clothing, and some held bloodied knives.

The Irish shouted at the Normans, but held back from their shields and spears. A stone clattered into a shield and Raymond whirled around. 'Stay where you are, don't let them bait you. Wait them out,' he ordered.

Another stone hit a squire on the helmet and he staggered back.

The Irish cheered but the man regained his place.

Milo approached the Welsh and shooed them away.

They dispersed, but left behind three of their number on the ground.

Bowman hadn't got up either, but that was self inflicted. 'I feel so bad,' he groaned as he looked up to the sky.

Richard patted him on the shoulder. 'You tried,' he said, 'you couldn't have done any more.'

The mob realised they could do no more either, and one-by-one they left the square.

Once their shouts faded away down the streets, Raymond ordered his men to pile up the bodies. A dozen Irishmen and women lay dead on the ground, some from poison, others from Welsh blades.

Raymond found Milo. 'What a mess,' he said.

'Waterford is like a pouch of tinder,' Milo said, 'waiting for a spark.'

'Maybe this was the spark and the fire just hasn't caught yet,' Raymond said. He noticed Richard and walked over. 'I might have known you'd be involved,' he said.

'We tried to stop it,' Richard brushed himself down.

'You did more harm that good,' Milo said, 'your friend should abstain from drink.'

Richard agreed with him but that wasn't the point. 'Cormac poisoned the well, he's the one who caused all of this.'

'I don't trust any of the Irish,' Raymond said, 'and Strongbow doesn't trust the Dubliners. Who is Cormac?'

'He delivered a message from King Dermot to us in Normandy,' Richard said, 'but got to Ireland without being part of our fleet. He rode into Waterford with the Countess.'

'Who in God's breeches is the Countess?' Raymond asked.

'A relative of the High King, Rory,' Richard answered.

Raymond shrugged. 'They are all the same to me, pagans we can't trust.'

'Come now cousin,' Milo said, 'leave the politics to Strongbow. We can tell him what happened here, and he can do with that information what he will.'

Richard rubbed his ribcage, breathing had gone back to being only mildly painful.

Bowman sat up and brushed his hair out of his face.

Raymond looked down at him. 'The two of you are to return to your lodgings. I do not want to see you or hear of you for the rest of the day. Stay out of sight, do you understand?'

Richard nodded and Bowman exhaled deeply and stood up.

'Go, now,' Milo said.

Richard pushed Bowman towards the street that would take them home.

As they walked out of the square, Richard's toe pulsed with each step. 'I think staying inside is a good idea,' he said.

Bowman passed wind loudly.

'Or maybe not,' Richard replied.

'I had been starting to like the Welsh,' Bowman said as they walked.

A woman poured a wooden bucket of human waste out into the street and Richard had to walked around it. It still smelt better than Bowman.

'Don't blame yourself,' Richard said.

'I wasn't,' Bowman said but his eyes were down by his feet.

'Tomorrow you'll feel better,' Richard put a hand on his shoulder, which meant raising it up, and his side felt sore to do it.

'I don't wish to drink that much ever again,' Bowman said.

Richard had to laugh. 'I've heard that before.'

'Children died, Richard, what sort of Irishman poisons a well that the children of his own people drink from?'

Richard took a deep breath and let it out slowly. 'The sort who wants to show us the type of resistance we're going to face,' he answered.

They got back to the house and shut the door behind them.

Brian's corner was empty, and Nicholas sat up on his bedding rubbing his forearm.

The monk crouched down by the bed and held a bowl out to the young man, who took it and started to eat.

'Where have you been?' Brian asked.

'Cormac killed some children and then there was a riot,' Bowman said as he threw himself back into his bed. He rolled over to face the wall.

'A riot?' The monk asked.

'Some Welsh killed some of the locals,' Richard said.

The monk looked up at Richard. 'More violence, then.'

'How are you doing, Nicholas?' Richard asked.

The young Martel swallowed some food. 'I've just stopped coughing up dust. Everything still hurts, though. I can only sit if I lean on one cheek.'

'You should thank your brother.'

Nicholas glanced over to the bed as if thinking about whether to correct Richard or not.

'You should all leave Ireland,' Brian stood up.

'I want to,' Richard said, 'I won't be able to sleep now, I'll be waiting for the Irish to come at us with knives in the night.'

'That would be bad,' Nicholas said.

The monk frowned. 'Would it?'

'We aren't that bad,' Richard said, 'and if you hate us so much, go and live with someone else.'

The monk's face hardened and he kicked his Papal banner

aside as he walked to the door and slammed it behind him as he left.

The day drifted by slowly as Richard tried to catch up on some sleep. When he dreamt fitfully of the two children in the house and their frightened mother, he gave up.

Nicholas rested more peacefully, and Bowman only stirred as the evening came.

'I suppose the monk isn't coming back,' Bowman said as he got out of bed.

'Looks that way,' Richard replied.

Bowman's eyes looked clearer and he moved more steadily. 'I'm so hungry,' he said.

Richard's stomach gurgled as if it were listening. 'They told us to stay inside all day.'

'If the sun hits the horizon,' Bowman said, 'then the day is over.'

'I don't think it works like that,' Richard pulled his cloak around himself anyway and fastened it with a round clasp.

'No one will notice us, maybe the beef is back in the square again,' Bowman found his own cloak.

'Fine,' Richard said, 'I haven't eaten all day, or drunk come to think of it.'

Bowman was out of the door first.

Richard checked on Nicholas, but he slept so Richard thought it best to leave him to it.

They walked back along the dim street as the members of the army started to take over Waterford again. Richard didn't see any Irishmen.

Bowman pointed to a sign hanging above the door of a house. 'Ale's here, I'm thirsty.'

'Not too much, though,' Richard said.

'You sound like my mother,' Bowman walked through the open door.

'Don't tell me,' Richard smiled, 'she was boring.'

'She wasn't,' Bowman found an unused cup.

Richard was glad Bowman was feeling better. The house had three sections that lay back from the street. They were poured some ale, again guarded by a Norman, and found a corner for themselves.

Bowman drank the whole cup dry. 'I needed that,' he said as he slammed it down.

Richard bit back the urge to tell him to slow down by drinking himself. Some of the Normans spoke about the locals and two wells that had been poisoned.

After another drink they left the alehouse to look for food. Groups of men wandered up and down the streets, a cat weaved between them, and laughter and shouting drifted over the rooftops.

Richard walked behind a group of four men with long hair down down their backs. They were the first native men he'd seen all night.

He nudged Bowman and nodded towards them.

'I'm getting bored of mentioning the thing about his ears,' Bowman said.

'I know,' Richard replied, 'what are the chances we'd see him again?'

Bowman snorted. 'Certain, I think.'

'The three men have become four, though,' Richard said, 'and he's probably about to poison another well. I don't know how many wells Waterford has, but we probably can't afford to lose another one.'

'Can we find the beef first?' Bowman asked.

Richard shook his head. 'I don't want the blood of more children on my hands.'

'I thought that wasn't our fault,' Bowman said.

Cormac and his associates turned down a smaller, darker, street.

Richard and Bowman let them go for a moment before following. The street was narrow and more of an alleyway between houses.

A dog barked violently at Cormac's party up ahead, and they swore loudly at it.

'That's going to bark at us, too,' Bowman said.

Richard groaned. 'What can we do about it?'

'If we'd gone to get food first, we could throw some over for it,' Bowman said.

It was too dark to see, but Richard knew he was grinning

smugly.

Two men walked past Cormac, towards Richard, and set the dog off again.

'Cormac didn't look back, I think we're safe,' Richard said, then stopped in his tracks because he was very wrong.

One of the two men who walked towards him in the dark alley was his uncle.

Luke stopped like a stone and his hand dropped to his sword.

Richard felt no fear, and that surprised him. Instead he gripped his dagger and his knuckles turned white on its hilt.

'You tried to stab me in the back,' he hissed, 'no, you actually did stab me in the back. You're nothing but a coward.'

Luke tensed. 'I do not know what you are talking about,' then he relaxed and laughed. The laugh sounded like Richard's father's laugh.

'Actually, why am I bothering denying it,' Luke said, 'you were a good boy, Richard, but now you are insufferable. All I have heard for two days is how you defeated three thousand Irish on your own. It makes me sick.'

Richard laughed.

Luke's eyes narrowed. 'Laughing now? Gone is the little boy who quaked at me back in Keynes.'

'Very gone,' Richard said and felt the truth of those words. Running away hadn't even crossed his mind, but a lot had happened since he'd fled from his uncle at Keynes.

'You murdered my mother,' Richard said, 'and I'm wondering if you did the same to my father.'

Luke's eyes didn't give the answer away, but there was pain behind them.

Bowman put his hand on Richard's arm. 'I'm all for settling this score, but we are trying to stop more children dying,' he said.

'What are you talking about? Richard?' Luke's companion asked. The man had a weathered face and was the oldest of the four of them.

'How do you know me?' Richard tensed his knife-hand.

'I served your father, I watched you grow up. I am Gerold.'

Memories flooded back to Richard, memories of a kindly man, older than his father. 'You taught me how to tie the horse knot,' Richard said.

Gerold nodded. 'After you tied your palomino colt to the barn door and he pulled the whole thing down because you couldn't untie him quick enough when he got his leg stuck.'

Richard laughed and for a moment his mind was back in Keynes, before his father left, when everything was happy.

'Richard,' Bowman hissed and snapped him out of it.

'Sorry, we have to finish this later, those Irishmen are off to poison another well,' he said.

Gerold watched Richard with keen eyes. 'How do you know?'

'Because we watched them poison the last one,' Richard said.

Luke drew his sword. 'That is the most cowardly excuse I've ever heard,' he said.

The blade was dark in the shadows, but its presence played on them all.

'I do not fear to fight you,' Richard said, 'but more than our lives rest on this. Put the feud aside and let us through.'

'I'm ending this now,' Luke said.

Gerold stepped forwards and put his hand on Luke's. 'William Keynes never once lied to me,' he said, 'and young Richard never did either. I do not think he has started now.'

'Let go of me,' Luke tried to push his retainer away.

'I shall have no part in a dishonourable family spat. If you fight, I will stand aside,' Gerold said, 'my sword remains clean tonight.'

'I am the Lord of Keynes, unhand and obey me.'

Gerold firmed his grip. 'I served your brother, and he never intended you to succeed him,' the old man was stronger than he looked, 'you were nothing but a hearth-son. I serve you now because you are of the right blood and sit at the high chair in the hall, but Richard has a right to challenge you. We all thought he was dead.'

'Just to be clear,' Bowman drew his dagger slowly and silently. 'Unlike your man, I will certainly be fighting alongside my young lord.'

Richard felt a pang of pride. He reached down to Sir John's dagger. 'Sheath the blade and stand aside, or Keynes gets a new lord tonight.'

Bowman grinned, and the light of the moon reflected off his

teeth.

Luke stepped back. 'You wouldn't murder a man in an alleyway, would you?'

Bowman stopped and looked at Richard. They both burst out laughing. Irrational, excessive, and vulgar laughter.

Bowman wiped a tear away with his dagger hand and the pointed blade glinted in the new moonlight. 'I did that just last night,' he said, 'or at least that's what I'm told I did.'

Uncertainty flashed across Luke's face for a moment. Then he ran. Luke left Gerold behind, ran past the dog that barked and lunged at him, and was soon lost in the darkness.

'I wish to talk to you,' Richard said, 'but we really do have a well to save.'

Gerold stepped aside. 'I look forward to it,' he said.

Richard and Bowman ran in the direction Luke had gone. As they went, the alleyway opened up into a narrow street.

'Which way?' Bowman asked, his dagger still drawn.

Richard looked left and right. 'Curse my uncle for delaying us,' he said to the moon.

Somewhere in Waterford a dog howled.

Richard took a deep breath. 'Brother Geoffrey would tell us to never choose left,' he said.

Bowman grinned, his eyes bright. 'So we're going left, then?'

'Of course we are,' Richard turned and jogged down the street. The street led to a well.

Bowman slammed to a halt beside Richard.

'If we ever meet that pretentious monk again, I'm telling him about this,' he said.

Three of the four Irishmen surrounded the well, one pulled the rope that raised the bucket. The fourth was looking down the road on the far side.

'What do we do?' Bowman asked.

'What else can we do?' Richard replied.

A moment later Sir John's dagger was in his hand and they were both running towards the well.

The Irish looked up at the sound of leather soles on dry earth only when it was too late.

Richard stabbed through the cloak of one and the man cried out as the knife found his stomach.

Bowman's knife found a neck, and the third Irishman released the bucket and it hit the water below with a echoey splash. The man who'd held it fled.

Richard's opponent flailed an arm at him and tried to draw his own knife. Richard had to plunge the dagger into his chest.

The fleeing Irishman knocked the fourth one into the wall and ran around the corner. The fourth man bounced off the wall and crumpled to the ground.

Bowman was on him in an instant, his dagger raised over his head.

Richard pushed his victim away and the man fell to the ground.

'You?' Bowman said.

Richard looked over.

'Don't kill me,' Brian the monk said from beneath Bowman's gory blade.

Bowman relaxed his grip on him. 'What in God's name are you doing here?'

Richard stood over the monk. 'Brian, you knew what they were doing, do you understand what this means?'

Brian started to cry. 'I just wanted the killing to stop.'

'By killing some other people?' Richard asked.

'Why not,' the monk wailed, 'isn't that what you do?'

Richard frowned as the man he'd stabbed groaned behind him.

'He's not dead,' Bowman said.

'I can see that,' Richard held his dagger out and approached the man on the ground.

'We can take him to Raymond and Strongbow,' Richard said.

The man rolled over onto his back and Richard could see his first stab had only caught his side.

'He'll hang you,' Bowman said to Brian, 'if you're lucky.'

Brian cried harder.

Richard couldn't understand it, maybe the monk had gone mad with grief. He crouched down by the Irishman and felt for weapons. He took out a knife and threw it to one side. 'Can you carry this wounded one?' He asked.

Bowman scoffed. 'I can, but I'll have to drag this one with me.'

Richard looked over to the monk on the floor. 'We can let him go, I don't think he'll be stupid enough to do anything like this again.'

Brian stopped crying. 'You'd let me go? Nicholas told me what you did to your Reeve, why would you show mercy now?'

'That was mercy,' Richard felt anger rise, 'he was a bad man. You are a good man overtaken by events. If I let you live, use your new time to do good.'

Brian nodded and Bowman let him go.

'Fine,' the blonde man said, 'we'll take that one only.'

The bleeding Irishman coughed, red in his mouth. 'I'll make sure the monk dies with me,' he said in bad Norman French.

'Why would you do that?' Richard asked.

'He has collaborated with the invaders so he is a traitor to his people. I never wanted him with us.'

'What now?' Bowman asked.

'Just keep your mouth shut about the monk,' Richard said, 'he doesn't need to die.'

The Irish tried to laugh but coughed up blood. 'He is a coward. He dies.'

Richard looked from Brian to Bowman to the man below him. He thought he heard an owl hoot in the far distance.

Richard made the sign of the cross with his dagger-hand and sighed at the contradiction of it.

'I deserve to die,' Brian said.

'There,' Bowman said, 'problem solved. Don't do anything stupid now, Richard.'

Richard didn't think any further. He brought the dagger down into the wounded Irishman's neck. With his other hand he covered the man's mouth and his last breath escaped in a sucking noise through his fingers. Richard felt the air rush by his skin and he shuddered.

Bowman cocked his head. 'Well, young lord, I'll admit it. It may have been stupid, but at least that wasn't boring.'

RIGHT OF PASSAGE

The first four days of the march north were easy. They rode a manageable distance each day to give the Welsh time to dig a defensible camp each night. The going was good as the late summer sun had kept the ground dry, much drier than usual according to Brian.

On the fifth day the army, strung out in marching order, came to a halt.

'What now?' Bowman watched a rider reach Raymond who led the vanguard towards Dublin.

Richard could only see the Big Norman's red cloak, still half the length it had been before Waterford, and couldn't hear what the rider told him.

'Maybe we're giving up and going home?' Nicholas asked. The arrow wound in his arm barely troubled him already, although he sat on his saddle at an angle due to the wound there. He'd physically recovered from the house collapsing onto his head, although he slept more than before. He spoke more, too.

'I doubt it,' Richard let Solis put his head down so he could investigate a patch of green ferns. The stallion ripped one out of the ground and started to pull it into his mouth.

'I prefer being in the rearguard,' Bowman scanned the gentle hill ahead of them.

'I'm not sure I want to fight under Sir Milo,' Richard said, 'I don't think he likes us very much.'

'I'm not sure Raymond likes us much better at the moment,' Bowman replied.

Their leader sent the messenger back down the army and turned his horse. 'The Irish have marched an army to block our way,' Raymond said, 'they say it is an army of four kings.

Strongbow is taking us around them to fall on Dublin by surprise,' he shouted. 'Pass the word along.'

'Who told us about the Irish army?' Richard asked mostly to himself.

'One of our pet Irish, I suppose,' Nicholas replied. The Dubliners who had gone to Waterford rode in Raymond's vanguard, often scouting ahead on their small horses. The march so far had been uneventful, and Raymond had sent them out more and more often as they went on.

'How far have we got left to go?' Richard asked Brian.

The monk rode behind them on the ambling horse of a knight who had died at Waterford. He looked unsteady on it, but the high wooden saddle had so far stopped him from spilling out. Brian's fingers clung onto the wooden panel that rose up to his waist as if he could fall at any moment.

'Three days on the route we have been on,' Brian said, 'but going around means going over the Wicklow Mountains.'

'Mountains?' Richard groaned. Thinking about it, he had only ever seen hills before, and riding up and down those slopes had taken enough effort. When riding on the flat you could daydream, but you had to concentrate on inclines, especially when the ground was stony or slippery.

'The mountains are bare and wet,' the monk added. 'The valleys are thick with trees and rivers. No one goes that way even on their own. I don't think an army can really go that way.'

'I think we're about to test that,' Richard pulled Solis's head up as the column moved on.

The horse walked on with a fern stuck out of his mouth.

'I'm just happy to be back in the open air,' Nicholas said, 'my memory of Waterford is hazy and confused.'

'I don't think Strongbow ordered us north on your account,' Richard said, 'we drank the last two wells dry.'

A gentle breeze ruffled Richard's cloak. A few days ago that would have been welcome, but now it felt ominous.

'It grates me that the one-eared man got away with the poisoning,' Bowman said, 'I wanted to settle that score before we left.'

'He's probably in the army of the four kings,' Richard replied. He realised that Sophie had been right about Cormac and his mind again drifted back to Yvetot, as it often had done while they marched. Had he been reckless in leaving the village?

Bowman rode in silence next to Richard as the vanguard crested the next ridge line. In the distance the green hills grew taller, the ones furthest away were larger and topped with brown rather than green.

Raymond pointed to them. 'That's where we're going, boys,' he said.

'It looks pleasant enough,' Richard said.

'Looks can be deceiving,' Brian muttered.

They rode up, gaining altitude and weaving through patches of some kind of bracken with bright yellow flowers.

Bowman turned to look back at the main body of the army that snaked up and down many hills at once. The blonde man snorted and Richard followed his eyes to Strongbow's banner. He could make out individuals, even across the valley. Strongbow rode on a fine grey horse at the head of his division, next him to was Eva.

'Forget about her,' Richard said.

Bowman ignored him as the hills grew steeper and the air cooler. The gentle breeze turned into a persistent wind and chilled the left side of Richard's face. It made his teeth cold.

'It feels like summer is over up here,' Nicholas held his cloak up to shelter his face.

'It is only going to get worse,' Brian said. He almost had to shout because of the wind.

'You seem to be enjoying our suffering,' Richard said. He didn't bother to turn round to see if Brian smiled in response.

Soon they had to drop into single file as the ground became harder to read. Richard dreaded to think how churned up the earth would be by the time the rearguard made its way up in his tracks.

They reached the brown-topped hills, where they were above the treeline. Unimpeded by any vegetation bigger than a fern, the wind only strengthened yet further.

'Is this even a track?' Richard had to turn his head to ask Bowman behind him.

'Barely,' the blonde man replied, 'and not for people.'

Richard's fingers grew cold on the reins so he hooked them

onto his belt and clasped his hands together inside his cloak. Riding in single file was lonely and the day seemed to last forever. They snaked around mountains and marched above lakes that filled the space between the peaks. Some of the mountains had rocky scree slopes that horses stumped and slipped on, while others were so steep most riders dismounted in case their horses fell. Solis kept his footing, but by the time they camped, the horse was exhausted.

The vanguard camped amongst a field of boulders on a plateau. Other hills and mountains rose to the sky around them under grey clouds. Some birds of prey circled overhead, but Richard didn't care what kind they were.

The night was uncomfortable despite the bed of moss Richard made for himself stuffed up against a stone larger than he was. He dreamt of the night his sister was taken, and afterwards the night he found her again.

The vanguard moved off well before dawn because almost no one had slept well. Up through the heather and over small streams they went, horses lost shoes, and men lost bodyweight as the cold ate into them. A small herd of cattle had been driven with the army to provide food, but the rumour went round that they had all escaped.

When they camped for the second night on a plateau that looked exactly like the last one, there was again no fire wood to burn for warmth or light.

Richard bedded down next to Bowman, half an eye on the hobbled horses that roamed around them looking in vain for decent grass.

Nicholas walked about looking here and there on the ground. 'Someone has taken my bed roll,' he said.

'Where did you last have it?' Richard asked from the stone he leant against.

'Right there,' Nicholas pointed to the mossy ground next to Bowman.

Brian walked over with a small bucket of water. 'This is all they have for us tonight,' he said.

Richard sighed. He'd had to retie his sword belt earlier that day to stop is sliding down his mail already, and he feared he'd have to tighten it again before they reached Dublin.

'I'd kill for an Irish cow,' Bowman said, 'my stomach feels like a rat is crawling around in it.'

'Prayer will fill your void,' Brian put the water down.

'I'll fill your void,' Bowman replied.

'Where am I going to sleep?' Nicholas threw his hands out.

'Are you sure you left it there?' Richard asked.

'Yes, on all that is holy,' Nicholas's face looked this way and that.

Bowman rolled over. 'Calm down, you're making me nervous. I'd bet you left it on your horse.'

Nicholas whirled around to him. 'You, you stole it didn't you?'

'Me?' Bowman looked down at his blanket and the cloak on top of it. 'If I have stolen it, where is it?'

'You've hidden it.'

Nicholas had a look in his eye that worried Richard. 'It will be around, calm down,' he said.

'Calm down? I'll calm down once that thief gives my bedding back.'

Richard pushed his blanket away. They slept fully clothed and armoured in case of attack. 'I'll look for it,' Richard said, 'please just sit down for a moment.'

Nicholas ran to Bowman and jumped on top of him. 'Where is it?' He shouted.

Richard ran over and tried to prise him off.

Nicholas flung an elbow at him, which caught Richard's nose. He reeled back and put a hand to his face. A smudge of blood came away on his palm.

Bowman pushed his half-brother away with his feet. 'What madness has got into you?'

Nicholas tumbled onto the ground and looked at Richard's face. His own softened. 'I'm sorry, I didn't mean that,' he said quietly.

Richard blew his nose onto the ground to clear it of blood. 'Just sit down,' he said.

'I am sitting down,' Nicholas turned to look where the fire should have been, 'sitting on the cold, hard earth.'

'Let me go and check your horse,' Richard said, 'if the two of you promise not to kill each other while I'm gone.'

Bowman shrugged.

His half-brother looked at neither of them and brought his knees up to his chin.

'Good,' Richard muttered and stomped off towards where they had let their horses go. He was grumpy enough already between his hunger and the wind without having to keep the peace. The sun fell halfway below a distant mountain to the west, casting an orange glow onto the clouds above. Richard saw Raymond and his followers unpack their pack animals and eat as a result. He cursed himself for not having acquired some more horses and packing some provision for themselves. He did however spot his own horse, the yellow coat rare in the hundred horses the vanguard had. He walked in his direction, sure that Nicholas's horse wouldn't stray far from their small sub-herd. A horse spun and kicked at another nearby and Richard took a wider berth around them, pushing around horse after horse, most of whom slept on their feet.

When he neared Solis, he saw Nicholas's horse next to him, his saddle still on, and a bedroll still tied to it. Richard took the saddle off the horse and carried everything back to their encampment.

The Welsh hadn't bothered to fortify it that night, but some men on horses were at least posted in every direction as lookouts.

Richard carefully placed the saddle down by Nicholas, and didn't say anything.

The captive knight looked down at the wooden saddle, the leather panels attached to its sides, and his belongings on its back. He reached over, took the blankets and made himself a bed, which he disappeared into.

Bowman looked at Richard as if to ask what to do about him, but Richard could only shrug back.

Even Raymond's food ran out the next day. He asked around for any sick men in the vanguard, then gave the last of his supplies to them.

Bowman claimed he was sick, but came away empty handed. 'You have to try,' he told Richard.

The next plateau was grassy but covered with cold streams

containing slimy, green coated stones. More than once they doubled back and took an alternative route, over what was really a huge peat bog.

Richard let Solis pick his way through the bog while he himself looked out at the landscape. It stretched further away than anywhere else he'd ever been. Richard wasn't sure if he was in awe of it, or worried about being swallowed up by it.

A merlin soared overhead and Bowman remarked that he'd never seen a wild one in the winter before.

That night, the rumour was that Strongbow had abandoned his tent due to a lack of pack animals to carry it.

'They should have kept the tent poles for firewood,' Brian said as they saddled their horses in the morning.

'We'll be burning lances soon,' Bowman mounted his horse, which now looked too thin for sustained combat.

Solis was younger, and only his quarters showed a faint hint of hollowing out. Richard pulled himself up and settled into his saddle.

Around him knights and squires readied for the march while the Welsh gathered their few things together.

A party of Irish horsemen walked through the camp, riding in from where the main division of the army had camped.

'Bowman,' Richard called, 'is that who it looks like?'

The big man stepped his horse sideways closer to Richard. 'It looks like Irish,' he said.

'Can you see the man with no ear with them?'

Bowman shook his head. 'It's that Countess, the one Brian was so fond of babbling about.'

'She's riding straight towards us,' Richard said.

'Then we had better not stare,' Bowman turned his horse around.

The noblewoman's dark eyes met Richard's and she stopped her trim pony next to him.

Richard thought about calling Brian over to translate.

'Richard, is it?' She said, the words tumbling in Norman French slowly from her mouth.

He nodded but it didn't sound like a question. 'Can I help you?' He asked.

Her mouth turned up into a faint smile. 'I hope so. Where are you from?'

That was a good question. 'Normandy,' Richard went with.

'Good,' the Countess replied, 'do you wish to settle here?'

'In Ireland?' Richard said, 'no, I am not here for land.'

The Countess said something in Irish but she looked pleased. 'You are here for money?'

Richard nodded, not quite wanting to say it out loud.

The Irishwoman nodded delicately back. She peered at Richard and didn't say anything for a moment. It made him want to move away, but he held firm.

'You are the knight who the princess wintered with in Normandy, yes?'

'I am,' Richard replied.

'Why did she choose such a lowly place?'

'What do you know of my land?' Richard asked.

The Countess smirked, but only for a second. 'Which one of your men looked after her?' She cast her eyes between Bowman, Nicholas and Brian. Her eyes did not linger long on the monk.

'I don't know what you mean,' Richard sensed his own eyes narrow.

'Don't you?' She said. Her hair blew in the wind and for a moment it covered her face.

'I really don't,' Richard pulled his reins up into one hand.

The Countess pulled her hair aside and sniffed. 'No matter,' her pony walked off and Solis put his ears back at it.

Her companions followed and Richard still couldn't see Cormac amongst them.

'What was that about?' Nicholas asked.

'No idea,' Richard said. He looked over to Bowman who made a point of walking his horse off without meeting his gaze.

Richard watched the Irish continue along the track and out ahead of the vanguard. Which seemed brave.

Brian hauled himself up into his saddle with more effort than he should have needed. 'You should watch her,' he said.

'I think she's watching me,' Richard replied. He had time to mull the encounter over as the vanguard marched deeper into the mountains. Darker clouds blew over them and the wind drove across their path.

'There's going to be a storm,' Bowman said when they let their horses drink from a stream.

Richard didn't need to be told that, and the thought of rain soaking through him wasn't a welcome one.

'Watch out,' Bowman glanced back down the track.

In his yellow surcoat, Alan and his two surviving knights arrived at the stream. Alan let his horse's head drop to drink.

Solis flung his head at him, teeth showing, and the other horse stepped back to drink at a safer distance.

'You,' Alan said, 'I've been looking for you.'

'Not very hard,' Bowman said, 'we've been in the same camp as you for days.'

The mercenary frowned, his cheeks burnt red by the wind. 'When we reach Dublin I will accuse you of killing Walter,' he said.

'Walter?' Richard asked.

'The man you or your friend killed,' Alan said, 'don't pretend you didn't. They never even found his body, I think you ate it.'

'That is a crime against God,' Richard said, 'if you accuse me I will demand a trial by combat.'

'There are new laws in England now,' Alan said, 'you will face an ordeal.'

'We're not in England,' Richard replied, his face still as his cloak rippled in the wind.

Alan swallowed.

'If anyone killed this Walter,' Richard continued, 'I'm sure it was deserved.'

Bowman grunted and lifted his horse's head up from the bubbling stream.

Solis started to eat grass instead of drink, so Richard left and followed Bowman.

The track curved around the side of a large mountain. Opposite, another loomed on the other side of a green, tree filled, valley. A third mountain towered directly ahead, and Bowman pointed up to it.

'What?' Richard asked.

'Look,' Bowman said.

'I can't see anything,' Richard said, 'other than the mountain.'

'There are horsemen up there,' Bowman said, 'can't you see?'

Nicholas stopped his horse so Richard caught him up. 'I can see them, too. Small horses, not ours.'

'Of course they aren't ours,' Bowman said, 'we're in the vanguard, no Normans are ahead of us. Idiot.'

Nicholas turned. 'I'm no idiot,' he shouted.

'Enough,' Richard pushed Solis between them, 'just carry on. I'm sure Raymond has seen them.'

Sure enough, Raymond led his division off the track, down the mountain and into the valley. Word was passed back that he wanted to confuse the Irish, but happily it also meant a respite from the wind.

Richard was glad when they reached the woods and the way flattened out. Green trees lined the route, but Richard could see that above them the mountain sides were steep and mostly impassable.

The valley floor was flat but wet, moss squelched out water when horses stood on it, and men were poked in the face by tree branches. Richard could hear the sound of a river flowing by to their left, and occasionally saw moving water through the tree trunks.

The going was slow because they followed no existing path. Frequently they stopped and waited to move off again as some obstruction up ahead was cleared.

Bowman stopped yet again as the path reached a cluster of mature beech trees. This time a group of Normans blocked the path in a group, and their chatter was loud.

'I'm not complaining about being out of the wind,' Nicholas said, 'but at least up on the hills we made half decent progress.'

Bowman opened his mouth to reply, but shut it again when he looked up into the beech trees.

Richard did so too and saw what had stopped the gaggle of men.

Raymond's voice boomed out from the front of them. 'God's teeth, what are you waiting for? Cut them down.'

Nailed to the thick, smooth limbs of the trees were Welshmen. Five men on five trees.

'A foraging party, probably,' Bowman said.

'How did the Irish know we'd come this way?' Richard asked.

'Do you remember what the natives did to us when we

rounded the cattle up on that hill?'

Richard did. He checked behind him without thinking about it, but all that was there was Brian's forlorn face.

'I'm done riding,' the monk said, 'I'm so bruised I can't sit any longer.'

'Walk, then,' Richard said. He had bigger things to worry about. 'If they know we're here,' Richard allowed his words to trail off.

Bowman slung his shield away from his back around to his side. 'Even up on the bogs our horses would be sure to have defeated any Irish attack. But here,' he scanned the thick woodland.

An archer stood on the shoulders of another and pulled one of the bodies off a tree. The man's eyes had been gouged out and shoved into his mouth. The nail holding one arm to the trunk refused to give way. The archer was passed a small hand-axe and severed the arm at the wrist with four hefty blows. The body fell from the tree with a thud, leaving one hand nailed to the old tree.

'Everyone else keep moving,' Raymond shouted, 'armour on and weapons ready. We'll return to high ground the next time we see a way up.'

'I've got a bad feeling about this,' Bowman said.

'When do you ever have a good feeling?' Richard asked.

'He's very negative,' Nicholas said.

'Not now,' Richard said, 'not when they're cutting men down from trees.'

As another body hit the ground, the vanguard started to advance again along the valley floor.

It started to rain. The drops were only heard to start with, pattering into the leaves that roofed the valley.

Richard draped his cloak over his shield and kept his attention on the trees around them. Under the canopy, light faded as the rain overhead intensified. The drops grew louder, and some started to infiltrate through and land on horses and men.

'I've decided that I don't much like Ireland,' Bowman said.

Richard tended to agree with him.

'What do you like?' Nicholas asked.

Richard hadn't seen the river for a while, and he couldn't see very far into the trees on his right, either.

'I like people who are not rude to me,' Bowman said, 'I cannot believe we share a mother.'

'That's about all we share,' Nicholas replied.

Between two trees, slightly back into the undergrowth, a straight line caught Richard's eye. Straight lines were out of place in nature.

'How about we share some silence,' Bowman said.

Solis turned his head to the right and his ears went forwards. 'Bowman,' Richard said.

'I'd like nothing more,' Nicholas said, 'but some thief keeps talking.'

'Thief?' Bowman laughed, 'you forgot your bedding. We all saw it, what is wrong with you?'

'Bowman,' Richard shouted.

Both knights looked at him. 'What?' Bowman said.

'In the trees,' Richard said, 'do you see anything in the trees?'

The blonde man squinted off to their right. 'Oh crap,' he mumbled.

A rhythmical thumping noise rang out all along the line of march and birds flew up from the trees causing a number of horses to jump.

'Not this again,' Richard said, 'it's the Irish.'

'Obviously,' Bowman said, 'and we've walked right into their trap.'

'And whose fault was that?' Nicholas said.

A horn blew behind them, but it didn't come from the path. A second long note droned out from ahead.

'What is happening?' Brian asked, holding his horse and walking along on his own feet.

'You're about to get your wish, monk,' Bowman said.

Brian furrowed his brow.

Bowman turned to look at him. 'A lot of Normans are about to die.'

'This feels too much like the Niort ambush,' Richard said.

This time though, the ambush was heralded not by arrows and rocks, but by thrown spears.

One spear hurtled out from the trees and flew between two

horses.

A Welshman lost his nerve, turned his horse, and tried to push his way back the way they'd come.

'I wonder if our pet Irish are still around?' Bowman asked dryly.

'Can we attack the ambush?' Richard asked.

'Can't you see the screens?' Bowman asked.

More spears erupted from the the dark woods. Most missed, but some hit horses.

Richard realised the straight object he'd seen was a screen, like the ones hunters used to funnel their prey. His eyes widened. 'They've blocked off the trees so we can't ride through,' he said.

A spear flew underneath Solis and skidded along the ground to the other side of him. The stallion snorted at it but kept walking.

Cries and shouts of men rose up from their left side, in the direction of the river that flowed parallel to their march.

'They're on both sides of us,' Nicholas said.

'We can hear that,' Bowman said, 'you don't need to tell us.'

Richard heard footsteps from the river, branches snapping. It still rained and drops now fell from the rim of his helmet in front of his eyes. The leather reins started to become slippery in his fingers.

Richard couldn't see more than a few men in front or behind them, but those in front started to move quicker.

'Maybe Raymond is trying to ride out of the ambush?' Richard said.

'Who cares,' Bowman said, 'let's go.'

'Wait for me,' Brian cried as he started to jog to keep up.

'Mount the damn horse,' Richard said, then had to turn away as they sped up.

Solis kept up with the horse in front, even as the occasional spear flew across his path. The stallion tried to jump one, which pushed Richard's head up and into wet branches that dragged painfully across his face.

When he could see again, he could see all the way ahead to Raymond's banner. Brushwood fences had been laid as a barricade directly in their path, and Irish warriors with spears and bows manned it.

Raymond jumped the barricade, as did some of his fellows. Others dismounted at the fences, fought with the Irish, and tore the barricades down. A Norman knight fell to a spear thrust into his face, but the Irish were cut to pieces as Raymond returned and charged them from behind.

Richard reached the broken barricade as the men on the ground threw them aside and remounted.

The sounds of battle rang out behind them.

'They'll be attacking the rest of the vanguard,' Raymond said, 'follow me.'

The big Norman pointed his horse towards the river to their left and battered his way through the foliage that was free of screens.

Richard urged Solis to follow him and the palomino bounded on. He knew Bowman would be behind, but couldn't check because he had to duck branches and swerve around trees.

A horse tripped in front and its rider cracked his head on a tree before the horse scrambled to its feet. The rider went limp and dropped his spear, but the horse carried on.

Richard felt leaves wipe his face, and felt the cold they left behind.

A moment later and he reached the river, which on another day he would have found beautiful. On the other side of it the bare mountain sloped up, thin grasses the only life that grew on its slope. Raymond splashed his horse across the river to get to the far bank, which was foliage free. Richard followed with the dozen other men who had kept up, and the icy water splashed up to his knees and chilled his feet.

Raymond galloped back along the far side of the river, right along the bank, and then plunged back in. Solis jumped half the river, but only half, and landed right in the middle of it with a great splash. A wave washed over Richard and it was so cold that for a moment he couldn't draw breath. He swore at his horse as it clambered out onto the other bank.

Solis shook. The saddle and Richard vibrated on his back as water flew from his coat. Richard looked back, Bowman was behind him. Alan and his knights had stopped on the far bank and didn't look like they were going to cross.

Raymond waited for no one, and now behind the ambushers, he charged his horse back into the trees.

The woods were a dark place to re-enter. Some knights rode ahead of Richard but between the trunks and leaves he could barely make them out. His lance caught on a branch and was wrenched from his hand. Richard drew the Little Lord's sword, and very nearly dropped that when Solis jumped a root.

Then he crashed into the Irish. Raymond rode through them and his lance pinned a man to a tree.

The Irish had charged the strung-out vanguard, who had stopped to fight back.

Richard flashed his sword down into a man's shoulder and Solis charged along the back of the enemy line. Richard cut down as fast as he could. He rode past more men than he attacked, but his blade found its mark often enough.

Loose horses bolted through the trees and one slammed into Solis and brought him to a stop.

A spearman lunged at Richard but caught only his shield.

Richard wasn't moving, which meant he was vulnerable, so he made Solis jump away from the danger. The horse bounded back into the trees just as a spear whistled through the air and stuck in a thick trunk beside him.

Richard made out the shape of horses moving towards him, and they couldn't be Norman. He put his sword away and grabbed the spear in the tree. If he was going to face cavalry, Richard thought he should do so with an appropriate weapon.

Another spear hit the ground nearby, and Richard made out three riders making for him. The Irish rode their ponies with no saddles. They wore shields and leather armour, and they looked furious. Richard pushed Solis right at them.

One threw a spear and it only narrowly missed.

Richard couched his spear under his shoulder and it became a lance. The Irishman in his path started to turn away, but Solis tracked him and they rode past each other at speed.

Richard's lance pushed the man right off the back of his horse and he hit the moss-strewn ground hard.

Richard saw movement in the trees ahead. More cavalry were on their way. He turned to fight the two other horsemen, but they'd come to a halt because Bowman and Nicholas were charging at them and their resolve had faltered.

Richard urged Solis towards them, un-couched the lance and threw it as a spear. The shaft cut through the air and hit one of the Irish square in the back. It threw him head first down the front shoulder of his pony.

His companion turned towards Richard, but Nicholas reached him and sent him tumbling from his horse, too.

'I wondered where you'd got to,' Richard said, 'but there are more coming.'

Bowman stabbed down with his lance to make sure one of the Irishmen was dead as their riderless ponies scattered.

'It's not cavalry,' Bowman said.

He was right. The shapes that moved through the trees morphed into men.

Rain hammered down onto the leaves above and it drowned out all other sound. Enough drops penetrated the canopy that it was hard to see through. He couldn't tell how far away they were from the main fighting.

'Do we go back?' Nicholas asked.

Richard shook his head and water fell from his helmet. 'This is a fight to the end. Charge when they are in the open.'

The three of them lined up and waited.

Solis pawed the ground, throwing a clump of moss up into the air behind him.

The Irish burst through the trees and into the small, uneven, clearing between them.

'Ten,' Nicholas said.

'We can all count,' Bowman said and spurred his horse.

Richard sighed and followed as Bowman charged on his own. Solis squealed as he launched and the Irish infantry slowed at the energy and size of the horses coming at them. The three horses charged with Bowman in front, their hooves echoed like thunder on the mossy earth.

The Irish stopped completely, and a few on the edges of their group took a step backwards.

Their opponents huddled in a clump, Richard followed Bowman right into them.

Richard lowered his lance and used Solis as a ram to split open their impromptu formation. His lance went through two men, broke, and his horse knocked one down as if he were made of leaves.

Out the other side, Bowman turned his horse for another run.

Richard turned in time with him, but Nicholas wasn't with them.

The Martel man's horse, riderless, kicked an Irishman who tried to grab his bridle, then ran off to the edge of the clearing, his reins dangling down by his hooves. Nicholas rolled on the floor in the midst of the half dozen Irish who were still on their feet.

Bowman and Richard charged.

The Irish were more spread out this time. Richard hit a man in the face with his broken lance, which pulled part of the skin and hair off his scalp. Richard threw the shortened spear at another man, but it bounced off his round shield.

Nicholas was on his knees when an Irishman swung a club and hit him in the head. The knight rolled over from the blow, but sprung to his feet with red rimmed eyes.

They reminded Richard of Eustace.

Nicholas hurled himself at the clubman and knocked him over.

Richard didn't have time to watch. He drew his sword and went in to help the Martel knight.

The knight needed little help though, as he rammed his fist into his opponent's nose. Stunned, he paused for long enough for Nicholas to whip out a knife and bury it in his open mouth.

A spear grazed Solis and Richard turned to hunt down the man who wielded it.

Seeing Richard's intent, and with a crazed Nicholas in their midst, the Irishman started to run for the trees.

Richard closed his legs onto his horse, and the stallion closed the distance to the fleeing spearman in two bounds. Solis grabbed his shoulder and the man screamed and dropped his spear as large teeth sunk into him.

Richard pushed Solis in his direction, and the horse dropped him, then he walked right over the spearman. Richard was quite sure the yellow-coated animal stomped down a back leg on the way.

Nicholas pushed a spear aside and stabbed a man in the throat. One speared him in his lower back, but the knight spun and charged him. Leaping like a cat, the hilt of his dagger broke the man's jaw.

Before Richard returned to the fray, Nicholas had gouged the eyes out of one man and left him howling on the moss, clawing at his empty sockets.

Bowman stopped after he successfully chased one spearman back to the trees. The spearman never made it.

Two Irishmen remained, panting, their escape clearly cut off by Richard and Bowman.

Nicholas laughed. Richard didn't think it was the laugh of a sane man.

The Martel knight, blood all over him, chased one of the spearmen. His companion, instead of helping, ran the other way.

'Do you want him?' Bowman shouted from across the clearing.

'No,' Richard shouted, 'you can if you want to.'

Bowman wanted to. His horse moved swiftly over the bodies on the moss, and the Irishman died under his lance.

The last spearman dropped to his knees when he somehow failed to outrun the mail-clad Nicholas.

Nicholas cackled, his eyes bloodshot, and his knife no longer silver. Someone's eye hung by a thread, all caught up in his mail shirt.

The Irishman cried out and held his hands up. He shook his head of long black hair even as Nicholas stepped forwards and slit his throat.

Bowman looked at Richard, his eyes asking a question.

Nicholas kicked the last Irishman to the ground and looked around for more.

'They're all gone,' Richard said, 'are you well?'

Nicholas looked up at him but his eyes were as glazed as they were red.

'He needs to stop getting hit on the head,' Bowman said.

'I'll show you what I need,' Nicholas pointed his knife at his half-brother.

Richard rode Solis between them. 'Enough,' he shouted,

'there is a battle going on, get back on your horse.'

Nicholas blinked and looked down at his knife. His eyes cleared and he looked up at Richard.

'Don't worry about it,' Richard said, 'I can still hear fighting, we need to help.'

Nicholas went to his horse, who was sniffing over the moss, and remounted. Richard led them back towards the ambush.

The vanguard had collected itself up around an oak tree along their route. The Welshmen shot arrows from behind a very thin wall of dismounted Normans, their horses held around the tree by the youngest servants.

Irish warriors swarmed the old oak tree and its defenders.

'Where's Raymond?' Richard asked.

Bowman pointed his lance down the track that ran along from the oak. Horses crossed back and forth along the track in the distance. Some were horses, and some were ponies with native riders.

'Who do we help?' Bowman asked.

Richard looked back to the oak where the Norman shieldwall held firm against the attack of their enemies.

'Help Raymond,' Richard said, 'then we can come back together and clear these natives away.'

Nicholas kicked his horse on down the track, and led the charge off to the cavalry battle.

'He's not getting there first,' Bowman let his horse chase him.

'Children,' Richard said under his breath as Solis refused to be left behind.

They tore across the now muddied track in the pouring rain and into the most chaotic fight Richard had ever been in. Normans chased Irishmen one way across the track, while the Irish threw spears at others going the other way. Horses stumbled and riders of both sides fell to the earth amongst the rain and the trees.

A small brown packhorse stood in the centre of the track, an island in the mayhem. Richard stopped by it and slid out three of the spears strapped to its back.

Bowman and Nicholas disappeared into the trees after the enemy.

Richard readied a spear to throw as an Irishman rode across

the track chasing one of Raymond's knights.

Richard tracked his target and flung the spear. It flew true and gouged the Irishman in his shoulder. He lost his seat but clung on to the mane of his pony despite the gash in his arm.

Richard readied another as Raymond's horse cantered towards him along the path, two Irishmen in hot pursuit. Raymond flew past Richard, who loosed his spear at his pursuers. It hit one man's helmeted head and his neck snapped with a crunching pop.

Richard had time to draw the other spear and hold it across himself like a lance. The second rider rode straight onto its wicked point. The man's eyes popped as his own speed impaled him on the lance. Richard's arm jarred with the force as he was pushed back into the curved wings at the back of his saddle, and his victim's pony rode off without him.

The man hung on the end of the spear for a moment before his weight pulled it to the ground and out of Richard's grip.

Raymond returned. 'We shall throws spears together one day,' he said, 'I wish to see how close you are to my range.'

Richard wasn't very interested in that. 'The Irish press our men around the oak,' he said, 'they need help.'

'It looks as though your men are finishing matters here,' Raymond replied.

Nicholas slashed his sword and a man fell from his small horse.

Four of Raymond's knights chased the last of the Irish back into the woods, but declined to chase them. All of their horses panted hard, and despite the rain, the steam from them all filled the air like a fog.

'Follow me,' Raymond ordered and started back towards the oak. Richard fell in behind him after he'd liberated another spear from the pack horse, who then decided to follow their new herd of horses.

Nicholas appeared alongside Richard, but his horse was lathered in sweat and Richard thought he'd been pushed too hard.

The vanguard still clustered around the big oak, rain pooling in the moss. Horses started to slip on it.

Richard couched his spear as the stream of Normans

cantered to the aid of their hard-pressed comrades.

The knights attacked the back of the Irish, who never saw them coming.

Richard's lance broke somewhere and his right leg smashed into someone's face. A moment later and the Irish were running for their lives.

The Welsh didn't cheer like they had at Baginbun Head, but drew their knives and ran past the mailed wall that had been protecting them. The dismounted Normans, exhausted from combat, stayed put as the Welsh cut down their attackers.

Richard drew his sword. Some of the scattered horsemen chased the natives down the track, others chased them into the woods. Richard cut at uncovered heads as Solis dodged trees, until they reached the river again and his sword arm ached so much he couldn't raise the blade anymore.

A few of the natives forded the river and started to climb the steep slope on the other side.

Alan and his two knights were still on that bank. They found their enthusiasm and charged at the fleeing enemy, cutting down a few of those who couldn't reach high ground quickly enough.

Solis's lungs worked so hard under him that Richard himself was moved up and down with each breath. The stallion lowered his head and his nostrils flared. The rain eased but drops still fell into the flowing river. Richard could only smell the warmth of his tired horse as the sounds of battle receded and he felt the danger fade.

He turned his back on Alan, and walked very slowly over corpses and back through the trees.

Bowman had stayed with the Welsh and dismounted.

Richard rode over to him and they nodded at each other.

He looked for Brian next, but the monk wasn't with the horses, and as the vanguard regrouped by the old oak, he still did not appear.

Nicholas did appear, almost dragging his horse that was not keen on moving any further.

Richard tucked his reins over the tall front of his saddle and left Solis alone next to Bowman's horse. They both dropped their heads, eyes empty, and started to slowly catch their breath.

A semi-circle of naked or semi-clothed bodies lay on the ground where the Norman wall had fought. No mailed bodies were amongst them.

'You made the right decision,' Bowman said, 'we lost more men to their cavalry.'

'Have you seen the monk?' Richard asked.

The rain had stopped but drops still made their way down through the trees. Everything was soaked and the ground squelched at every step.

'No.'

Nicholas hauled his horse over. 'I think this horse is older than I was sold,' he said, 'he's tired already but we only chased some Irish around the woods a bit.'

Richard chewed his lip and waited to see if Bowman would start an argument with him.

Bowman walked away.

'All the horses are blown,' Richard said, 'you did a lot of fighting. And you never bought that horse, Guy of Lusignan gave it to you.'

Nicholas shrugged. Blood covered him in a way that it covered no other living man in the clearing.

Raymond noticed him from his horse. 'Ah, a man who likes to get stuck in,' his eyes moved to the treeline where Alan and his knights emerged, 'we need more men who get stuck in, and less who appear once the battle is over.'

Welshmen started to lead pack horses from up the trail with bodies slung over them.

'We should get going,' Raymond said, 'but we need to bury our fallen first.'

Richard felt the water in the moss start to seep into the soles of his leather shoes. They wouldn't dry out now until he held them up to a fire. He sighed.

'Don't lose heart, boy,' the big Norman said, 'this was everything they had. You can wait at the oak until the rearguard passes by. Join them at the back, it should give your horses some time to rest. I'll take some of the rearguard up to the front with me to replace you.'

'Doesn't your horse need a rest?'

Raymond laughed. 'I'll just swap to another. You really should have more horses between the three of you. You look like merchants. Poor merchants.'

Richard wondered if Solis was now so tired he'd let Richard ride another horse. Maybe if Brian still had his horse he could swap for a while.

Strongbow rode along the track at the head of the main division a short while later. His seventy fresh knights made Richard feel a lot safer as they marched past in silence, their eyes inspecting the aftermath of the battle.

Eva was with him and rode her small horse, her face sticking out from under her cloak. Her eyes and Bowman's met as she went by, but neither said a word.

Behind their archers on foot, more pack animals carried the bodies of those who had fallen to the Irish further back along the path. They were deposited with the growing pile of bodies next to a large hole the vanguard's archers dug with all the energy they had left.

Richard was suddenly glad of the cold rain, because it meant those bodies wouldn't smell before they were buried. He stood by their horses and waited for the monk.

'Why are you bothering?' Bowman asked when he returned, 'he tried to poison us.'

'He didn't mean it.'

Bowman snorted. 'How can you not mean to poison someone? You're soft on him, young lord. Remember what happened when you were soft on the Reeve?'

'I was never soft on the Reeve, I was fair.'

'Fair is soft,' Bowman said, 'be careful or one day you'll be chopping his head off, too.'

Richard shuddered at the memory. 'The monk owes me his life, I think he has the honour in him not to try to take mine.'

'We need to get out of this land,' Bowman pressed his foot into some moss and water squirted out around it, 'it's worse than Wales.'

The rearguard and Milo arrived a good time after Strongbow had passed through. Milo regarded the scene with what looked like disinterest, and after speaking to Raymond, half a dozen of his knights all went with his cousin. That only left five or six with Milo, and Richard recognised one as his uncle.

'We'll ride behind him,' Bowman said, 'then we can at least see where he is.'

Raymond cantered off with his fresh knights to get back out in front of Strongbow.

'We'll wait for the burial to be complete before we carry on,' Milo declared to the clearing.

The occasional drop of rain still fell through the trees, but all the water was now on the ground or saturating the chilled air.

Richard could see his breath, but couldn't feel his toes.

A handful of wounded Welshmen walked off down the track, leaving behind three with bad leg wounds. Milo ordered them to be strapped to pack horses, and their journey would be extremely uncomfortable from then on.

Still the odd Welshman walked into the clearing from the path.

'Those stragglers won't make it to Dublin,' Bowman said.

'Not if there's Irish shadowing us,' Richard said.

Nicholas helped strapping the wounded men onto horses before he remounted his own. He rode over with a smile. 'I'm looking forward to seeing Dublin,' he said.

Bowman shook his head and made the sign of the cross. 'What is wrong with you?'

Richard coughed. 'I've never seen you make the sign before.'

'I've never been in the presence of an evil spirit before,' he replied.

Nicholas looked back at his half-brother. 'What are you talking about?'

'Exactly,' Bowman said, 'it has left him now.'

'Rearguard,' Milo shouted, 'form up.'

Richard patted Solis on his neck, apologised, and got back onboard.

The stallion snorted and yawned.

'Richard, you and your knights ride at the front with me, the others at a distance at the back. The squires in the middle.'

'So much for keeping an eye on Luke,' Richard mumbled.

'Thank God for your double mail,' Bowman said, 'you can ride behind me and protect my back.'

'That's not funny,' Richard walked Solis up to Milo.

The Norman's sunken eyes greeted him with emptiness. 'This was a well planned ambush,' he said.

'It was,' Richard said, 'we lost a few knights.'

'Too many,' Milo said, 'but you need to stay alert. There are only a few of us and the enemy are surely not all dead.'

'We gave them a good beating,' Bowman said, 'they won't be stupid enough to try again.'

Richard hoped he was right as they left the old oak and the bodies of at least a hundred of their army behind them.

Milo led them through the barricades that the vanguard had pushed aside, the bodies of the Irish infantry still littering the ground. Not all of them were dead yet, and some moaned as Richard rode by. Their death would be cold, lonely, and slow.

Richard's sympathy was limited as the chill spread up his toes and foot. He couldn't even feel the stirrups. He looked down to check, and sure enough, his feet were still in them.

Richard peered into the dripping woods as it thinned out. No more brushwood screens or natives lurked as the track started to ascend.

Milo paused once they had ridden a short way from the trees and into open ground. 'We'll wait for stragglers,' he said.

Richard didn't mind waiting a bit because it meant his horse would have a chance to eat. The odd Welshman and even Norman squire trudged past, most gave thankful nods to the rearguard that had bothered to wait for them.

Just as Richard thought Milo's patience was on the edge of running out, the small frame of the monk slogged out of the trees. Without the horse.

Brian reached them out of breath and looked up at Richard. 'More death.'

'That was not our fault,' Richard said.

'You are in Ireland, are you not?'

'What's wrong with you, monk?' Milo asked, 'get on with you, we're not waiting for anyone else.'

Brian turned back to the woods. 'I'm the last one, but it felt like someone was watching me,' he said.

'The paranoia of a churchman,' Milo scoffed, 'move on.'

Richard saw nothing in Brian's eyes. He leant down and stretched out a hand.

'Really?'

Bowman coughed. 'Watch him, young lord.'

'Come on,' Richard said, 'you can't walk the whole day and we can't leave you behind.'

Brian considered the hand.

Milo turned his horse and Richard saw his uncle and the five knights who rode at the very rear.

'Although,' Bowman said, 'if your uncle is going to stab you in the back, maybe having the monk there is a good investment.'

Brian glanced at the blonde man, then accepted Richard's offer despite the joke. Richard pulled him up and he sat on the rump of his horse. Brian's arms clenched around Richard's waist.

'Don't grip so hard, I can't breath,' Richard said.

The monk changed nothing. 'How about now?'

Richard sighed and asked Solis to walk. The stallion lurched off awkwardly, but once he'd noticed the extra weight it didn't seem to bother him.

A warning cry rang out from the knights at the rear.

Richard turned his head but couldn't see past the monk. Who smelt strongly of wet wool. Richard had to turn his horse instead to see the source of the alarm.

The five knights at the rear, including his uncle and Gerold, faced back to the woods.

Out of the woods, from the path they'd just left, Irish cavalry spilled onto the open ground.

'This is a bad dream,' Bowman moaned.

'Form a line,' Milo shouted loudly. His bannerman next to him held aloft his flag of red with white chevrons.

The squires gathered into a line around the five rear knights, bumping into each other and jostling to find a place.

Milo pushed his horse into the front and couched his lance. 'Charge.'

Richard and his companions were still behind the line, Milo's charge coming to early for them to join it.

'We can charge,' Richard said, 'but don't chase them, our horses will give out, and then we're dead.'

Bowman's face steeled as he joined Richard in a canter towards the wood. The ground was lumpy, streams ran down the hill, and rocks were hidden under blankets of moss.

A horse in the line ahead slipped, tripped, and spilled its rider.

The Irish rode towards them in open order, spears held above their heads.

The Norman line crashed towards them but gaps opened up as horses swerved around stones.

The Irish threw their spears at long range and turned their hardy ponies around. The spears hit a few horses and two squires were unhorsed.

'They're baiting us,' Bowman shouted as the cool air stung Richard's ears under his helmet.

Richard knew he couldn't fight with the monk on his back and found himself easing his horse's pace. He didn't want Solis to break a leg, either.

Nicholas roared by, sword drawn.

The Irish stopped, threw more spears, then started to funnel back onto the path through the trees. Their spears were hurled at a close range this time. One spear point burst out of the back of a knight.

Milo shouted something and his horse pulled up. Some of the horsemen stopped with him, others didn't hear or didn't care, and chased the Irish back into the treeline.

Nicholas cantered straight past Milo and disappeared into the woods.

Bowman reached Milo and the half of the Normans who rallied to him.

'They've used up their spears,' Milo said, 'and they won't close with us. We can continue our march. Those damned fools shouldn't have gone back into the woods, I'll have their heads.'

Shouts echoed from the trees and echoed off the mountain sides above them.

Horses snorted and some of the fresher ones pawed the turf.

The knights and squires who had chased the Irish, which Richard thought must include his uncle, started to come out of the woods. They came at full speed.

The horses around Richard saw them coming and grew

either nervous or excited. Some spun around on the spot and one reared up.

Only five riders emerged from the trees, Luke first amongst them. Behind them the Irish came, swords and axes in their hands as their small horses pushed on.

Milo swore.

'Idiots,' Bowman mumbled and adjusted the grip on his sword.

'Hold the line,' Milo said, 'they won't close.'

The Irish pursued Luke and the other survivors right into the Norman line. Their horses bolted to their friends in the open ground, and the five horses collided with the rearguard and caused chaos. Horses kicked or bit each other despite being on the same side. Others jumped away from the energy of the frantically bolting newcomers.

Solis spun on the spot and Brian very nearly fell off as Nicholas's rejoined them.

Richard saw his uncle fly by with his sword in his hand. Solis spun again but he saw Luke swing the sword at Bowman as his horse bolted on. The sword sliced Bowman in the small of his back, cutting halfway through his cloak, and cut into the rim of his shield. Luke kept going, out of control, and his horse took him off in the direction of the rest of the army. A handful of squires lost control of their horses and they all went in the same direction.

Richard clamped his legs on and shouted at Solis to calm down.

The Irish horsemen stopped before they got too close, then rode back towards the woods.

'I'll have their heads for this,' Milo shouted, 'this is what ill discipline does, had we been facing knights, we would all be lost.'

Bowman put his sword away and tried to feel where the sword had hit him.

'The coward,' he winced when he found the spot.

'Did he get through the mail?' Richard asked.

Bowman's hand came up red. 'He saw your monk-shaped armour and struck me instead,' he shouted, 'this is the monk's fault.'

Brian mumbled something behind Richard but clearly had no idea what was going on.

'Form two companies,' Milo shouted, 'one rides while the other watches the rear.'

Richard pushed Solis on, determined to be in the first group to ride away. 'How bad is it?' He asked.

Bowman shifted his shoulders around. 'I don't think it's deep,'

'What happened to you?' Milo asked.

'A family matter,' Richard replied for Bowman.

Milo didn't care, he divided the surviving rearguard up into two and the first company started off in the direction of the main division. Richard saw Gerold in the other group.

'He has to die, your uncle has to die,' Bowman said, 'before one of us does.'

Richard nodded. 'I know.'

'He can't leave Ireland alive,' Bowman said, 'this has to stop.'

'I know.'

Nicholas rode up, his sword in hand and covered in fresh blood. His horse had streaks of blood coming out of its nostrils.

'Easy on him,' Richard said, 'you might have killed him.'

Nicholas looked down. 'I didn't realise,' he said, 'I don't know what came over me.'

Milo called up his bannerman and they crested the next hill.

Over the hill the landscape changed. To his right Richard saw a huge body of water as far as he could see, and straight ahead the hills gave way and lowlands stretched out to the horizon.

'That's the sea,' Milo said, 'and at the end of that plain lies the City of the Black Pool.'

'The what?'

'Dublin, boy,' Milo said, 'Dublin is at hand. The city is ours by right of passage through these mountains. We will repay our lost blood with theirs, as God intends.'

Behind Richard, Brian groaned.

CITY OF THE BLACK POOL

The first thing Raymond asked them was where the Papal banner was. The whole army regrouped at the foot of the Wicklow Mountains, and it was in a sorry state. Men and horses were wounded and tired, supplies missing, and most of their Irish allies had vanished.

Brian slid off the back of Richard's horse and rubbed his rear. 'I don't remember when I lost it,' he said.

Raymond, his cloak now but a collection of jagged red streamers on his back, frowned. 'Then you will go and get it back.'

'It isn't even really from Rome,' Brian fell to his knees on the damp grass.

'Pull yourself together,' Raymond said.

'He's had a hard time,' Richard said, 'he's only a monk.'

'If you're going to defend him, Richard, you can go back with him to find it.'

'The Irish will be all over the hills,' Richard said, 'we can't survive going back.'

Raymond sighed. 'The monk should have thought of that before he lost the symbol of our legitimacy.'

Brian looked up at the large Norman. 'I am not afraid to die for my God,' he said, 'but dying in the hills and not bringing back your banner serves no one.'

'Our God will not allow His banner to fall into pagan hands,' Raymond started to walk away, 'so he will keep you alive. Don't come back without it.'

Brian stood up. 'He does know the Irish aren't pagan, doesn't he?'

Richard shrugged. 'I don't think it matters much to him.'

Bowman had sat silently on his horse until now. 'Why did you have to drop it? It is men like you that gives the clergy a bad name.'

Brian bunched his fists. 'I'm a man of peace, but that doesn't mean I won't strike you.'

The blonde man laughed at him. 'Come on, I'd like to see you try.'

'Enough,' Richard said, 'what are we going to do about the banner?'

Brian looked at his toes.

'If we ride back up there, we'll die,' Bowman said.

'If we stay here, Raymond will kill us,' Richard said, 'who do we fear more?'

'Up the mountain we go, then,' Bowman said, 'although dying here would be a lot less tiring.'

'Maybe we don't have to do either,' Richard said.

The monk looked up. 'We need the Papal banner if we want to live,' he said.

'No,' Richard said, 'we don't need THE Papal banner, we just need A Papal banner.'

Bowman grinned. 'Maybe there is a God looking after us. I knew I followed you for a reason, young lord.'

'We'll find a horse for Brian, then ride up the hills,' Richard said, 'once we're out of view of the army we'll head towards the coast. Then we'll find a local to buy or steal some white linen from.'

The three of them retraced their steps with Nicholas, riding back up the incline and away from the safety of the army. No one spoke. Richard peered over the crest of the first hill almost expecting to see an army of Irishmen facing them.

When the hills revealed themselves as empty, Richard felt a bit better. They followed the next hill round to the east, towards the sea and away from the army.

'I don't like it up here, we're too easy to see,' Bowman said.

'Me neither,' Richard replied, 'we'll descend as soon as we can find a way down.'

Brian's horse plodded along the grassy hill behind everyone else. He'd been given the thinnest, least well looking spare horse. The emaciated animal showed how unimpressed it was by walking as slowly as it could get away with.

The hills quickly smoothed out towards the coast and seabirds started to appear overhead. The land became greener and soon they rode through hedged pastures.

'Cattle,' Bowman pointed to some tracks in the long grass.

'We'll leave them alone this time,' Richard forced a smile.

The next pasture led to a cluster of roundhouses, their conical roofs still alien and strange to Richard's eyes.

'Shall we try there?' Bowman asked.

'We might as well,' Richard turned back to shout at Brian, 'can you speak to them for us?'

The monk never said yes, but dismounted nonetheless once they reached what Richard supposed was a hamlet.

An old man was helped out of the largest roundhouse by two young women. They wore simple green tunics and all had long hair. They reminded Richard of his villagers in Yvetot, except that these people had fear in their eyes. In Yvetot it looked more like hatred.

'Do you think they've ever seen mail before?' Nicholas asked.

'I doubt the local nobles visit a place like this too often,' Richard said, 'they look terrified.'

The women helped the old man down to his knees and he spoke in Bowman's direction.

'What are they saying?' Richard asked.

The monk pointed at Bowman. 'They think he's the leader.'

'I told you before,' Bowman said, 'these Irish are a wonderful people.'

'Whatever you say,' Richard said.

Brian stopped pointing. 'They think you're going to burn their hamlet down,' he said, 'and the elder is offering his life to spare his family.'

'Is everyone here his family?' Nicholas asked, 'there must be a dozen houses.'

'Extended family, probably,' the monk said, 'what do you want me to tell them?'

'If they give us a banner we won't burn their hamlet down?' Bowman suggested.

Richard scratched his forehead. 'Of course not. They won't

have a banner anyway, will they?'

'What are we going to do, make one?'

Richard nodded. 'We are, actually. Ask them if they have white linen, and red and blue thread.'

Brian did and relayed the reply. 'They have some cloth. They offered to make a flag for you if you spare them.'

'How long will that take?' Richard asked.

'He said two days.'

Richard groaned. 'We don't have that long. Can't they do it any quicker?'

The monk and the elder talked to each other, then one of the young women started to cry.

'They have no one else to help,' Brian said, 'they still think you're going to burn everything.'

'Can you sew?' Richard asked him.

The monk nodded. 'Who can't?'

'Tell them we'll sew it ourselves,' Richard said, 'although if they can give us a little food and drink we'll be very grateful.'

'Keep them scared,' Nicholas said, 'they'll give us their best food then.'

'Or poison us,' Richard replied.

Brian paled, and after another conversation pointed to the big roundhouse. 'We can sew in there, they shall bring us food.'

The woman stopped crying and put her hands together in prayer as Brian told them they wouldn't die that day.

'They have a paddock for horses at the back of the village,' Brian said, so they put their horses away and entered the roundhouse.

A small fire burnt in the middle of it and the smoke seeped up through and out of the roof, which kept it dry. It was more spacious inside than Richard had expected, but darker than he would have liked for their task.

They sat down on two benches until one of the Irish women brought in a length of linen. It was thick enough to use for clothing, so they cut enough to make a double-sided square. Brian dished out small bone needles and linen thread.

'I can't believe you're making me sew,' Bowman dropped a small ball of linen thread and it bounced on the ground and tangled up.

'Probably the most civilised thing you've ever done,' Nicholas said.

'I bet you enjoy sewing,' Bowman picked up the mess of thread and sighed.

'We just need a red border and a blue cross,' Richard said.

'And some streamers,' Brian added.

'It doesn't have to be great, it just has to look like the old one,' Richard said.

'Raymond will notice if it's wrong,' Bowman said, 'he's not stupid.'

'Raymond only cares that a banner arrives. He is clever enough to know it doesn't have to be real or perfect, not when the first one wasn't.'

Nicholas never sat down. 'I'm not doing women's work.'

'Go and watch the horses, then,' Richard said, 'make sure we aren't surprised by the Irish.'

Nicholas stomped outside.

'We're better off without him,' Bowman said.

Richard stabbed his finger with a needle and swore. 'Maybe, he has changed since Waterford.'

'He's dangerous,' Bowman said.

Richard sewed part of the red border and his fingers started to ache almost instantly.

'He's unpredictable, too,' Bowman added.

'What can I do about it?' Richard dropped his needle and it fell into his double layer of mail. He sighed. The thread had fallen out and he couldn't even see the needle amongst the metal rings.

It wasn't long before Richard needed a break. His spine felt compacted and his thumb was almost numb. He couldn't sew like his sister had been taught, but like most young boys, he had been taught enough to repair his own clothing.

Richard went outside. He walked between some of the roundhouses and wondered where all the menfolk were. Maybe they had been called up into the army of the four kings, or maybe they were just attending to cattle somewhere. He didn't know, but the thought unsettled him.

A few pigs slept in a pen, which he smelt before he saw, and a young dog chased an older sibling around, but otherwise the hamlet was all silence.

Richard wandered on until something stopped him in his tracks.

A small group of Irish horsemen surrounded Nicholas, and one of them was speaking to him. Something told him not to rush in, so Richard pressed himself against the wall of the nearest roundhouse and stuck his head around it to watch.

The small Irish horses were ridden by men who looked like those who had spent the last week trying to kill him. The one who spoke to Nicholas, however, was a woman. Richard recognised her speckled blonde hair, and then her voice. When he stilled his breathing he could just about hear her.

'You are a long way from home, Norman,' the Countess said.

'And yet I stand here unafraid,' Nicholas stood tall. He wore his mail shirt and had his sword by his side.

Richard saw something of Eustace in his defiance.

'Would you be more afraid if I told you that we followed you here?'

Nicholas remained perfectly still.

'I have heard a tale of one of your knights. I think one who is somewhere else in this hamlet.'

'I'm not overly fond of stories,' Nicholas replied.

'This one is not really a story,' she said, 'it is a truth. Although stories can be just as damaging. Maybe more so. This truth will be more damaging that most.'

'What do you want?' Nicholas asked.

'To set the truth free.'

'What are you talking about?'

The Countess slid off her saddleless pony and Richard found it harder to hear her.

'This truth has the power to free a land, to free a people,' she continued, 'but to do so it must be revealed in the right way. By the right person.'

'I don't think I'm the right person,' the Martel knight said.

'Oh, but you are,' the Countess replied, 'your little trio is quite famous. Did you know that King Rory has placed a bounty on all of your heads?'

Nicholas's hand shot to his sword.

The Irishwoman laughed, a gentle laugh. 'You think I need

Rory's money? I am not here to collect your head, Norman, but to use it.'

Nicholas stared at the woman and let go of his weapon. 'What do you want?' He asked.

'You know the truth I speak of, of course you do,' the Countess said, 'I simply need you to tell de Clare.'

'Strongbow?' Nicholas asked, 'I've never spoken to him before. And I still don't know what you're talking about.'

The woman sighed at him. 'I know some Normans are not very bright, but do not make me spell it out for you. I know who your brother is.'

'Half-brother.'

The Countess paused for a moment. 'I know who he is and what he did before the invasion. Strongbow, however, does not.'

Richard's stomach tightened. He knew Bowman was going to get himself killed for what he did with Eva, but this could drag Richard down with him.

'Why would Strongbow listen to me?' Nicholas asked.

'Because you are one of the four who held the fort at Baginbun, and slayed a thousand of my countryfolk.'

'I think it was more than that,' Nicholas replied.

Whatever Nicholas was, Richard thought, he was no coward.

'You are lucky that my men do not understand you,' the Countess said, 'or they would kill you where you stand.'

'They can try, there's not even ten of them.'

She sighed. 'Bravado does not interest me. Tell Strongbow about your brother, all of Ireland knows you hate him.'

'Hate is a strong word,' Nicholas said, 'he's just a liar and a thief. But so are half the men in the army.'

'You have been seen fighting each other,' the Countess said, 'tell Strongbow and free Ireland from a dark future.'

Nicholas laughed. 'Just kill me, Strongbow won't believe anything I say.'

'He will.'

'Why?'

'Because you are his brother.'

'Half-brother.'

She rubbed her forehead as she shook it. 'I am willing to make you an offer, but do not test my patience,' the Countess said.

'An offer?' Nicholas asked.

'Land,' the Irishwoman replied, 'land and the right to build a castle on it. Near Dublin. Once Strongbow and his army have gone, the Norman lords who got here before him will stay. Some of them have imported their families already and you can be one of them, a landed knight. A lord.'

Nicholas scratched his chin.

'All you need to do it tell Strongbow a single truth,' she said, 'which I am told you knights hold very dear. And pay homage to King Dermot and King Rory, of course.'

'Is King Dermot part of this?' Nicholas asked.

The Countess laughed. 'Now he is a clever Norman,' she said, 'but forget about King Dermot, he is none of your business.'

'What lands would you give me?' Nicholas asked.

Richard groaned inside.

The Countess smiled. 'Near here, near the coast. Rich pastures with fat cattle, and close enough to Dublin to be close to power. You will build a dynasty.'

Richard cursed the woman. Nicholas was a man from two families who was an outsider to both. That sort of man must yearn for his own family, somewhere to belong.

Nicholas sniffed. 'Your offer is generous.'

'You even get to keep your head when we drive the Normans into the sea.'

'I don't think you'll do that,' Nicholas said, 'unless you have a hundred mailed knights hidden in a bog somewhere.'

'We have an army of four kings, and your army is about to anchor itself to Dublin's walls,' the Countess walked back towards her horse. 'We will crush you against those walls and chase the survivors into the sea. The waves will wash red with blood and the Normans will leave the way they came. Wet, bleeding and unwelcome.'

Nicholas looked around the roundhouses and Richard ducked his head back for a moment. He peered back as the Countess vaulted onto her horse. That was how all the Irish got onto their horses, but something about the way she did it troubled Richard.

'Well?' The Countess asked the Norman beneath her, 'do you

wish to die under Dublin's walls, or rule outside of them?'

'I think given the choice,' Nicholas said, 'I would much rather rule.'

'Good,' she turned her pony away, 'tell him tomorrow when you rejoin the army.'

Nicholas didn't reply as the Irish group turned and left the hamlet.

Richard stopped watching and quietly walked back to the big roundhouse. He entered it to find Brian finishing a length of red stitching, and Bowman throwing a bone needle across the house.

'This is much harder than it looks,' the blonde man said, 'and I thought we'd be done by now.'

'Only a while longer,' the monk said without looking up. His eyes were a hand's width from the fabric

'The monk is enjoying it,' Bowman said, 'which means it is no fit task for a real man.'

'We need to finish it,' Richard said. He sat down and carried on stitching. He used the dull monotonous job to give himself time to think. Nicholas had agreed to betray them all, he'd heard it with his own ears. What was Richard going to do about it? Did Nicholas mean to go through with it? How could Richard stop him if he did? He could accuse the Martel man publicly, but the proper process for that ended in a judicial duel. No, Richard thought, he did not fancy fighting Nicholas. Bowman might do it for him, but the likely outcome there was one dead man and one so wounded he would die of his injuries.

Richard rammed the needle into his thumb and swore. The bone needles were very nearly as sharp as the iron ones from his childhood, and this one drew blood.

'See,' Bowman said, 'we shouldn't be doing this.'

'We shouldn't be doing a lot of things,' Richard mumbled.

Bowman cocked an eyebrow at him but didn't press the subject. As it grew dark, the banner was completed, with Brian having done almost all of the work. Nicholas came back inside eventually, but Richard found himself unable to look at him.

The Irish villagers dropped food off in the roundhouse, then scurried out as fast as they could.

The night was the most comfortable any of them had spent

245

since Waterford. A roof and a fire meant they all slept deeply, so deeply that Richard didn't dream.

The new day brought fog.

They packed their things and Brian attached the new banner to a hoe he found outside.

'You're stealing that, are you?' Bowman asked him as he mounted.

Brian turned his nose up to him. 'The Papal banner must fly high, these farmers will understand.'

'Never trust an Irishman,' Bowman said to Richard, 'like I've always said.'

'You haven't,' Richard replied and Bowman laughed.

Nicholas tied his bedding to his saddle alone, neither joining in with the laughter nor speaking to anyone.

'Go on then,' Richard said to the monk, 'you ride in front with your banner high and show us the way to Dublin.'

'Do you know what it means?' Brian asked.

'What?' Richard asked

'Dublin.'

'No,' Richard replied, 'it's Dublin, it's a name.'

'No,' Brian said forcefully, 'Dublin is your name for it.'

'Is your name a long Irish name we won't understand?' Bowman asked.

'It is known as the City of the Black Pool,' Brian said, 'two rivers meet outside the walls and a tidal pool throws up black water.'

'So?' Richard asked.

'It is a bad place, a black place,' the monk said, 'it is full of sin and I do not care for it.'

'Good thing we don't care what you think, then,' Bowman said.

Dublin was not large, and when they arrived to the south of the city, it was blanketed in the same thick fog that had hampered their whole journey.

'I expected it to be bigger than Waterford,' Bowman said when they finally saw the walls. Except, due to the fog, they couldn't quite see either end. The walls were stone, tall, and punctuated by gatehouses.

'They're already building ladders,' Bowman pointed to the west, where the Welsh dragged their first ladder towards the city. The fog was so dense Richard couldn't see how many Welsh were building ladders further away from the city, but he could hear axes biting into trees.

They rode closer to where the majority of the army were digging a trench towards the castle. The knights and squires were busy making camp.

'Can you see Raymond's banner?' Richard asked. He looked to Nicholas, but the knight just stared at the walls.

'Over there,' Bowman pointed.

They found the large Norman holding his helmet by its laces, his eyes on the walls.

Brian rode out of the fog and Raymond turned to admire the gleaming Papal banner. He started to laugh. 'My boys,' he said, 'not in a year of Sundays did I expect this.'

Brian looked Raymond in the eyes. 'Someone needs to bring God to this place,' he said.

Raymond stopped laughing and wiped a tear from his eye. 'God can find his place here once the city is taken. But he shows his favour by coming to us with such a clean, fresh banner. Truly this is a time of miracles.'

Brian shifted in his saddle, but he could just have been sore.

'Strongbow is out there in the murk,' Raymond pointed towards the obscured part of the walls, 'negotiating a truce. He thinks the army is not fit to attack.'

Richard watched as Milo and his retinue laced their helmets and slung their shields behind Raymond.

'You don't look like you're settling in for a truce,' Richard said.

'Keen eyes, boy,' Raymond chuckled, 'but we're Norman, and we can fight even from our deathbeds. We'll show my cautious lord how fit we are.'

'You'll defy Strongbow?' Richard asked.

'He defied the King,' Raymond shrugged, 'and when we're successful he'll hail us.'

If, Richard thought.

The first completed ladder was dropped off and Milo's men were joined by other knights who heard Raymond.

The big lord turned to them and his voice boomed across the

damp air. 'Our Lord shows his favour. A miracle has occurred. Behold the Papal banner,' he pointed up at Brian.

The monk tried to sit up as tall as he could in the saddle, but his face reddened as two dozen hardened knights looked up at him and cheered.

'God is with us,' Raymond said, 'and we shall introduce the Irish to him.'

Brian's lips tightened.

A rider emerged from the fog at an amble and came to a stop next to Brian. 'They have agreed a truce,' the rider said, 'there is to be no fighting. You are to prepare to camp.'

Raymond glanced back at his men. None unlaced their helmets.

He placed his own onto his head and tied it on. 'What do you say?' He asked them. 'Do we stick to a truce that makes a mockery of your strength, or do we follow God's will and take Dublin?'

'Take Dublin,' roared the reply.

Raymond turned to Richard. 'See? I am a man of my men, and my men wish to attack. What can I do but lead them?'

Richard shrugged.

'You can get off your horse and follow me,' Raymond said, 'the fog and the truce will cover our approach. Quickly, to the walls.'

Richard dismounted as Raymond approached Brian.

'I want you to take that banner to Strongbow,' Raymond told the monk, 'tell him it is a gift from me, and he can enter Dublin behind it.'

Brian showed no reaction as he turned his horse slowly away and he and his banner faded into the fog.

Richard hobbled Solis and they heaped up their saddles and bedding. They checked their equipment and put their helmets on. Richard was annoyed by the extent of the rust that crept across his mail shirt, and the pommel of the Little Lord's sword hadn't been spared either. The blade at least shone clean, although the edge was pocked with dents and rough to the touch.

Milo barked orders and some knights picked up the ladder.

'Aren't we waiting for more ladders?' Richard asked.

'Better to be ready with one ladder,' Raymond said, 'than late with twenty.'

Eight knights, all fully armed, picked up the ladder. Richard recognised his uncle and Gerold among them. Their white shields with the blue line marked them out even in the fog. Richard looked down at his own shield, which was identical, and shuddered.

Raymond ordered the ladder to advance. The Welshmen that had been at Baginbun Head followed it, bows strung and arrows in their hands.

The company moved over the grass quietly, the only sound that of footsteps, clinking mail, and rapid breathing.

Richard followed behind the archers, not in any rush to die for Raymond's glory.

'It's too quiet,' Bowman said, his sword in his hand.

'There is a truce, there shouldn't be any noise,' Richard said, 'but keep your voice down.'

Similarly to Waterford, some poorly constructed houses had been built outside the walls, and the ladder aimed at a gap between two of them. The knights slowed as they drew close and everyone looking up to the walls, waiting for a storm of arrows or spears. The Welsh, well within arrow range, nocked their arrows and waited for someone to show themselves.

The ladder reached the foot of the wall and the knights lifted it up. Luke was at the bottom of it when it bumped onto the stone wall and he started to climb it first. Milo was right behind him.

To Richard's right, a boy appeared in the doorway of a house and pointed at the ladder. He shouted something in Irish.

A Welsh archer shot him in the chest and he fell back into his ramshackle home. It was followed by his mother's scream.

Inside the city someone shouted an alarm.

'Up the ladder,' Raymond shouted, 'they know we're here.'

Dogs started barking from the shanty town and some of the Welsh took it upon themselves to pour into the houses and silence everyone they found. The screams of men, women, and children cut through the fog, and Richard shivered.

Nicholas watched the carnage and shook his head. Richard wondered if that was a sign of his intention to go through with the Countess's deal.

A horn sounded from inside Dublin just as Luke put his hands on the battlement and jumped over it.

An arrow whistled off the wall and into the throng of Welshmen. They started to shoot back in the direction it came from with a great twang of bowstrings.

'Safest place is in the city, now,' Bowman ran forwards to the ladder.

Richard agreed as more arrows flew through the air and thinned the ranks of the Welsh archers.

Milo jumped onto the wall as defenders rushed towards him and Luke from both sides. Luke started fighting one way, Milo the other.

'Up we go,' Raymond shouted and climbed up ahead of Bowman and Richard.

The sound of their hooves echoed in the fog and a company of horsemen raced through the shanty town. Strongbow led them, and rode over the twisted body of an Irish woman who had tried to flee the Welsh. 'There is a truce, by God,' he shouted, 'what are you doing?'

'They're on the walls,' Bowman shouted back, 'can't you see?'

Strongbow's face boiled but then his eyes saw that Norman knights were indeed on the walls. He swallowed. 'God's legs. Raise the army, onto the walls, attack.'

Richard leapt onto Dublin's walls behind Bowman. 'You're feeling brave,' Richard said.

'Why, because I went up the ladder before you?'

'No,' Richard replied, 'because you shouted at Strongbow.'

'Who is he anyway,' Bowman mumbled and pushed his way along the wall.

Luke was that way, so Richard went towards Milo instead. He could see into Dublin now, although not far as the fog shrouded the houses and rooftops.

A handful of defenders faced them on the walls, but down below Richard saw no one to resist the Norman tide.

Milo punched along the wall on his own, carving a path through the dozen poorly armed men who tried to stop him. He reached a gatehouse and Richard followed him into it. He found a windlass of rope in the small chamber, the rope running down through a hole in the stone.

'Turn it, open the gate,' Milo ordered and ran down to ground level.

Richard turned the wheel and the gate below opened.

Nicholas reached the chamber. 'It's over already,' he said, 'Strongbow is waiting to march in.'

Cheers rang from outside, so Richard climbed back up to the top of the gatehouse to watch Strongbow enter Dublin beneath him.

He rode a white Italian warhorse, and Eva was already beside him. She wore a bright red dress and had been mounted on a black English horse. She sat awkwardly in the saddle but held whatever her true feelings were quite hidden.

In front of them, Brian the monk held his farmer's hoe with both hands, the bright new Papal banner held aloft in victory.

Brian's eyes looked empty, but only Richard noticed at him. He wondered if this was how Brian had wanted God to enter Dublin.

Richard watched them ride into the town and down the street. A defender lay in the gutter as they went, guts spilled out amongst the filth, his lungs still just about moving. Milo and his men moved ahead of the procession, going from house to house to check for armed men. Richard spotted Nicholas amongst them.

Church bells rung in the distance, the alarm being sounded far too late to save the city. The church bells, he thought, sounded just like the ones in England or Normandy, was the same God already here, too?

Without a better idea of what to do next, Richard descended the gatehouse and followed Strongbow's company into Dublin. He walked behind the twenty knights and squires de Clare had mustered in the few moments he'd had. He stepped around their horse's droppings, but that was better than walking in the filthy channels down the side of the street. The twenty horses left a trail all the way to Dublin's large church. Near it stood the city mint, and into that Milo and his men poured.

He found Brian discarded at the door of the church. The monk stood still, looking up at the tall spire, the banner held so low the streamers dragged on the ground.

'I'm a marked man, now,' Brian said.

'No one will remember you, you're safe enough,' Richard sheathed his sword.

'I'm not sure that's really what I wanted to hear, either,' Brian said, 'but pride is a sin so I will bare it.'

'Thank God we took the city this easily,' Richard said.

'The Lord gives and the Lord takes away.'

'What's he going to take for Dublin?' Richard asked.

'Don't ask me. Ask the bishop in there.'

'Do you think Raymond will believe the Irish have bishops if he sees one with his own eyes?'

Brian sighed. 'It hardly matters. Ireland is lost.'

'I don't know,' Richard looked at the buildings around the church, 'it looks like Ireland needs saving. Most of these houses are no better than the wattle and daub roundhouses we got the banner from.'

'We were doing perfectly well before you arrived,' the monk held the banner out to Richard.

'Then why were you standing on the beach to welcome us?'

Brian sighed. 'Because the Church of Rome is the true church. Rome's monks and nuns must come to Ireland to spread His word.'

'What did you think would happen?' Richard asked, 'and now I think of it, why did you also say your name was Magnus.'

'Because I'm from the Ostmanstown here in Dublin,' Brian said.

'Then you should thank God with me for how easily we gained entry,' Richard said, 'there could be a lot more blood in the streets.'

Brian sniffed as the fog swirled over houses in the distance. 'I can show you an empty house where we can wait out the celebrations,' he said.

Richard nodded. 'I want to lie down again,' he said, 'and I need to dry my mail out by a fire then find a barrel to roll it in.'

Brian raised the banner back up and turned away from the church and mint. Richard followed him to a building which had a sunken cellar to support a second storey above the ground floor. It was a better building than many in the city.

The church bells rung again, Richard assumed as a

celebration this time.

'I'll check it's still empty,' Brian ducked into the house.

Richard waited outside, unsure why he had to, as a band of Welsh roved down the street looting houses.

They walked by Richard and left his house alone.

A pair of dogs howled to each other across Dublin as another group of men walked down the street. This time they stopped at Richard, and in the grey light of the fog, he looked twice when he saw the long black hair of Cormac and his beady eyes stare back at him.

'There you are,' the messenger said.

The four men with him had dour faces, which contrasted sharply with the cheerful looting of the Welsh who came before them.

'You'll hang for poisoning the wells,' Richard said.

Cormac smirked. 'It is not me you should be worrying about,' he said.

Richard's hand dropped to Sir John's dagger.

The Irishman laughed. 'You think you'll survive a knife fight with us?'

Richard didn't. 'Who do you serve?' He asked.

'My people,' Cormac replied.

'The people who invited us in, or those who wish us to be pushed out to sea?' Richard asked.

'That is neither here nor there. I have a message for you.'

'From who?' Richard asked.

'The people of Ireland.'

'Fine, what's your message?'

'Are you fond of the monk in the house?' Cormac asked.

Richard shrugged. 'He does moan a lot. But that can't be your message?'

'If you don't do what we ask, he'll die first.'

'What do you want?' Richard remembered the offer Nicholas has received, 'or are you offering me land if I betray my brother-in-arms?'

Cormac laughed. 'The time for deals and offers ended when your men broke a truce and scaled the walls. Your army might fall apart if Strongbow dies, but he has to die soon. You will see to that.'

It was Richard's turn to laugh. 'Have you seen the man? He'll squash me like an ant. You might as well kill me now and at least save my reputation.'

'If you wanted to save your reputation, you should never have come to Ireland,' Cormac said.

Brian reappeared from the house. 'It's empty,' he froze when he saw who Richard spoke to.

'Go back inside,' Richard said without turning around.

'No,' Cormac said, 'he can listen. It is his head that will roll first if you do not comply. A death he would deserve.'

Richard felt the monk's eyes on the back of his head. 'Maybe someone did notice you and your banner,' Richard said wearily.

'If Strongbow is alive by the end of tomorrow,' Cormac said, 'the two of you won't be.'

The Irishman ushered his companions away into the fog, leaving Brian looking at Richard questioningly.

'You don't want to know,' Richard told him.

'He wants you to murder Strongbow?'

'Obviously I'm not going to even try,' Richard said, 'but we need to do something about Cormac. The Countess is behind it.'

'I told you she was a witch,' the monk said.

'We need to find Bowman and Nicholas,' Richard said, 'things are getting complicated and we need to do something.'

Richard left Brian to look after the house and went back to the church. Riders rode up and down the streets shouting orders not to kill or loot. The knights were allowed to force locals out of their houses for the night, but the Welsh were to spend the night outside the walls and as far away from trouble as possible.

Richard found Bowman leading their two horses into Dublin.

Bowman grinned at him. 'There are a few benefits to being a knight,' he said, 'no more sleeping with the common folk for me.'

'You aren't really a knight, remember,' Richard said.

Bowman handed him Solis. 'You can keep saying it,' Bowman said, 'but my spurs still shine in the sun.'

'We need to talk.'

Bowman lost his grin. 'What's happened?'

'A lot, actually,' Richard said, 'someone followed Eva back to the barn.'

'Who?'

'Either Cormac or someone who told him about it,' Richard said.

'Can a man have no privacy anymore?' Bowman asked.

Richard looked up and down the street, which was full of Normans. 'Not when it was a princess. The monk has found an empty house for us, it's better if we talk about it there.'

Brian's house had a courtyard behind it with a pig, so the horses were put in there and Bowman followed Richard inside. Bowman's horse sniffed the pig, then ran back and wouldn't go anywhere near it.

Brian had lit a fire and the interior, although sparse, was now warm.

'He should leave,' Bowman gestured at the monk.

'Cormac has threatened his life too,' Richard said, 'so he's involved.'

'When did he do that?'

'Before I went looking for you. Cormac is here in Dublin.'

'Good,' Bowman said, 'then I can kill him.'

'That might actually be our best plan,' Richard said.

'He had many men with him,' Brian said, 'and killing is a sin.'

Bowman laughed. 'We're beyond sin. Besides, our Irish so-called allies are out to ruin us, so neither Strongbow nor God will mind if Cormac dies.'

'We should do it quietly, though,' Richard said.

Bowman coughed in surprise. 'Young lord, are you actually agreeing with me? Agreeing to murder?'

Richard sat down on a long bench and looked into the fire. 'It might be him or us who has to die, and I'm choosing him. Although, this is entirely your fault.'

'Me?' Bowman scoffed, 'Cormac poisoned the wells and he's the one making threats.'

'You slept with the princess.'

Brian's head popped up out of his cloak. 'Sorry?'

'Everyone seems to know,' Richard said, 'except for Strongbow, it seems. And that could change soon. I also need to tell you something about Nicholas.'

'I already know he's not to be trusted and half of his blood is bad, what more do I need to know?' Bowman said.

'The Countess made him an offer yesterday.'

'What?' Bowman walked over to Richard and sat down on the bench facing him. 'Yesterday? Why are you only telling me now?'

'We were a bit busy with the banner and storming the city,' Richard fought the urge to look away from the blonde man.

'What did she offer that bastard?'

'To be a lord in Ireland,' Richard replied, 'if he told Strongbow about you and Eva.'

Bowman looked around for something to throw but nothing was within his reach. 'I'll kill him. Dirty, treacherous, bastard. I should kill you for not telling me sooner.'

'How do you know he accepted the offer?' Richard asked.

Bowman stood up and stomped around the chamber. 'Of course he did, he's a Martel, remember? All they want is land and power. He hates me, why wouldn't he accept?'

'You pulled him out from under the collapsed house at Waterford,' Richard said.

'He's a Martel, he doesn't care about that,' Bowman grunted in anger, 'and I don't think he even remembers it.'

'What is going on?' Brian asked.

'Shut up,' Bowman told him, 'I need to kill the bastard before he gets to Strongbow. But I need to warn Eva first.'

'Someone is going to tell Strongbow eventually,' Richard said.

'Exactly, she needs to know.'

'You'll get yourself killed.'

Bowman found a dry log and threw it at the hearth. It knocked a flaming log from the fire and it tumbled across the room in a shower of sparks.

Brian rushed to stamp out the embers scattered around the floor. The bright yellows on the dark earthy ground flashed and pulsed, and Richard wondered if that's what the night sky looked like in hell.

Bowman walked towards the doorway. 'It doesn't matter what happens to me, Eva must survive,' he said.

'Calm down before you go and do something stupid,' Richard said.

'Calm down? How can I calm down,' Bowman pulled the door

open so hard that one of its big iron hinges half pulled out of the wall.

Brian stamped out the last of the embers. 'We'll have to fix that,' he groaned.

'You should have told me sooner,' Bowman left and slammed the door shut behind him and the second hinge almost snapped.

Brian looked at Richard.

'This is bad,' Richard told him, 'he'll be dead by the time the fog burns off.'

'Then you should stop him,' the monk replied.

'How? I can't control him.'

'How sure are you that Nicholas has betrayed us?' The monk asked.

'It's *us* now, is it?' Richard raised his eyebrows.

Brian shrugged. 'My countrymen want to kill me, and the Normans want to kill my countrymen. No Norman would mourn my death so it seems to me that you are the only man in Ireland who has done anything to keep me alive.'

'Then maybe you can help. Find Nicholas and talk to him. He won't suspect you, so try to find out if he's hiding any guilt,' Richard said.

Brian nodded. 'I'll do my best.'

'I'll see if I can get to Eva first, as it would be better if Bowman doesn't get near her.'

Richard got up from the bench and left the house. He didn't know where Eva was, but the church seemed to be the centre of the city, so he went back there.

The sun had started to win its battle against the fog, and a blurry yellow light pushed through the white gloom. It cast an eerie white glow over houses and the people in the streets.

Strongbow's yellow banner with its red chevrons was held by a guard outside the church, so Richard walked up to the doorway. The church may not have been Canterbury Cathedral, he thought, but it was still stone and tall.

The guards didn't try to stop Richard entering, he supposed because he was clearly not Irish.

The interior of the church was the busiest part of Dublin. Benches and desks had already been set up in the nave, and clerks and lawyers were hard at work. They shouted over to each other and bustled back and forth with parchment and ink.

Beyond them Strongbow sat by the cloth covered altar, giving an audience to local men. Some had long hair and looked Irish and some looked more like the men from Waterford.

Dermot stood beside and behind Strongbow, and said nothing to anyone.

A delegate knelt down and held his hands up to Strongbow.

The Norman got up, placed his hands around them and said something to him.

Richard spotted some doors at the back of the church and slowly walked towards them. No one paid him a second glance and a loud group of knights entered the church which drew everyone else's attention.

The first door led to a small chamber where the church bells were rung from, so Richard carried on and into the next one.

That chamber had all the trappings of a rich churchman's bedroom. A bed in the corner was accompanied by a table full of golden and silver crosses and plates.

On the bed, lying down with her eyes to the ceiling, was Eva.

Richard half thought that her belly had swollen since Waterford, but he wasn't sure.

Eva turned her head. 'You? I did not expect to see you ever again.'

Richard shut the door slowly behind him. 'We have a problem.'

Eva pushed herself up. 'I am so very tired, Richard, I do not need problems.'

'I'm sorry,' he said, 'crossing the Wicklow Mountains must have been tiring for you.'

Eva sniffed. 'I am no stranger to discomfort, but that was an unpleasant time,' she said.

'This is also an unpleasant time,' Richard said, 'I don't want to waste time, either. Someone saw you go to the barn in Wales.'

Eva's eyes widened and she hushed Richard. 'Quiet now. Who?'

'I think Cormac,' Richard said, 'or at least he knows about it.'

Eva swore in Irish. 'I have heard whispers about him. I was told he was seen near the weapon store at Waterford before it was fired.'

'He is not your father's man,' Richard said, 'I've seen him with the Countess.'

'That bitch,' Eva's face flashed red, 'she wishes to see me and my father in the ground.'

'I heard her say she wants to drive the Normans into the sea.'

'Of course she would. Either we rule Ireland, or her beloved Rory does.'

'The problem is that they are using their knowledge of the barn to blackmail and bribe us.'

'Us? What has happened, Richard?'

'She's offered Nicholas land if he tells your husband about the thing that we aren't talking about.'

'And will he tell my husband?' Eva asked.

Richard shrugged. 'I'm going to look for him next to find out. Bowman is looking for you to warn you, then will try to kill Nicholas.'

'But he's his brother.'

'Half-brother,' Richard said, 'and that blood bond might be weaker than you'd think.'

'I can handle my husband,' Eva rubbed her belly, 'he is absolutely sure this is his.'

'So he is ignorant of how long that takes?'

Eva nodded and smiled. 'All men are ignorant of these things,' she said, 'at least until they've had a child.'

Richard thought back to Sophie and his twins. He really should be at home.

'Thank you for your warning, Richard.'

'Cormac came to me earlier today,' Richard said.

'There's more?'

Richard nodded. 'I'm afraid so. He told me to kill your husband by the end of tomorrow, or he'll kill me.'

Eva let herself fall back onto the bed. 'Men. Always killing.'

Richard noticed the crossbow leant against a wall but decided not to mention it. 'Obviously I'm not going to, but I can't tell Strongbow about it, either,' he said.

'Cut that traitorous swine's other ear off,' Eva said, 'and I'll make sure my husband starts to hear things about the Countess. He'll hear so much that he'll decide for himself that

259

she is our enemy.'

That sounded like the best idea, Richard thought.

'You should go,' Eva said, 'it would be a scandal if anyone saw you alone with me.'

Richard grinned. 'At least you're already pregnant.'

Eva frowned at him from the bed. 'A joke? Now?'

Richard blushed. 'I'll try and keep Bowman away from you, but I will more than likely fail,' he said.

'Thank you for coming,' Eva said, 'now go.'

Richard left her chamber, passed through the bell chamber and back into the church. Men still queued up to pay homage to Strongbow, and no one saw him slowly walk back towards the nave. Richard noticed that Dermot was not taking anyone's homage as he slipped out of the church altogether.

The sun had burnt through even more of the fog by the time he got back out into the fresh air. He could see the big yellow disc high in the sky, a patch of brighter light surrounded it.

Richard had to find Bowman, but if Bowman wasn't already at the church, maybe he had gone to deal with his half-brother instead.

Richard walked towards the walls and the gate that led out to the army encampment. Carts rumbled into the city and men on horses rode back and forth.

He found Nicholas before Bowman. The Martel knight stood on the walls looking out into the fog that still hung over the plain outside Dublin. Richard only recognised him because he'd rested his white and blue shield on the wall. Richard climbed up the staircase in a gatehouse and walked along the top of the wall until he reached him.

'Your brother wants to kill you,' Richard said.

Nicholas kept staring out of the city. 'No greeting first?'

'It's a warning,' Richard said, 'although I'm not even sure if I should be trying to stop him.'

Nicholas turned his head very slowly. 'And why would you let him kill me?'

Richard sighed. 'I saw the Countess in the hamlet. I heard everything. Why did you accept?'

'There were ten Irishmen with spears and swords standing around me,' Nicholas said, 'I had to at least tell them I would accept.'

'If you accepted under duress then why didn't you tell me about it?'

Nicholas looked back over the wall. 'My half-brother wouldn't have believed me, would he?'

Richard chuckled. 'That is fair. But you should have come to me.'

'You hate half my blood just as much as he does,' Nicholas said.

'I do need to keep you alive though, don't I?' Richard said, 'at least until you've paid your ransom.'

'True.'

'How do I know you're telling the truth to me now?' Richard asked.

'An oath taken under duress is not legally binding for a reason,' Nicholas said, 'probably in Irish law as well as ours. So you will just have to trust me.'

'There is not a lot of trust going around right now,' Richard leant on the wall. He could see the houses outside Dublin, but not the camp beyond.

'We need to get paid and leave Ireland,' the Martel knight said.

Richard made the sign of the cross. 'I'll pray for that,' he replied.

'So, what are you going to do?' Nicholas asked.

Richard drummed his fingers on the stones. 'It would be best if your brother doesn't find you for a few days.'

'That could be a problem.'

'Why?' Richard asked.

Nicholas turned his head the other way along the wall.

Richard followed his gaze. 'If you run, I'll try to stop him,' Richard said.

Bowman strode along the wall. He pointed at Nicholas and shouted. 'You.'

'Hurry, go,' Richard said.

Nicholas turned and faced his half-brother instead. 'I'm not running, because I'm not guilty,' he said.

'He'll kill you.'

'Something has to eventually,' Nicholas left his right hand on

261

the wall, far away from his weapons.

'Bowman, wait,' Richard shouted.

'I'll throw him off the wall,' Bowman stopped before Nicholas and pushed a hand into his chest. Nicholas recoiled backwards but held himself tall.

'Throw me then, I've had enough of this land, nothing good is here,' Nicholas said.

Bowman paused, his angry eyes searched his half-brother's face. 'You would betray me and Eva to our deaths?'

'He said he accepted under duress,' Richard said.

'And you believed him, a Martel?'

Richard bit his lower lip. He really had no idea what he believed.

Bowman pushed Nicholas back again. 'You almost had me, I almost believed you might be more of your mother than your father.'

'Stop it,' Richard said, 'if you're wrong, we can't undo killing him later. It's better to wait. If he really meant it, I'll happily let you kill him.'

Bowman thought about it for a moment. 'No,' he drew his dagger, 'we'll never trust him now.'

'I need his ransom,' Richard said, 'wait until we've collected it.'

Bowman's dagger slashed through the air before Richard even realised he'd attacked.

Nicholas tried to dodge it, failed, and the blade bounced off the mail on his upper arm.

'Hold still and take it like a man,' Bowman snarled.

'Stop, now,' a voice shouted up from within the city. Raymond's voice.

Richard saw the large Norman pointing up to them. 'I've had to break up five fights already today,' he shouted, 'if that knife isn't put away now, there'll be a third man hanging from a gatehouse at dawn.'

Bowman stepped back but kept the knife pointed at Nicholas.

'Put it away or I'm coming up there,' Raymond said.

'Come on,' Richard said quietly, 'there's no point in both of you dying.'

'I don't want to hang a knight,' Raymond said, 'we have few

enough as it is, but don't think that will stop me, so help me God.'

Bowman put the knife away but didn't take his eyes off Nicholas. 'You're dead,' he whispered.

'As you are all so full of energy,' Raymond said, 'you can join me at dawn. We're raiding north, and I wanted that monk and his banner to join me anyway. We're going to show the pagan monasteries of Ireland the power of the Pope and his banner.'

FIRE AND BRIMSTONE

Bowman and Nicholas rode out of Dublin at opposite ends of Raymond's company. Apparently they were going to Meath, and as the sun rose in the east Richard deduced that Meath was to the north west.

The company was purely Norman, except for Brian and Dermot, so Richard at least didn't have to worry about Cormac slitting his throat. He did worry about Bowman slitting his half-brother's, though.

Richard rode with Raymond and Nicholas at the head of the party, followed closely by Alan and his last knight, one having managed somehow to die during the assault of Dublin. Bowman rode on his own at the very rear of the column as it snaked through the green countryside, presumably so he could keep an eye on all those who might wish him harm.

Raymond ignored Dermot even when he tried to explain what an ancient earthwork on a distant hill was. The grass covered mound could be seen from far and wide, and looked to Richard to be an ideal site for a castle.

Twenty squires rode with them, and three largely empty carts trundled behind. Richard assumed this raid was to gather supplies for the army, but when a monastery complex loomed into view ahead, he started to question his theory.

The church at the centre of the complex was of stone, but the outbuildings and barns were wooden. The fields around it had been recently harvested, and a respectable herd of cattle were in a pasture by one side.

Richard expected they would round up the cattle and return to Dublin, but Raymond instead turned to Brian. 'I want you to keep that banner up and follow us in,' he said.

Wearing his mail and with the remnants of his tattered cloak still on his shoulders, Raymond turned to the company. 'We bring God to this pagan land, we fight for the church. These pagans despoil this sacred ground and must be cleansed by iron and flame. Burn everything, kill everyone, and put everything of value into the carts.'

Some of the squires cheered or praised God.

'This is a monastery,' Richard said to Nicholas, 'we can't burn it.'

Raymond heard him. 'This is an Irish monastery, boy,' he said, 'not one of Rome. It must burn so it can be rebuilt and populated with good monks from England.'

Raymond drew his sword and led the company up to the complex gate. A low wall ran around the property, where everyone dismounted.

'I can stay with the horses,' Richard offered.

'Scared of a little blood?' Raymond asked.

'Scared of eternal damnation,' Richard replied.

Raymond laughed. 'You can hold the horses this time, but for the next monastery you're joining in.'

'The next one?'

Raymond shook his head. 'We're not out here to collect cattle, we're out here to make a point to the natives. Their own King sanctioned this. He's right here with us.'

Richard looked at Dermot, who nodded back. 'This is Rory's land,' Dermot said, 'and it should burn.'

Richard dismounted and started to find places on the boundary wall to tie horses to. A few squires stayed with him as everyone else walked up towards the holy building.

Bowman went last, his sword out and his eyes on his half-brother, making Richard wondered if they would both make it out of the complex alive.

In the end, they did. The company stormed in and monks screamed for mercy as they died. Some tried to run, but the squires with Richard remounted and chased them across the fields. None got very far.

Flames soon sprouted from the outbuildings, and even the church itself was alight before long. Squires carried out silver cups and a jewelled golden cross, but apart from a few barrels of drink, that's all they bothered to save from the fire.

Alan returned to the horses out of breath, his bloody sword still in his hands. Richard almost asked if killing monks was too much hard work for him, but held himself back. He ignored Alan and looked back to the palls of smoke that drifted up into the grey sky. Richard wondered what he was doing there.

Brian stood in front of the church the whole time, his banner aloft as the carnage unfolded around him. Once everything was either dead, on fire, or sometimes both, Raymond pulled the monk back towards the horses.

The carts partially loaded, the company continued moving north west, driving deeper into Irish territory.

Dermot rode silently as the dark smoke faded over the horizon behind them and Richard expected he might be having second thoughts.

In the early evening, the next monastery they sighted looked much the same as the first. It was situated on a low hill, and a cluster of roundhouses sat next to a wood on the other side of the road.

Everything was green and peaceful.

This time though, as the horses were held together, Raymond ordered Richard to go in with them.

He didn't draw his sword, and stalked up the hill at the rear of the company with Bowman. 'You'll need your sword, young lord,' he said.

'I won't,' Richard replied, 'why are you joining in?'

'This is our job,' Bowman said, 'it's what we're being paid to do.'

A shudder went through Richard as he realised that the looted goods in the carts might be what they ended up being paid with.

'Do you really want to be paid for this?'

'We have the Papal banner,' Bowman grinned, 'so we do God's work.'

Raymond banged the pommel of his sword on the church's door. His squires spread out and started to enter outbuildings.

A monk opened the church door and received Raymond's pommel in his face for the trouble.

Alan dragged a monk out of another doorway but the monk

clung on to the frame. Alan's companion cut at one of his wrists and the monk's grip was lost in a spray of blood.

Raymond called back to Richard. 'Into the church with me.'

Richard followed, still without drawing a weapon.

The tall Norman spotted three monks praying on their knees, facing a cross on the altar.

Raymond approached as their prayers grew louder.

Richard walked down the nave but stayed as far away as he could as Raymond lifted his sword. It came down and sunk into the neck of the first monk. His body convulsed in a short spasm before it slumped onto the stone floor.

The second monk held firm and kept praying in loud Latin.

The third however, a man with a weathered face and grey hair, got up and ran past Raymond.

'Richard, kill him,' Raymond said.

Richard folded his arms and looked his commander in the eye.

The monk ran past and towards the open door, his freedom in sight.

Nicholas stepped into the doorway and the monk slammed to a halt in front of him.

A swing of Nicholas's sword later, and that monk too lay dead on the church floor.

Raymond pointed his sword at Richard. 'There will be a consequence,' he said before bringing his sword down in a wide arc vertically onto the final monk's skull.

His head split open with a crack and thud.

Raymond twisted the sword and prised part of the skull off. When the body hit the ground, brain leaked across the holy building.

Raymond strode out of the church, barging Richard out of his way with his huge shoulder.

Richard regained his balance and followed him, not keen on remaining in the desecrated church any longer than he had to. He stepped over the body of the monk he hadn't killed and back out into the open air.

Which wasn't so open anymore. A fire had been started in a barn full of hay and straw, and the dry material had caught quickly.

Richard locked eyes with Brian, who stood with his banner fluttering in the weak breeze that fanned the flames of the fire.

Brian saw Richard held no weapons. 'You can't stop it,' he said, 'but thank you for trying.'

Raymond watched Alan enter the church. 'I want all the rest of the monks brought out here, we need to send a message,' he said.

Richard didn't like the sound of that, and something on his face must have given it away, because Raymond stormed over. 'Boy, never disobey me. If I tell you to kill someone, you kill them.'

'You're not my lord,' Richard said, 'and those aren't pagans. They pray to a cross the same as you or I.'

'They are heathen swine, but I don't care if you don't want to kill them. I'll just dock your pay. It isn't like we need your help, monks aren't hard to kill. Even Sir Alan is managing it.'

Monks started to be dragged out into the central yard of the complex. Some other men were dragged out too, along with a group of four nuns who lived on site to pray for the monks who prayed for everyone else.

'Kill them all,' Raymond ordered, 'and arrange their bodies in a huge cross on the ground. Use our monk as the middle point.'

A squire hauled a monk over and slashed his throat with a knife. The man held his throat but could do nothing to stop the bleeding. The squire pushed him over and laid him out in a line from Brian.

The next monk was pushed to his knees next to Brian. The doomed monk looked up with hatred in his eyes, and spat at Brian. A dagger plunged into the man's neck and he died with Brian unable to take his eyes off him.

Nicholas added a nun to the cross as the four lines of still-warm bodies started to be laid out.

Bowman contented himself with theft and at least stayed clear of the courtyard as monks and even nuns were put to the sword.

Richard could taste iron in the air and blood started to run and pool in depressions in the ground. He had his usual vision of the burning village of Fallencourt, and then the mounds of bodies the Martels had heaped up in Brittany. Richard realised

Nicholas would have been involved in that as he added another monk to Raymond's macabre work of art.

Richard took Brian by the arm and walked him back towards their horses. 'You don't need to be there,' Richard told him.

Brian didn't reply, and when Richard looked over there were tears in his eyes. Brian moved the banner so it was between him and Richard as they went to stand by the horses and carts.

The carts gained some more valuables, which were covered with canvas sheets to protect them.

Raymond led the company north again, and Richard went to ride with Bowman at the rear.

'I think he just likes seeing blood,' Bowman said as they passed a gently flowing river.

'I liked him after Baginbun,' Richard said, 'but you can't kill monks.'

'The bastard enjoyed doing this work just as much,' Bowman said, 'I noticed that.'

Richard didn't say anything because he had hardly been able to miss it himself. The image of the three slaughtered monks in the church stuck in his mind, and it stayed there as they made camp in a cluster of trees that night.

Squires were posted and fires were dug into pits to make them harder to see in the dark. Richard slept armoured and with his weapons on him, but no attack came. Wolves howled in the darkness, but Richard knew they wouldn't come near. His father had once told him about a man he'd met who trapped wolves in England by filling pits full of pitch for them to get stuck in. That memory made Richard feel even worse about being in Ireland. If he was going to be away from his family, he should at least be in the Holy Land searching for his father's truth.

Richard slept awkwardly, and dreamt of the time a monk had flown from a tower at Castle Tancarville. When he woke he checked his hands, and sure enough, the scars from the hot iron were still there.

There was moisture in the air as they set off towards the next monastery. It never quite managed to rain, but the floating water made everything feel damp by the time the sun started to go down and Richard saw the light from fires on a hill.

The trackway ran besides a shallow stream on its left with a tall bank on its right. Long grasses grew on the bank, though Richard reckoned Solis could climb it easily enough. Across the stream lay a small wooden bridge, just big enough for a man, that led up to the raised mound from which they'd seen firelight.

The company stopped and Richard rode to the front to ask who they would be butchering this time.

Brian nodded at the mound and the building atop it. 'That is Saint Ciaran's Well,' he said, 'and the monastery that serves it is just along this track.'

'Preposterous,' Raymond said, 'worshipping a well?'

'Saint Ciaran, actually,' Brian replied.

'Whoever that is,' Raymond laughed.

The well was housed in a wooden building from which the glow of a fire shone.

'Alan,' Raymond said, 'would you go and put whoever is tending that fire on it?'

The mercenary grinned, and he and his companion crossed the bridge and climbed the small hill to the well. The light had faded enough that Richard couldn't see who was around the fire, but he heard their cry for help. The fire half disappeared as a body was flung onto it, but soon enough the flames grew up around it.

Alan walked down the mound cleaning his sword.

'This isn't what I signed on for,' Richard said.

'It is exactly what we signed on for,' Bowman replied.

'I forgot,' Raymond shouted over the stream to Alan, 'you need to throw the body into the well.'

'Shouldn't we let it burn first?' Alan shouted back.

Raymond nodded, got bored, and ordered the company on. 'We can sleep in the monastery tonight,' he said, 'once we've cleared the vermin from it.'

'We can't spill blood there tonight,' Brian said.

Raymond laughed. 'And why not, young monk? We all know we're emptying these places of life so English monks and nuns can be sent to replace them. How did you think we'd be making room?'

'Today is the ninth day of September, it is Saint Ciaran's feast day.'

'Is it?' Raymond grew more animated, 'that means a feast will be ready and waiting for us.'

The squires who heard liked that idea, although Dermot frowned.

Raymond ordered the company on, Brian not moving his horse until the carts rolled by and he started to feel very alone. Richard went back for him as the fire on the mound flickered brightly as it caught the dead minder's clothing.

'He died of plague,' Brian said.

Richard looked up at the fire. 'I think he died of sword,' he replied.

'No,' the monk said, 'Saint Ciaran. He died of plague.'

'So? All of his monks are going to die of fire or having their guts emptied all over their monastery. None will live long enough to die of plague.'

Richard didn't hear a response. 'I'm sorry,' he said.

Brian stayed silent as Raymond led them to the compound of Saint Ciaran's monastery. By now he didn't need to give orders, Alan rushed through the gate behind him, Nicholas not far behind. Dermot stayed on his horse and looked less enthusiastic this time around.

Bowman passed his reins to a squire. 'At least we'll eat well tonight,' he told Richard as he arrived.

'I'm not sure I'll be hungry,' he replied.

The walls around this complex were taller than the others and Richard couldn't see over them. The gate was just as undefended however, and the raiders poured in. The carnage began and Richard waited with a glum Brian by the gate. A squire stood with them, which at least meant Richard would have no need to harm any of the monks if they tried to escape. This time, most of them boarded themselves up in the chapel at the heart of the compound, Richard saw them run from their hall, across the courtyard, and into their place of refuge.

Raymond ordered the door barred and the building fired. Squires piled up some kindling and straw under one of the walls, and soon flames licked up the chapel and those inside began to wail and claw at the door.

Raymond left two squires to keep a watch over the fire,

and ordered everyone else to enjoy the feast the monks had so kindly prepared for them. Dermot sat in the hall already, drinking to avoid seeing the chapel torched.

Richard was the last into the hall for Brian hadn't even bothered to put on the pretence of obeying Raymond, and was nowhere to be seen.

The big Norman cared little however, and was hugely happy with what they found in the hall. Honeyed drink filled cups and roasted beef filled platters next to boiled eggs and enormous wheels of cheese. The bread was a little lighter than the dark bread of home, but Richard had little appetite for any of it.

Bowman pushed a cup along the table to him. 'This will make you feel better. Or feel less, perhaps,' he said.

Richard drank the sweet liquid and after the second cup his vision started to lag behind where it felt like it should be.

Raymond yelled for someone to close the door because the sound of the church combusting started to seep through and spoil his feast.

Another cup was pushed Richard's way and soon he was floating in a world of numbness.

Nicholas started singing with Alan and Raymond, which brought scowls from Bowman. He drank more than Richard, but didn't seem to be any the worse for it.

Richard remembered nothing more from that point on, until he woke up with a headache as a cockerel heralded the sunrise.

He was still sat at the feasting table, half eaten food scattered across it and men sleeping all over the floor. Bowman wasn't there so Richard got up and thought to look for some fresh water. The monastery would have its own well, maybe the stream even ran straight through it on its way to Saint Ciaran's well, he thought.

Richard opened the door and stepped out only to be greeted by a scene of utter devastation. He'd forgotten about the chapel. The husk of the building was charred back and white with smoke still steadily rising up into the cool morning air. At some point the monks had tried to escape the fire through a collapsed wall, for their bodies lay around the wall where the squires had cut them down. They were blackened too, and

Richard could smell them. Had he eaten from the feast, he would surely have thrown it all back up there and then.

Bowman jogged up from where the carts had been parked. He gasped for breath. 'We are not alone,' he said.

'Who is here?' Richard asked. His eyes ached, too.

'I don't know,' Bowman said, 'more Irish. They are standing in one big line all around us.'

'What?' Richard felt a chill and suddenly a lot more awake.

'I'm going to tell Raymond,' Bowman rushed back towards the hall.

Richard made the sign of the cross and said a prayer begging for forgiveness. Then he went to stand by the church, because from its modest mound he could see over the compound wall. Sure enough, when he got there, he could see the figures of men all around the monastery. They weren't in a single line as Bowman had suggested, but in groups, watching the Normans inside.

Brian appeared, his eyes darting from one group of distant Irish to the next. 'The wolves, Richard, did you hear the wolves?'

'I heard some last night,' he replied.

'They were a sign,' the monk said, 'the wolves, don't you see?'

Richard shook his head. 'Calm down, tell me what you're talking about.'

'They are Fian, young men clad in animal skins who act like animals. The Lord is using them to punish us.'

'What or who are the Fian?' Richard grabbed the monk by his shoulders. 'And take a breath.'

Brian filled and emptied his lungs slowly to steady himself. 'They are the young men yet to inherit, or those who will never inherit. They form warrior bands who roam the land in the summer, trading pelts and hiring their services out.'

'What services?'

'Guards, cattle raiders, warriors.'

Richard let the monk go. 'What are they doing here?'

'Avenging the monks we murdered.'

'How did they know to come here?' Richard asked.

'Maybe this group of them, this Fianna, saw the huge chapel on fire last night,' Brian said, 'although the church have been trying to stamp out the Fian way of life. There are barely any bands left.'

'So it's just a coincidence,' Richard said to himself, 'they might have seen the fire and come to investigate.'

'Or God sent them.'

'But the church doesn't approve of them, that's what you just said.'

Brian shrugged. 'The Lord works in mysterious ways.'

Richard had always thought that saying was just an excuse. He squinted out over the walls at some of the Fianna. The biggest group included three men who wore great sets of antlers on their heads, and he thought two others wore the pelts of wolves as cloaks and hoods.

'They actually look like pagans to me,' Richard said, 'Raymond is going to love this.'

Dermot left the hall before Raymond, spurred on by Bowman's report, where he took one look at the Irish surrounding him, and ran back inside.

Raymond emerged only once he'd fully dressed for battle. 'Monk, where's your banner?' He called out.

Brian closed his eyes for a moment before tramping off to retrieve it.

Alan and his knight left the hall armed and the squires were not far behind.

Raymond considered the Fianna at the walls. He sniffed loudly. 'We faced worse odds on the promontory. They look like boys. We have the walls and enough food to last a month. We'll stand watch all day, and at dusk we'll storm out. They won't be able to follow us in the dark, and their small horses won't be able to keep up anyway.'

Richard nodded, the plan gave their horses the day to rest. The compound had a decent stable block and a store of horsebread, which was the first supply of such they'd found since Waterford. The Fianna didn't seem to be in any hurry to storm the walls, so they waited.

They all waited, waited for dusk while standing in the compound and watching the Irish who watched them back. Sometimes a group left, sometimes it appeared somewhere else, but a few of the company at a time went back into the hall to eat and try to relax.

When it was Richard's turn he found relaxing difficult. He found some horsebread and carved the same charm into it he had used long ago. He fed it to Solis and noticed that the monks had five horses of their own in the stables. He thought he'd try to claim one as a pack animal if he could. The carts had stayed outside the gate, and the Irish eventually helped themselves to the treasure that sat within them.

Raymond watched tight-lipped as the Fianna stole everything the company had itself stolen, but didn't see the need to risk his men to stop them.

Richard found Brian rocking in a corner of the hall when he got back in.

'The church calls them Sons of Death,' Brian said, 'an eye for an eye, the bible says.'

'Everything will be fine,' Richard said, 'we'll punch a hole in their circle tonight and ride straight out. You'll be surrounded the rest of us, you'll be fine.'

'Promise you won't leave me behind,' the monk's eyes were wide and childlike as he looked into Richard's.

'I swear it,' Richard replied.

Dermot continued to drink in the hall for most of the day, and Richard tried not to think about why the only two Irish men in the company were quite so frightened.

As the afternoon turned into the evening and the grey sky accelerated dusk, Raymond walked round from man to man and spoke to each of them.

To Richard he nodded. 'Once we're through them, we'll take the second most direct road back, they won't expect that. If you get separated, ride away from Dublin for a while before you turn back to it.'

Richard nodded back.

'Every man should take some food, enough for two days,' Raymond said.

'You think this will go wrong?' Richard asked.

Raymond tapped the pommel of his sword. 'This is what those of us in the brotherhood of knighthood are for, Richard. We learn Vegetius and we think about how we fight. That is why our kind rule land from Dublin to Jerusalem. Those who see our way of war as a simple, brutish charge of horsemen know nothing.'

Richard knew how long it took to learn to ride in a charge, and knew he wasn't perfect at it. 'Are we abandoning the carts?' Richard asked.

'There's nothing in them to save, and they are just bits of wood,' Raymond replied.

Yes then, Richard thought.

Raymond went on to the next man so Richard went to find Bowman.

In the hall, he found Bowman as he crammed a whole wheel of cheese into a linen bag.

'That's not two day's food, is it?' Richard said to him.

'No, but I'll be able to sell it in Dublin,' Bowman replied, 'and maybe earn us the very first coin we've had out of this whole venture so far.'

'The Irish don't use coins, that's what the monk said,' Richard replied, even though he'd seen a mint in Dublin.

'Then I'll swap it for something I can sell in England.'

Richard got out his own bag and swept some more cheese into it.

Bowman watched him do it and chuckled.

When Nicholas entered the hall his eyes fell on the table first.

Bowman noticed him. 'When we ride out of here, I want you in front of me so you don't stab me in the back,' he said.

Nicholas held his hands up. 'You're the one who threatened to kill me.'

Bowman walked around the other side of the table towards the door. 'And I still intend to.'

'There are enough people for you both to fight outside the walls,' Richard said, 'when we get back to Dublin we'll work out what to do about Cormac and the Countess.'

'Kill them,' Nicholas shrugged.

Bowman stopped at the door and looked back at Richard to hear his reply.

Richard looked for a cup still full of the honey-drink but failed. 'At the moment I don't have a better idea,' he said.

Bowman smirked and went outside.

Richard hadn't seen the sun all day, and the evening

encroached quickly once he'd gone and readied Solis for their breakout. Richard got on him and realised immediately that the Fianna would see what they were about to do.

Squires mounted up around him, and Alan lurched into his saddle nearby. The horse grunted as he landed on its long-suffering back.

Brian wedged the Papal banner into the ground to help him get onto his horse.

The Irishmen outside the monastery gathered a spear's throw from the gateway and started to block the road in both directions. Their round shields locked close together and their ranks were soon three deep.

The junior squires handed lances up to the company and all the knights formed up behind Raymond.

'Richard,' the big Norman shouted, 'you're next to me.'

Nerves ate into his stomach and his guts stirred and gurgled. Bowman and Nicholas fell in behind, then Alan and his knight, and then the squires. Brian was somewhere but Richard only had thoughts of what might happen to him or his horse.

His mind jumped back to the mutilated veterans of Lillebonne and their missing limbs and mangled stories. Charges like this were how men ended up like that. Richard's drinking the night before came back to haunt him and he tasted acid in the back of his mouth.

Raymond started off down the gentle slope that led to the open gate in the compound wall.

Jeers and hooting noises came from the Fianna. Some howled like wolves.

The road went left and right, and the Irish had shield walls blocking both. Richard realised that the squires at the rear of the company were just as much in danger as he was if the company got stuck.

Raymond reached the gate and stepped his horse sideways to make room for Richard.

Richard pulled up alongside and they turned right and started to walk towards the shieldwall.

'You and me, Richard, this is our battle,' Raymond said, 'you might be headstrong and self-righteous, but I wouldn't want anyone else next to me now.'

Richard felt himself blush, but his guts were water and he felt his stomach starting to cramp.

The Irish in their path, six men wide from bank to stream, waved spears and axes in the air and shouted and sang.

Solis arched his neck and strained to charge. 'I'm ready,' Richard held him back.

'Charge,' Raymond couched his lance and Richard launched into a canter alongside him.

They reached full speed in two bounds, rode knee-to-knee, and crashed into the shieldwall.

Solis's front feet, moving together, hit the top of the shields in front of him and pushed the men holding them down. Richard's lance skated off a shield and up into a warrior's face to burst out of the back of his unprotected skull.

Solis landed onto something that squelched and bounded off into the third rank of the defenders. They never had a chance to step back, and as quickly as Richard's lance pushed a young man onto the ground, they were through and onto the open road.

Raymond's knee still pressed into his. 'Keep going, we need to make room,' he cried.

Solis flew along the road and Richard heard the noise of battle behind him.

Hooves clattered on earth and Richard risked turning to look back.

The shieldwall had split in two and all the Norman knights were through. The squires were half through, but the second shieldwall was closing in and the last few squires looked like they were going to get caught.

Brian was too near the back of the company.

Richard pulled Solis around in the harshest way he'd ever done.

Raymond was about to shout at him when a spear darted down from the top of the bank at him. It scrapped his back and tore more of his tattered red cloak.

Stones flew down and Richard realised there were slingers on the top of the slope.

Bowman cantered past and a stone rang on his helmet. Richard went the other way, back to the shieldwall, and left

Bowman to his luck.

The warriors wearing antlers ran down the hill and leapt onto the first squires who emerged from the shieldwall.

Richard focused on Brian as the column broke apart and more Irish poured down the bank.

The battered shieldwall closed the gap on the road, even though they were only one rank deep now, and Brian and four squires were now trapped between it and the approaching second wall.

Regretting his promise not to leave the monk behind, Richard lowered his lance and charged the thin line of Irishmen from behind.

Between Solis and the lance, half of the six warriors in the wall fell to the ground and Brian's eyes found Richard as their horses nearly collided.

The monk's horse spun, snorted and reared up as the second shield wall skewed the rearmost squires.

'Go,' Richard said, 'you're holding his reins in fear and holding him back. Point him down the road and let go.'

Brian nearly fell out of the saddle as the horse reared higher.

Richard swore at him. He threw his lance aside as Brian's horse landed and bumped into Solis. Richard drew his sword and slashed out at Brian's reins.

One leather rein snapped. The horse, the pressure on its mouth released as the surprised monk dropped the other one, bolted down the road after its friends.

Brian screamed as it jumped through the three surviving men from the shieldwall and took him away through the melee.

The only squire between Richard and the second shieldwall had his horse killed from under him, and they came for him next. Richard couldn't save the doomed squire so he pushed his horse to follow Brian's.

Solis grunted with exertion and used his chest to clear an Irishman from his path. Richard didn't like being the last man in the company. Spears and stones were thick in the air as squires fought above the bodies of their dead and dying comrades.

Richard's horse jumped the body of Alan's last companion

who lay sprawled across the road clutching a wound in his stomach, and then he saw Bowman on the ground.

The blonde man's helmet was gone but he still moved.

Solis flew down the road and didn't want to turn around.

The rest of the company cantered down the road towards safety. All except Nicholas, whose horse hared past Richard and towards his half-brother.

The Irish noticed him and the arrows, stones and spears all started to fly at him. His horse slammed to a stop and Nicholas jumped from the saddle. Half of the Fianna ran down the road from the monastery towards him, seeing their chance to kill one last Norman.

Most of the rest launched missiles, but one of the warriors with antlers on his head ran towards Nicholas and Bowman with a knife in his hands.

The man wore nothing on his torso, and Richard pushed Solis towards him.

The warrior turned to face him and Solis baulked at his antlers. Richard realised his stallion wasn't sure if he was looking at a man or a deer, and either way he wouldn't charge home against him.

Richard tried to dismount quickly, but one foot caught in a stirrup just as Solis spooked away from the antlers. As the horse turned, he flung Richard through the air and he landed right on the surprised warrior.

Richard's sword wasn't in his hand anymore, but the Irishman's knife cut through the air and scraped down Richard's chest.

The warrior looked up at him as they hit the ground and halted. The man's brown eyes were wide and Richard wondered if he'd ever fought a mailed man before. Richard reached up to the antlers and pulled violently on a tine. It snapped with a crack and Richard plunged the separated point down into the surprised warrior's neck.

Richard pushed him away and jumped to his feet.

Nicholas slapped Bowman in the face and the stunned man shook his head and looked around.

'Don't expect thanks,' Bowman got up to his knees, 'this just means we're even.'

Nicholas saw the young men who started to charge down the bank towards then, as well as the men from the shieldwall who still ran along the road towards them.

'We need to go,' Nicholas shouted, 'get on my horse.'

Bowman straightened himself up then staggered sideways with a hand on his head.

Solis came trotting back towards Richard now that the antlers lay still on the ground. Richard gave him a sour look. 'Idiot,' he muttered under his breath.

The two men wearing wolf-pelts sprinted down the bank with a war cry that made Richard hesitate.

They were going to reach Nicholas and Bowman.

Richard started to run back towards them. His horse shook his head and followed at his shoulder.

Richard forgot he only held a shard of antler as a weapon as one of the wolf-men changed direction to face him.

Nicholas picked Bowman up and helped him to his horse. The animal had stayed put, but it watched the men that ran towards it with its head up in the air and its eyes wide.

The wolf-man lunged at Richard. After the antler-man, Richard simply ignored the knife as it thudded into his stomach. His antler however, sunk into the side of the warrior's forearm and he dropped his knife.

Richard stabbed down again and the antler went into the Irishman's open mouth, through his tongue and snapped his lower jaw.

His scream forced Richard to wince, but he kicked the man away who sprawled onto the road.

Nicholas had got his half-brother onto his horse and pulled the reins to get it moving in the direction the company had gone. He slapped the horse on its flank and the animal kicked out at him as it accelerated.

It galloped past Solis, who thought about chasing but didn't, and in a flash Bowman was clear of the Fianna.

Richard and Nicholas, one horse between them, were not.

The second wolf-man jumped onto Nicholas and they rolled on the earth.

Warriors swarmed down the bank and they didn't have long until they would be overwhelmed.

281

Richard charged towards Nicholas as he fought. Richard brought his antler down onto the the wolf-man's neck, but the hide kept it out and it slipped from his grasp.

The wolf-man turned his head to see what had hit him, which gave Nicholas enough him to grab his head and almost wrench it from its body.

The wolf-man went limp and Nicholas ripped the pelt from his back.

'You're thinking of trophies?' Richard gasped, 'now?'

Nicholas grinned, and his eyes were somehow red, green, and glazed at the same time. Half a dozen men from the Fianna jumped the last part of the bank and attacked.

Two went for Solis with spears, but the horse danced sideways away from them as if they were the tusks of a boar.

The other four tried to kill Richard.

He pulled his shield around and drew Sir John's dagger. He braced.

Nicholas ran past him and threw himself at the warriors, all far younger than him, and three bounced off his mailed chest. Nicholas's sword killed the fourth before Richard took his chance and sprung at the three men on the ground.

He hesitated for a second when he saw their age, their youth. Then he remembered he was barely any older himself and stabbed one to death.

Nicholas killed the other two before Richard had even looked up.

A spear swept sideways through the air and left a long wound along the palomino horse's front shoulder.

The two spearmen had hurt his horse. Richard felt a pure rage he'd never felt before. When the pilgrims had stolen his horse in Kent, when he was just a child, Richard had felt fear and pain. Now he was different, and the spearmen died under his dagger in a spray of blood, a shard of skull and a burst eyeball. When he was done, Richard's face was wet and blood stung his eye that had the scar across it.

Nicholas turned to face what remained of the Fianna, maybe thirty young men who howled for blood and vengeance for their fallen comrades.

Richard watched Nicholas hold his sword out and bellow at

the attackers. Richard thought about escaping and looked back at his horse. Blood ran down his yellow coat so Richard couldn't think of escape anymore, fresh rage pulsed through his veins.

Richard ran to Nicholas and stood alongside him.

The Martel knight didn't acknowledge his presence as their lungs heaved together, and with death all around them, and without having to exchange a word, they both charged at the Irish.

The Fianna did not expect that. As the two mail-clad knights charged them, their advance faltered. Richard jumped the body of a squire.

Nicholas roared his war cry, which was, 'Martel,' and those at the front of the mass of warriors stopped. The rest bumped into them and their cohesion was lost.

Richard and Nicholas flew into them, blades flashed and the Irish fell back in confusion.

He felt blows on his body and arms, but Richard would make them pay for cutting his horse. He'd seen smaller wounds corrupt before, so he dealt bigger wounds back to his opponents.

Nicholas fought as if a wild animal. He'd tied the wolf-pelt around his neck and the black fur shone with red droplets of blood as Nicholas's victims fell around him.

For a glorious moment Richard thought they could kill all thirty of them. Euphoria flushed his rage out as his dagger pierced an eye socket.

Then his arm started to get tired. He tried to raise it up but it didn't go all the way.

Nicholas's blade swung through the air beside him, but some of the Irish were about to get around behind them. Richard's euphoria evaporated.

A spear jabbed through the throng and hit the nasal guard of Richard's helmet. The metal bent back inwards onto his nose and crunched the cartilage.

Richard pulled his shield around to knock the spear away, but an axe bit into the top of it and a chunk the size of his hand was cut away.

Nicholas killed a man and his victim fell onto the warrior who attacked Richard. His spear was knocked over and the blade dug into the thigh of the Irishman next to him.

Richard killed both of them but something heavy knocked his shield and he slipped on the road. He fell backwards, hit his head on the earth and his helmet jarred his head.

A warrior lunged at him so Richard kicked his leg out and knocked him over. Richard hit him with his bad toe, only recently healed, and pain shot up his leg.

Two more Irish stood above him ready to strike and Richard sense his death. A cold sensation filtered through his mind and he wished he had never come to Ireland.

The earth shuddered. His back flat on the ground, Richard felt the earth vibrate through his whole body.

The two Irishmen standing over him looked down the road.

Richard lunged and sunk his dagger into one of their thighs.

Hooves echoed off the bank in what was now nearly full night, and the Fianna started to run. Most ran up the bank, Nicholas chased and killed one who was not fast enough.

Raymond and Bowmen were the first to appear. Their horses cantered along the road and they chased the warriors who tried to flee along it.

Solis ran after them and disappeared into the dark.

'So much for loyalty, Solie,' Richard mumbled as Nicholas returned and held a hand down to him.

Squires stopped at the bank as the Irish vanished over the top of it.

'You came back for me,' the gore-covered Martel knight said.

Richard clasped his hand and groaned as he was pulled up to his feet. His mail would need heavy repairs now, as well as work to clear the rust from it. His right arm felt as if it wanted to drop off and he put his dagger away without cleaning it.

A wolf howled across the fields and Richard looked at the blood-speckled pelt on his captive knight's shoulders. 'I think that suits you,' he said.

Nicholas's eyes returned to normal.

'Your brother came back for you,' Richard said, 'as you returned for him.'

'It's not me you need to convince,' Nicholas replied.

Raymond and Bowman rode back along the road, white steam rushing from their horse's nostrils.

Solis trotted along happily behind them, noticed Richard and walked over.

Richard inspected the wound on his shoulder. It was long and a finger's width deep in the centre. That worried him.

Raymond eased his horse to a halt. 'If I had thought we could just kill them all, we would have stayed and fought,' he said. There was blood on his horse's chest, but it hadn't come from the horse.

Bowman's black horse snorted loudly, but the blonde man didn't look too steady in the saddle.

Raymond watched him sway slightly, and his own horse was just as covered in sweat. 'We don't need to risk a night ride now, we can go back inside the monastery tonight. The Irish are scattered.'

Richard was glad of that. He ignored Bowman and Nicholas for the moment, and led his horse back to its stable. He had seen wounds being treated in Brittany in all manner of ways, but the method he could apply here was wine. He fetched a jug of light-coloured wine and poured it as slowly as he could along the gash in the horse's shoulder. Solis winced when it reached the deepest part, and the wine washed more blood from it until the whole side of the horse was covered in blood tinged wine. Richard also knew that horse droppings should be removed from stables as soon as possible, so cleared those out before we went back to the hall to see to himself.

Bowman lay on the ground along the side of the hall on no bedding, his eyes closed.

Dermot went back to the honey-drink, as did Nicholas.

Richard found some water to wash his face, and as the cold liquid splashed down him it left puddles of red on the floor. His eye itched and he had to stop himself from scratching it.

Nicholas still wore his wolf-pelt, which Raymond admired. 'You look terrifying, that is for sure. The churchmen back in Dublin will disapprove of it,' he grinned.

Nicholas looked indifferent. 'They can disapprove all they want.'

Richard sat down and found some cheese that had avoided being stuffed into a bag earlier in the day. He started to eat but wasn't hungry.

Everyone in the hall was covered in cuts and bruises, but it was obvious that most of the squires hadn't survived. Alan sat at the end of the big table on his own, mournfully looking at his empty plate.

'Has anyone seen the monk?' Richard asked loudly. He felt bad he'd only just thought about him.

'He came back,' Raymond said, 'he's in the compound somewhere trying to sew his reins back together.'

The last remains of his energy seeped out of Richard's limbs and he decided to go to sleep.

In the morning they stripped the bodies along the road of weapons and armour, and loaded everything into the carts. The monastery's horses were tied to the back of them, and they left the compound and its charred chapel behind them. Which was just fine with Richard, seeing as the bodies outside it had started to smell.

The company rode back towards Dublin with watchful eyes on their surroundings, everyone marched ready to battle.

'He came back for you,' Richard told Bowman, 'why would he have done that if he meant to betray us?'

Bowman coughed. 'To make his betrayal all the more complete,' he replied.

'You can't believe that,' Richard said, 'you would be dead on the road if it wasn't for him.'

'Don't exaggerate.'

Richard felt better about Nicholas, but a niggling thought at the back of his mind still agreed with Bowman.

'We need a plan for when we get back to Dublin,' Richard said, 'there could be a horde of Irishmen waiting to slit our throats in our sleep.'

'Slit theirs first,' Bowman answered flatly.

'You've been in Ireland too long,' Richard said.

'We all have. These Irish should have solved their problems themselves instead of dragging us into it.'

'That's it,' Richard said, 'that's what we need to do.'

'What? How did you get an answer from that?' Bowman asked.

'The Irish can fix this problem for us,' Richard said, 'I need to speak to Brian.'

Richard waited by the road for the monk to catch him up. Green hills rolled into the distance and fluffy white clouds drifted by overhead.

Brian held his reins away from Richard. 'Do you know how long it took me to find something to make holes in the leather?'

'It saved your life,' Richard said, 'you ride like a frightened child.'

The monk frowned. 'I'm not a knight.'

'You fought well enough on the ramparts at Baginbun,' Richard said.

'God fought through me,' Brian replied.

'We need you to do something now, though,' Richard said, 'something brave.'

'It isn't for God, though, is it?'

Richard shook his head and tried not to laugh at him. 'If Cormac murders me, Bowman kills Nicholas, and Strongbow hangs Bowman, who will be left to look out for you?'

'The Lord above.'

'Oh, did he cut your reins for you?' Richard asked wryly.

Brian sighed. 'I'm not going to kill anyone for you,' he said.

'Of course not, we just need you to ride back to Dublin next to King Dermot.'

DOWN WITH THE KING

Raymond walked into Dublin's church after telling the rest of the company to wait outside it.

Richard Dismounted and led Solis over to one of the large water troughs that was kept topped up with water in all towns and cities.

Richard watched Solis, who seemed not to care about his wound, drink. 'I'm worried about what Raymond might tell Strongbow.'

'I think they both have bigger things to worry about than your disobedience,' Bowman said.

Richard hoped so. He flexed his right arm out, but his muscles felt empty and tired.

Nicholas adjusted the wolf-pelt on his shoulders. 'She doesn't look happy,' he nodded over towards the church as Eva left it.

A crier stood up on a wooden platform in the square and started to shout local news out in Irish.

Eva walked through the crowd that started to built up for him, her red dress enough for the lower classes to step out of her way.

Bowman took his horse away from the trough.

Eva greeted them with an unsmiling face. 'How many men did you lose in your battle against the warrior monks of Meath?' She asked in Richard's direction.

Richard tried to pull Solis away from the trough but he refused and put his head down for another drink. 'We fought through a Fianna,' he said, 'and lost more than half our company.'

'Do you think that might be God's judgement for your desecration of our holy sites?'

Bowman went to speak to her but backed off as her face grew only darker.

'We didn't know we'd be burning monasteries until we'd already left,' Richard said.

Eva cocked an eyebrow at him. 'Just following orders?'

'Something like that.'

The princess looked over towards Bowman. 'The Irish healers and the bishop both agree I shall be having a girl,' she said.

Bowman looked up at her, licked his lips, then asked quietly. 'And what might you be thinking of calling her?'

Eva watched the blonde man for a moment. 'I shall be suggesting Isabel.'

Bowman took a sharp breath.

'That does not mean he shall accept it,' Eva added.

That didn't matter to Bowman, the message was clear and his face lit up.

'Keep him quiet,' Eva said to Richard, 'but I thought he should know.'

Richard's mind worked for a moment to remember the significance of the name, but he remembered the answer in Bowman's bright, child-like eyes.

'You shouldn't be seen near us,' Richard said.

'My husband threw me out of the church so he could speak to the Norman giant without me,' Eva said, 'which does not build trust.'

Richard wondered if she had the right to complain, but didn't voice that thought.

An Englishman whose slender body and nervous eyes marked him out as a servant rather than a knight approached them from the church. 'You are to enter now,' he said.

'Who, me?' Richard asked.

The Englishman nodded.

'What about me?' Bowman asked.

'Lord de Clare asked for all the knights from the Meath raid.'

'What about me?' Eva asked, 'or am I still outcast?'

'You are not a knight from the Meath raid,' the Englishman shrugged.

'I'm coming back anyway,' the princess pushed her way back

through the crowed listening to the crier and into the church.

Richard soon joined her, just as Strongbow finished shouting at her to get out or be marched out by guards. Eva left by herself and glowered at Richard on her way.

Bowman gawped at her and started to speak.

'Whatever you want to say,' Richard hissed at him, 'it has to wait until we're not here.'

Bowman almost bounced on his feet as he walked down the nave with Richard to see Strongbow.

Richard expected him to announce that due to Bowman's barn related antics in Wales, they were all now going to die. He stood with slouched shoulders to await their fate.

'I have a job for you,' Strongbow said instead.

Richard wasn't ready for that. 'A job?'

Strongbow leant to one side on his chair and looked at Nicholas. 'Why are you dressed like some pagan savage?'

The Martel knight stroked the fur that sat on top of his mail. 'I like it.'

Strongbow considered him, groaned, and spoke to Richard instead. 'No matter. I need men who can kill, and no others have proved so capable at that than the three of you.'

'Anyone in the army can kill monks,' Richard replied.

Strongbow's face darkened and his hand curled around the armrest of his ornately carved chair. 'I don't need monks killed, I need a king killed.'

Richard's mouth flapped open as the words hung in the high ceiling of the church. Unlike his previous visit, no one else was inside the cavernous space, just Raymond and Alan, who had followed them in.

'Which king?' Nicholas asked.

Raymond choked down a snort of laughter and turned it into a cough. 'That is a good question,' he said.

'The deaths of any of them would be beneficial,' Strongbow mused for a moment.

Richard looked down at the two wolfhounds that had curled up together at their lord's feet. One snored softly.

'High King Rory?' Richard asked.

Strongbow smiled faintly. 'It would take an army to cut

290

through to him,' he said, 'my target is far less capable.'

Bowman's eyes widened and Richard tried to elbow him without it being obvious.

'King Dermot?' Richard said.

Strongbow nodded.

'Why?'

'Whisperings in dark places,' Strongbow said, 'that is what kings have to contend with, and whispers can be deadlier than swords.'

'Are you a king now, then?' Bowman asked.

Richard stood on his foot and the blonde man grunted.

Strongbow's eyes bored into Bowman. He sniffed loudly. 'If you succeed then I will be. Dermot plots to kill me and by doing so seals his own fate. He is killing himself with his betrayal.'

'We are not killers to be hired out,' Richard said.

'Are you not?' Strongbow laughed, 'I thought that is exactly what you are. You sailed all the way from wherever it was to fight here for money. Kill one man on top of the mountain of bodies you have already harvested, and you will be rewarded accordingly.'

If one killing meant Nicholas could earn his ransom, then they could leave Ireland very soon. 'But it is no small thing to kill a king,' Richard said.

'They die like other men,' Strongbow said, 'now go and find him. Raymond tells me King Dermot failed to reach the church with you, so he has already slipped away. He will be in the city somewhere, find him and kill him.'

'Be quick about it,' Raymond added, 'and if it isn't obvious enough, no one can know of this.'

'What about red balls, here,' Bowman pointed at Alan.

The mercenary stood dead still, unsure of what to do.

'He'll have to go with them,' Raymond said to his lord, 'if he's involved then he won't open his mouth tonight when he finds some drink.'

'I care not,' Strongbow said, 'so long as Dermot dies. All of you, go now, hunt him together. Failure is not acceptable. But make it look like an accident.'

When they left the church, Alan started to jog awkwardly

towards his horse. 'I'll have no part of this, not with you,' he said.

'Get him,' Richard said.

'You get him,' Bowman replied.

Nicholas ran off after Alan and grabbed him by his cloak. The knight looked round at the dead eyes of the black wolf on Nicholas's shoulder and gave up his attempted escape.

'We like this idea as much as you do,' Richard said, 'but you heard Strongbow, you have got to come with us.'

Eva saw them leave and started to go back in a second time.

Bowman turned to follow but Richard caught his arm. 'You need to pull yourself together, people will start to notice.'

'She needs to know what I'm thinking,' he said.

'You tell me all the time how we don't live in a romance,' Richard said, 'you need to take your own advice or you'll be swinging from a rope before sunset.'

'If Cormac doesn't beat Strongbow to it,' Bowman snapped back.

Richard stopped in his tracks. He'd forgotten about that. Now they'd returned to the city, his deadline to kill Strongbow would be enforcible again.

'What happened to your plan with the monk?' Bowman asked.

Richard glanced at Alan. 'Not with him here.'

Brian had held their horses while they had been in the church. 'You all look excited,' he told them.

'Worried,' Richard replied, 'Strongbow has given us a task.'

Brian frowned.

'Don't worry, no more monks,' Nicholas replied, 'which is a shame because they were at least easy to kill.'

'God will judge you,' Brian said to him.

'What about you, monk? You stood and watched,' Nicholas said.

Brian looked into the empty eye sockets of the wolf-pelt and looked away towards Richard. 'What is the task?'

Richard checked no one was too close, then walked up to the monk. 'We have to kill King Dermot.'

'Kill,' Brian shouted then checked himself down to a whisper, 'kill the King?'

Richard nodded.

'You cannot do that, all kings are anointed by God. Hell awaits king-killers.'

Richard let out a deep breath. 'If we don't kill him, Strongbow will send me to hell right now. If we kill Dermot, I'll still be alive to get to the holy land and cleanse my soul of this new sin.'

Brian opened his mouth to argue but Richard saw defeat in his eyes.

Bowman retrieved his reins and his horse from the monk. 'I've thought about it,' he said, 'and I actually agree with the monk.'

'You do?' Richard asked, 'about what?'

'We can't kill the King.'

'Why not? You don't care about him,' Nicholas said, 'it would be just another crime to add to your list.'

Bowman growled at him. 'I'll turn your skin into a pelt if you don't shut up,' then turned to Richard, 'Dermot is Eva's father. I can't kill him, he's my father in law.'

Richard stared at him for a moment, dumbfounded. 'You're not married to Eva,' he eventually said.

'I will be.'

Nicholas bent double with laughter.

'You won't be,' Richard said, 'ever. What is wrong with you?'

'I can't kill her father,' Bowman continued, 'what would Eva say?'

'She'll never know, and you may well never speak to her again. You'll certainly never share a barn with her.'

'A barn?' Alan asked.

Richard cursed himself. 'Enough,' he said, 'we're doing what we have to. But it will take us days to search Dublin, how do we find King Dermot before the sun goes down and Cormac's knives come out?'

Brian held Solis's reins out to Richard. 'You don't need to search for him in Dublin,' he said.

Richard took the reins and the yellow horse came and rested his wet chin on Richard's shoulder. 'Why not?'

'Because I know where he is.'

'What?' Bowman asked, 'are you the confidant of the King of Leinster now?'

'I am, actually,' the monk grinned in self-importance, 'Richard told me to speak to him on our return from Meath, so I did.'

Bowman tilted his head. 'Fancy that, a useful monk,' he said.

'As the only man in the company to speak Irish,' Brian said, 'he told me all sorts of things. I think he was just happy to have someone to talk to.'

'Where did he go?' Richard asked.

'I don't know if it's good or bad,' Brian said, 'but he's not even in Dublin.'

They borrowed a packhorse stolen from the monastery of Saint Ciaran, and loaded it with enough food for the five of them for two days.

Their small company rode north along the coast and out again into lands no Norman army had secured. They spent the night by a brook that bubbled gently and kept Richard awake. It was not warm enough to go without a fire overnight, but due to their vulnerable number, Richard didn't allow one. He shivered as he tried to sleep, but even though when the sun came up the next morning, he was tired, he didn't regret it.

'How far away is he?' Bowman asked later that day.

'The monastery of Saint Columba is just over the next ridge,' Brian said, 'or at least I think it is.'

'I'm sick of monasteries,' Bowman said, 'although the food in the last one was good.'

'I don't think we'll be pillaging this one,' Richard replied as the wind pulled at his cloak. The breeze blew off and out to the sea that had been on their right side since Dublin. A small fishing boat bobbed on the mild waves in the distance, and dark coloured seabirds swooped overhead.

Alan rode at the rear, which Richard didn't mind because it meant he couldn't hear what the rest of them said. They hadn't told anyone they were leaving Dublin, but Richard assumed Raymond would work it out once he realised they'd taken a packhorse. He did worry Raymond would take their departure as desertion, but decided to trust Brian and hope for the best.

Behind the next ridge was no monastery, or any building at all, only a valley that sloped down to a wide estuary.

'We follow the estuary in,' Brian said.

'How sure are you?' Bowman asked, 'as sure as you were before?'

Brian nodded, although there was no alternative to following his directions.

At the top of the next small hill, Brian pointed ahead and grinned. 'See, I was right all along.'

The monastery of Saint Columba was grander than those they had torched in Meath. Its multitude of stone buildings nestled in a valley between two green and shallow hills. Surrounded by a wall and with paddocks on their approach, they rode closer to get a better look.

'How do we know this is the right place?' Nicholas asked as the wind tugged on his wolf-pelt and its hairs blew back and forth, 'or if the king is even here?'

Richard pointed at the paddock. 'Do you see the grass?'

'Are you reading the future in grass, now?' Bowman asked.

'No,' Richard replied, 'it's long and tufted with many types of grass growing.'

'So?'

'There are many horses in the paddock and had they been there all summer, the grass would be short and trimmed. Those horses have not been in there for very long.'

'With thoughts like those, you should have gone into the church,' Bowman grinned at him, 'but I still hate horses.'

'You can't still hate him,' Richard glanced down to Bowman's black horse.

Bowman shrugged. 'We've come to an understanding,' he said.

'So we think King Dermot is here,' Nicholas said, 'how do we make it look like an accident?'

'Probably by not walking in with that stupid pelt on your shoulders,' Bowman said to him.

'Actually,' Richard said, 'that might be exactly what we should do.'

As Brian went into the complex to check if Dermot was really there, Richard and Nicholas stripped down to their waists.

'This is a stupid plan,' Bowman watched with his hands on

his hips.

'So what's yours?' Richard asked as he dropped his mail shirts into separate linen bags and tied them to his saddle. He shook the bags around to grind a bit of the rust off them, but it was a token effort.

Bowman didn't reply because no one had thought of a better idea of how to get Richard and Nicholas into the compound below them.

'You can't complain,' Richard said, 'you've got the easy job.'

'I'm not complaining,' Bowman said, 'I need to consider my safety now I'm going to have a child. I can't go charging into battle like you anymore.'

'Like me?' Richard said, 'I actually have two children. You just are one. Just stay here and have the horses ready for whenever we come out. Knowing our luck, we'll be leaving while being chased.'

'Last time you ran from a monastery, it was red balls here who was chasing you,' Bowman chuckled to himself.

'That was a nunnery,' Richard replied.

Alan crossed his arms and walked off. Which was fine by everyone else.

'You're too big to pass for Irish, anyway,' Richard said, 'and too blonde.'

'If I was Irish I'd be even more offended by what you're doing,' Bowman said.

'Well you aren't, so stay quiet while we go and do the hard work. If we come back empty handed, and Raymond thinks we deserted, we'll lose our heads.'

Nicholas put the wolf-pelt back on his bare torso so the head sat on his, and the front paws tied together around his neck.

'Why can't he go with you?' Bowman pointed to the large mercenary.

'Have you yet seen an Irishman with a belly as big as his?' Richard asked.

'The King his here. We should go,' Brian came back, 'arriving too late in the day is suspicious.'

Nicholas hung his sword belt over his saddle and looked at his half-brother. 'This had better be here when we return, I know how much you like stealing sword belts from my family.'

'It isn't worth stealing,' Bowman started to tie his reins to a tree so he didn't have to stand around holding horses all night.

Brian led the two stripped-down knights towards the monastery. In the darkening sky, the fires in the buildings leaked yellow light from doorways and gave their struggling eyes something to aim for.

'I'm not so sure this was a good idea,' Richard said as they reached the paddock.

'It was your idea,' Nicholas replied.

A horse sleeping by the fence woke up in a start as they walked by, and hurtled off along the pasture in a flurry of hooves. It reached the main herd of twenty or so animals and they all tore off around the paddock together.

Richard could only see their shadows in the distance, but when they stopped he heard their snorts and a cough.

'This way,' Brian found a gate in the wall and they entered the compound.

The hairs on Richard's arms stood on end, and he shivered by the time the monk led them into a large building that turned out to be a dormitory.

A monk greeted Brian slowly and with narrow eyes, and Richard tried to look relaxed as they exchanged words in Irish. Too many words for Richard's liking. He knew Brian was telling them their story, that he and Nicholas were the leaders of a Fianna who wished to change their ways and learn of the true Christ. To cover their lack of Irish, Richard had dreamt up the idea that they had taken a vow of silence until the word of God had revealed itself to them.

The local monk looked at Richard's scar that ran across his eye, and noticed his missing finger. There was a faint purple patch on his chest from the bruising he'd received at Waterford, and a scar where the crossbow bolt at Castle Josselin had nearly killed him. The monk seemed satisfied by his marks, and the presence of the menacing animal skin draped over Nicholas was enough to make the monk look away with a wrinkled up face.

He led the three of them into the hall where a lively party filled Richard's senses.

A long hearth burnt brightly and threw heat out of the

doorway and up into the ceiling. A thick mat of freshly cut reeds covered the floor, over which two cats chased a single, doomed mouse. Richard felt sorry for the mouse, then realised that tonight, he and Nicholas were the cats.

Five musicians plied their trade so loudly that everyone had to shout at each other over the tables of food that were as rich as anything Richard had seen in Normandy.

Some monks sat at the table, and a number of richly dressed Irishmen ate alongside them. At the head of the table, sat an already drunk Dermot. His eyes were blurry, and while he spoke he waved around a silver cup that sloshed red wine all over himself.

Richard wondered what they had found worth celebrating, but at least he was too drunk to recognise them.

Their host monk went to the head of the table and whispered into a senior monk's ear. That monk was tall and thin, his check bones high, but the cheeks themselves eroded by time. His eyes settled on Richard for a moment before he pointed to the very far end of the table.

Richard and Nicholas were led there and left to eat some bread, no one offered them anything better. Brian was invited to sit with the monks, where he was given drink and decent food. He seemed to enjoy himself while Richard and Nicholas could only exchange a glance and maintain their vow of silence.

The feast wore on long enough for most of the monks to retreat to bed. Dermot got to his feet, shouted something loudly, to which the nobles laughed, and staggered towards the door.

Richard nudged Nicholas, who was nearly asleep.

Dermot left and Richard gave him as long as he dared before going out after him. Stepping out into the night felt like a bucket of cold water being emptied over his head. His bare chest stung from the iciness of the dark and he had to catch his breathing to restart it.

Nicholas came out behind him, and Richard envied his warming animal pelt.

Richard followed Dermot around the corner of the hall and a cat ran across the ground in front of him with a mouse in its jaws.

The King of Leinster stood against a building and emptied his bladder.

'Now?' Nicholas asked?

Richard shook his head. 'It needs to look natural. He needs to be in his bed.'

Dermot finished and lumbered into the compound's tall church.

Richard wasn't keen to murder a king in a church, but he pushed that thought aside and crept in behind his target.

Dermot leant against the wall part way down the nave and started to snore.

'Can we kill him and put him in his bed?' Nicholas whispered in Richard's ear.

Richard shook his head. 'What if there's more than one bed in the rooms back there.'

'But what if there's someone awake?'

Richard didn't know, neither choice was exactly good.

'We can't wait all night,' Nicholas said, 'we need to be gone from here before anyone realises.'

Richard looked out of the door and back to the sleeping monarch. Maybe they could crack his head on the floor? Maybe suffocate him and drag him off to bed?

Before he could decide, Dermot jolted himself awake and started to sway as he walked to the far end of the church.

Richard followed him into a chamber which had a bed and a desk. On a shelf on the wall a fine array of cups were displayed. A large glass jug stood in their centre, full of a dark red liquid.

Dermot fumbled at his cloak, failed to undo the pin, and had to drag it over his head to peel it off. He grunted as the pin dragged across his face and he threw the cloak with force onto his bed. Except it missed and landed on the floor. Dermot spun around and came face to face with Richard. His eyes blinked and he rubbed one of them. Then they froze and widened.

Richard lurched forwards and held a hand over the King's mouth.

'What now?' Nicholas asked as Richard forced the old man back until he fell onto his bed.

'I don't know,' Richard said, 'something that looks like an

accident.'

Nicholas looked around the room. 'Like what? We don't have a lot to work with here.'

The King struggled and clawed at Richard's hand.

'Just suffocate him,' Nicholas stood over and watched.

'He can breath through my fingers.'

Nicholas picked up the cloak from the floor and shoved it onto the King's face. 'Use that.'

Richard released his grip so he could use the fabric instead.

Dermot yelped loudly in the moment his mouth was free before the woollen garment was shoved in. He kept struggling.

'I think he can breath through this, too,' Richard said, 'we might just have to hit him over the head with something.'

Nicholas looked around the chamber again. 'Hold on,' he said.

He returned with the glass jug and held it over the struggling King's head.

'What's that for?' Richard asked, 'are we going to make him drink himself to death?'

'No,' Nicholas said, 'if you hold his nose shut I think we can drown him.'

Richard saw the wine stains all over the King already. 'Fine, try it,' he said and gripped Dermot's nose tightly through the cloak.

The King cried out as Nicholas started to pour the large jug. The red wine started to splash onto the cloak as Dermot's legs kicked out into the air.

The wine poured and the King breathed in the liquid. He coughed out and some flew around the bed, but more kept coming and he spluttered.

'I think it's working,' Richard said.

'We're nearly out of wine,' Nicholas said.

The last of the wine left the jug and flowed into the King of Leinster's wool-covered mouth. He lay still.

Richard waited a moment and slowly released his fingers. No air came in or out and Dermot remained motionless.

'I think we've done it,' Nicholas held the jug away.

'We've killed a king,' Richard said softly. Red wine had splattered over his uncovered body and he tried to wipe it off but could only smear it. It looked a little too much like blood.

'How will Strongbow know he's dead?' Richard asked.

'I think the traditional way is to bring his head,' Nicholas replied.

Richard pulled the cloak off Dermot's wine-stained face and flinched at his bulging eyes. 'We don't have anything to saw his head off with. It's also barbaric.'

Nicholas frowned. 'You are right, though. He will want proof. Maybe a hand?'

'No,' Richard said, 'unless you have an axe hiding in your underclothes?'

'A finger then? I could probably snap a finger off.'

'I can't believe we're talking about snapping a king's finger off,' Richard said.

'He's wearing some gold rings,' Nicholas pointed to the man's hands, 'I'm taking them anyway, they're probably worth four of my ransoms.'

Richard nodded. 'I'll agree to that. Maybe hide one away for ourselves, then.'

Nicholas grinned and started to slip the rings off.

Dermot's hair was spread out behind him on the bed. 'Some of that might be good, too,' Richard said, 'maybe we can use a candle from the church to burn a lock of hair off?'

'That's disgusting, it'll smell terrible.'

'You wanted to saw his head off,' Richard said.

Nicholas put the rings on his fingers and picked up a golden cross from the desk. 'Should we say something?' He asked.

'What?'

'A man has just died,' Nicholas said, 'should we say a prayer?'

Richard groaned. 'We should get out of here, I don't think the prayers of his murderers will count for much.'

Nicholas turned the golden cross over in his hands. It had a red jewel in its centre.

The body on the bed gasped for breath, a loud, sudden, rasping sound.

Richard screamed.

Nicholas screamed and struck out with the gold cross.

Dermot went cross-eyed as the cross hit him between the eyes and he collapsed back to bed. His last breath sucked out of his lungs and the sound of it held in the air.

Richard's eyes stayed wide.

Nicholas looked at the cross and down at the king.

'Why did you do that?' Richard asked.

'I don't know, I thought he was going to jump up at us.'

'There's a red mark on his head now,' Richard said.

'He's covered in wine anyway, no one will notice,' Nicholas said.

'They will if they wash his body.'

'I think we should go now,' Nicholas turned and walked out of the chamber.

'What about the hair?'

Nicholas went back and lent over Dermot. 'I don't think we have time to burn it.' He held the cross down over the King's face to pin it to the bed, and with his other hand he grabbed and handful of long hair and tugged. No hair came out so Nicholas let some go of some and tried again. The second tug ripped and snapped some hair and a loose handful came out. As he held down the body, the golden cross crunched down on Dermot's nose. When the cross lifted, it was red and crumpled.

'Is that enough?'

'It will have to do,' Richard said, 'let's go.'

The Martel knight left with his trophies.

Richard went to follow but the desk caught his eye. A stack of parchment lay on it, and he scooped it up before he followed his companion out of the chamber and the church.

Nicholas walked towards the gate.

'We can't go yet, we need to fetch Brian,' Richard said.

Nicholas stopped and looked up into the sky. 'Why do you care about that monk so much?'

'He saved all of us at Baginbun Head,' Richard said, 'and I promised I'd keep him safe. We'll go back in for him.'

'You're covered in wine,' Nicholas said, 'which looks like blood in the dark.'

Richard swore. He didn't feel cold this time, even outside he felt warm, warm and worried.

The old monk who had banished them to the bottom of the hall emerged from it, then Brian ran out after him. The young monk tried to hold him back but the elder one shrugged him off.

He stopped when he nearly ran into Richard. The old monk frowned at his wine-stained chest, and then his eyes went to Nicholas, who held the golden cross behind his back. The monk barked something in a harsh tone.

'He wants to confiscate the pelt,' Brian said.

The old monk froze and turned very slowly towards Brian, who had given his warning not in Irish, but Norman.

The monk looked back at Nicholas.

'He's not having my pelt,' Nicholas said, 'I'll fight them all for it before I give it up.'

'We're supposed to have a vow of silence,' Richard said.

The old monk's eyes lowered to the rings on the Martel knight's visible hand. The light from the hall glinted in the gold.

Richard's shoulders dropped.

Nicholas looked him in the eyes. 'This is where we run?'

'This is where we run,' Richard started first. He ran past his accomplice and looked back only to check Brian was following.

The monk thought about it, then his legs took him away from the hall and out into the dead of the night.

Richard ran towards the gate but skidded to a halt when he saw a stable block. Nicholas bolted past him as Richard went along the five stable doors and flung each door open. The horses inside took a moment to realise their new situation, but as Richard started off again towards the paddock, they ran out into the compound and unexpected freedom. One nearly barrelled into Brian, who fell over to avoid it, but then Richard was sprinting along the path next to the paddock and back up the slope towards their horses. The cold air burnt in his lungs, and he couldn't see if his footing was good or not, but he had to keep going.

Nicholas was ahead and shouting to Bowman and Alan.

Richard ran past the gate into the paddock and stopped. Back inside the compound he could hear loud voices and shadowy figures moved in the dark. A crow landed on the wooden fence of the pasture and cawed at him.

'Shut up,' Richard told the bird and opened the gate. He assumed the horses would find their own way out as Brian caught him up and kept going.

Richard reached Bowman as the last horse was untied.

'They're coming,' Nicholas shouted and he vaulted up onto this horse.

Alan appeared out of the dark trying to rearrange his clothing.

'We don't have long,' Richard said to him and went towards Solis. His horse started backwards at him for a moment before realising who it was, and gave Richard a face full of snort in return.

Alan ran at his horse. He half stumbled, threw a hand up to balance himself, and his horse reared away from it. It pulled free from Bowman's grasp, walked backwards on its hind legs and spun.

Richard was already on top of Solis as Alan ran after his horse.

Brian mounted and Bowman handed Richard the rope that led their packhorse.

Alan ran into the dark after his own horse as Richard saw men running along the paddock path and up the slope.

'Go,' he shouted.

He kicked Solis on and they cantered past Alan who ran on foot after his mount. He looked to have enough time to recover it.

The horse stopped as three Irishmen with drawn swords reached their waiting place. Alan tripped on a root which only made his horse jump away from him again.

Richard turned Solis to go back for him and let go of the packhorse.

The large man got up and started to run, but the Irish gained on him.

Richard rode towards him but had to look around his saddle to see where his sword hung. In the dark he had to feel for it.

As his hand felt the familiar texture of the leather grip, the Irish found Alan. The mercenary ran, his lungs bursting and his face red, as a sword thumped into his side. He fell over and in a flurry of blows and piercing screams he was dead.

Richard whirled Solis around and cantered away after the rest of the group. Alan's horse bolted to them and ran with them, as did the packhorse with its rope trailing behind it.

They quickly dropped to a walk because faster was dangerous, and Richard caught his breath as well as the packhorse. Alan's horse slowed with them and walked close behind Solis, its breathing heavy and nostrils flaring.

'Where's red balls?' Bowman asked.

'Dead,' Richard said.

'What about the King?'

'Dead,' Richard said again.

'Well, probably,' Nicholas laughed to himself.

Bowman nodded in the gloom. 'If they're both dead, I'd say that this venture went better than we could have possibly hoped.'

LONG LIVE THE KING

Halfway back to Dublin and now they rode with the sea to their left. The horses grazed by a stream as Brian read out the letters that Richard had removed from Dermot's chamber.

'I was hoping for something more sensational,' Richard said when he finished.

Bowman repacked some horsebread and held a piece out for his horse. Alan's horse had followed them the whole way back, walking loose, and it tried to muscle its way in to take the horsebread. Bowman shooed it away.

'There's nothing here that links King Dermot to the Countess,' Brian said.

Richard went over and inspected the parchment. The black scrawls across it meant nothing to him, but he wanted to look at them all the same.

'I'm ready to go,' Bowman tied the lace on his linen bag.

'We might as well,' Richard said, 'I was just hoping these letters would help Strongbow to go after Cormac and the Countess.'

Nicholas, his armour back on beneath his furs, was already on his horse, and he pointed out to sea. 'Sails,' he said.

'More fishermen, I expect,' Bowman put his foot in his stirrup.

'I don't think so,' Nicholas said, 'I think they're looking for something bigger than fish.'

Richard left the letters and went to look out over the cliffs. White breakers broke up the blue and grey carpet of the sea that stretched out to the horizon. Richard counted the ships. Thirty he thought, but he was sure he could sees a few more sails over the horizon itself.

'Longships,' Bowman said, 'could be English.'

Richard frowned. 'That many, here? And sailing south?'

'You might be right, young lord,' Bowman's face hardened.

'We best get back to the city, then,' Richard said, 'before they get there.'

They rode south in parallel with the ships for some time, and eventually pulled far enough ahead that they lost sight of their sails behind them.

Alan's horse walked with its nose just above Solis's tail, and the stallion occasionally kicked at it in annoyance. Every time he did, it jolted Richard in the saddle.

When they crested a hill with a large stone cross on it, Brian insisted Richard looked closely at it.

'It's just a cross,' Richard said, 'and we need to get back.'

'But look,' Brian said, 'can you see the patterns on it?'

Richard rode Solis up to the weathered monument and squinted at it. The stone was inscribed but weathered by wind and rain. Weeds grew up at its base, but the shapes on it did not look like anything he'd seen in England or Normandy.

'See the interlocking lines?' Brian asked, 'that's the old Christianity, the bad type.'

'It seems that no one is taking care of this one, so maybe you don't need to worry about it so much.'

Brian shook his head. 'The roots run deep. This is a cross of the Norse, of my ancestors. Of the men who sail in those ships. They might worship Christ, but they are doomed to suffer in Hell.'

Bowman waited on the track. 'We don't have time for this,' he said.

Richard turned Solis away from the cross, just as the horse stuck his nose out to sniff it. The horse ignored Richard and licked the moss that grew on it.

'If the ships aren't ours, 'I'm guessing that army isn't either,' Nicholas said.

Richard looked inland to where the Martel knight pointed.

A string of horsemen moved south on a hillside in the distance. There were easily a hundred of them but they didn't look be in any hurry.

'Those horses aren't Norman,' Richard said, 'if we're unlucky we might already be too late.'

They cantered back along the dirt track to Dublin as fast as they could. When they sighted the city walls, their horses were lathered in sweat, but no Irish army stood in their path. The city gates lay open, and their Norman appearance meant the Welsh who guarded them let them in without interest.

Richard led their party straight to the church where Brian again was tasked with minding the horses, including Alan's.

A gathering of people, mostly with long hair and cloaks of Irish length, stood before Strongbow's chair at the end of the church.

The lord himself sat with his head resting on his hand. The droning of the bishop besides him sent him to sleep, and his elbow slipped off his armrest. Strongbow's eyes jumped back to life and he noticed Richard push his way through his audience.

'The Irish are coming,' Richard shouted.

Strongbow fanned his arm out. 'They're already here.'

'No,' Richard said, 'an army is marching south. We arrived back barely ahead of them.'

'What do you mean? I thought you were in Dublin?'

Nicholas's wolf-pelt opened up a path through the Irish for him. The golden cross was wrapped up in his bedding, but almost all of the rings and the lock of hair were in the hands he held up to the Norman lord.

'You are the King of Leinster now,' Richard told him.

The bishop gasped.

'Quiet,' Strongbow said, 'and do not translate this to them.'

'He was in a monastery to the north,' Richard explained, 'and we saw an army on our return.'

Strongbow's hand clenched the armrest. 'This is the moment, this is the moment where the fate of Ireland hangs in the balance. If we can see off the Irish from Dublin and hold it, then we prove our divine right to rule.'

Nicholas offered up the hair to Strongbow, bowing as he did so.

'It is unseemly for this savage to offer a trophy of an unlawful killing,' the bishop protested. He was Irish, but his hair was short and he had no beard.

'The last King of Leinster was involved in the raising of this army Richard speaks of,' the new King of Leinster told him, 'and he has been punished for his treason. We will speak of this after the Irish have been repelled.'

A door creaked open at the back of the church, the door that led to the bell chamber, and Eva's beyond it.

She emerged wearing a red dress, although it was a new red dress with silver thread sewn along the sleeves and neckline as borders.

She walked to Strongbow, but before she sat down, her eyes fell on the rings Nicholas held up to her husband.

Strongbow turned his head to her, and for the first time Richard had ever seen, she didn't know what to say.

Bowman had been standing right behind Richard, but he sensed the tall man step back.

Eva glanced at her husband. 'Why are those here?'

Strongbow stood up so he could look her in the eye. 'Your father was involved in a plot, I'm afraid, and an Irish army he mustered is about to arrive at our gates.'

Eva held her breath.

'It was treason, my dear.'

She slapped him so quickly Richard never saw her arm move. Red nail marks blossomed on Strongbow's cheek.

The new King stayed perfectly still. 'I will forgive that,' he said, 'such news is terribly hard to hear, and I know you and your father were close.'

Eva, eyes unblinking, turned to Richard. 'You,' she saw the hair and her voice wavered, 'did you do it?'

Richard could hear Bowman sniff behind him.

Nicholas looked at Strongbow. 'Do you want these or not?'

Tears flooded from Eva's eyes.

Strongbow slowly, very slowly, took both the hair and the rings. He turned to his outraged bishop. 'Keep these safe,' he passed them over.

'You,' Eva said to Richard, but she was really looking over his shoulder to Bowman, 'anyone but you.'

Strongbow frowned at Richard.

'She wintered with me in Normandy,' Richard replied, 'with me and my wife.'

'I see,' Strongbow replied, 'you should have said so and I

would have found someone else to perform your task.'

Richard was quite sure Eva had already told him about it.

'You are nothing but swords for hire, base men with no honour,' Eva spat at them, 'dogs of war good for nothing but begging for scraps from their master.'

'You should leave us,' her husband told her.

Eva spun around, her dress whirled with her and she ran back towards her chamber.

Strongbow rubbed his face and nodded at Richard. 'I will not forget your service, but now we must prepare for an attack.'

'There is another thing,' Richard said, 'there was a fleet sailing south, too.'

'A fleet?'

'Norse ships, long, like our old sort. I counted at least twenty or thirty,' Richard said.

'The Norse kingdoms still rule the seas to the north of here,' Strongbow sighed, 'and Dublin was a city they founded. They must have made common cause with the Irish.'

Richard nodded back because he had nothing to add.

'Find me Raymond,' Strongbow said to the bishop, 'we must gather supplies and see if we can clear the city ditch out. Find me a ship and a clerk, I must send word to England. It is time King Henry learnt that he must now deal with me as a King to a King. But I will also need his help to fend off the myriad of other kings that seem to sprout from this land.'

Richard wondered if he could write a letter home while he was at it, but Strongbow waved the bishop away and picked up his sword belt that rested on the altar.

'The three of you can rest your horses and selves for the day, but everyone else is to work while we still can. Was there not another knight who went with you?'

Nicholas shrugged. 'No.'

The new King thought for a moment, then shrugged. 'Go then, I have a kingdom to defend.'

They went back to Brian's house in the Ostmanstown area, with their newly won horse and saddle in tow. Richard had decided to give the packhorse back.

Bowman remained silent, and when they arrived he busied himself lighting the hearth with an iron striker and a stone.

Richard lay down flat on the floor, his back ached and it felt like the right thing to do. 'We are using this house like it is yours, Brian,' he said, 'who does it belong to?'

The monk spread Dermot's letters out over the table, pushing wooden bowls and cups out of the way. 'I suppose,' he said, 'because it *is* mine. I've never really thought about it.'

'Who owned it before?'

'It's my family's, I grew up here.'

'Oh,' Richard saw no belongings anywhere, 'where are they now?'

'Gone,' Brian peered at a letter in the poor light, 'they fell foul of the old Christian laws. I don't want to talk about it.'

Richard didn't want to push him, either.

Bowman got a spark to land on the clump of silver birch bark and reed down he'd placed in the hearth. The down caught, then the bark, and then the small sticks layered on top. Quickly the dried wood flickered in yellow flame and the house brightened up.

'We've checked the letters already,' Richard said.

Brian put one aside and read another one. 'We might have missed something,' he said, 'and I know we really need something that proves the Countess is plotting against Strongbow.'

'You're a monk,' Nicholas took off his animal skin and laid it on a bench, 'can't you write?'

Brian looked down his nose at him. 'That would be dishonest. A sin.'

Richard thought about it. 'Is it, though?' He asked, 'if we use a forged letter to prove a crime we know for sure has taken place.'

Brian licked his lips. 'I suppose that is less of a sin. Less of a sin that killing a king.'

'Don't remind me,' Richard felt his back release and got up.

Brian went down into the basement that was below ground level, and came back with an ink well and a quill. He tore off some unused parchment from one of the letters and started to write, his eyes so close to the parchment that his nose almost rubbed the ink.

'What are you writing?' Richard asked.

'Leave it to me,' the monk said.

Bowman sat back as the fire took hold. He stared into the yellows and oranges and the smell of smoke filled the house.

Nicholas stood up with the jewelled cross and turned it over in his hands as the fire reflected off it.

'Someone will notice you've got that,' Richard said.

The door flew open and cool air rushed in, making the young fire dance and jump.

Richard's hand went to Sir John's dagger, but by the time he gripped it, five men where in the house, and behind them came Cormac. All had knives drawn.

'Nobody move,' Cormac said.

Brian slipped the letters together into a single pile.

'What are you doing there?' Cormac said to him.

Nicholas waved the cross in his face, it looked like a weapon, but Richard thought it was actually a clever distraction.

Cormac snatched it and his eyes stuck on the red jewel. 'What are poor men like you doing with something like this?'

Brian very slowly stepped away from the table.

'What do you want?' Richard asked.

Cormac looked up from the jewel that shone in his eyes. 'Have you forgotten our deal?'

Richard shook his head. 'The sun isn't down, so I still have time,' he said.

'Do not try to fool me,' the Irishman lowered the cross, 'the Countess wants to see you.'

'Me?'

'Walk out with us or we'll burn the house with your friends inside it. I have twice as many more men outside.'

Richard looked to Bowman who shrugged. 'I'd be quite happy if you killed Strongbow,' he said.

'Hand your weapons over,' Cormac instructed.

Richard saw no way out so he gave his sword and the dagger to one of the Irish. Once all the swords and knives were in the hands of the enemy, Cormac beckoned Richard outside with him.

In the street he saw a cart drawn by a small horse, and perhaps a dozen more Irishmen. The next thing he saw was the inside of the hood that was shoved over his head. The world went black and Richard felt his legs being picked up. He cried out but stopped when he was thrown into the cart and he felt a knife being pressed into his neck.

'Stop squealing,' Cormac said, 'the Countess might want to see you, but if you fight back and have to die, then I will not suffer for it. Do you understand?'

Richard understood very well and kept quiet. The cart rolled along the street and he felt it turn left. The next turn was right, and Richard tried to keep track of which direction they were going. Just as he lost track, the cart halted and rough hands grabbed him and dragged him along the ground by his legs. His head bumped on stones or rough ground, then bumped down what was unmistakeably a set of steps.

The hood was removed after he was dumped rudely onto a floor.

Richard blinked as light flooded into his eyes and the smell of urine and rats filled his nose.

In front of him, with a cloth over her mouth, sat the Countess. A fire gave the only light, and Richard could sense Cormac's presence behind him.

'I am glad to see you again,' she said, 'although I had hoped it would have been as friends.'

Richard rubbed the back of his head. 'I'm not usually friends with people who keep trying to kill me and my countrymen.'

Cormac kicked him between the shoulder blades and Richard was thrown forwards.

'Now, there's no need for that,' the Countess said, 'I am sure I can have a conversation with this Norman without the need for violence.'

'I'm not Norman, I'm English.'

'You are not,' she said, 'you are one of them. But you could still be useful to me. Do you know I rule alone, without a male guardian?'

Richard flexed his shoulders. If he ever got the chance, he'd repay Cormac for that.

'Of course you do,' the Countess continued, 'everyone knows. But, if we fail and your Normans spread out across our land like a plague, then I will need to change. I will need Norman allies. I might need a Norman husband.'

Richard laughed. That was not what he'd expected to hear. 'I don't think that will work, I am already married.'

'An inconvenience at most,' she replied, 'and my offer is real. Do not mock me.'

'I am married in the eyes of God,' Richard said, 'and you cannot force me to marry you, such a marriage is not legal where I am from.'

The Irishwoman smirked. 'A small matter. This is my peace offering, Richard. Accept and you and your friends will live, whatever fate holds in store for Ireland. Reject me, and Norman blood must flow.'

Richard let out a heavy breath. 'I never chose to be married, but I am, and I can't chose to unmarry either. You'll just have to kill me.'

It was her turn to laugh. 'My dear Richard, it is not you who has to die. But if you are rejecting me on grounds of piety, maybe you are too dull to be my husband. Very well, your fate is your own. Do you remember our original deal?'

'It wasn't really a deal, was it?'

Cormac kicked Richard in the small of his back.

'Enough,' the Countess shouted, 'Richard, you will kill Strongbow now. I mean now. If you do not go straight into the church and stab him in the neck, your friends all die.'

'He'll kill me, and even if he doesn't, I'll never make it out of the church alive. Find someone else,' Richard said.

'It matters not if you survive, you rejected my offer so you will die. But I leave you the choice of who dies with you, your friends or the butcher of the Irish.'

Richard's mouth was dry. What choice did he have. 'Fine, give me a knife, then.'

The Countess smiled. 'Such a shame. You would have made a good husband.'

The hood went down over his head and the world went dark again. He groaned and he was dragged back up the stairs, more painfully than the way down, and thrown into the the cart. It drove around Dublin in what felt like circles, before someone crudely dragged him off the back. He landed with a thud on the road, and Cormac whipped the hood off.

'Go straight to de Clare. He doesn't live through the night,' Cormac dropped a knife onto the ground for him and climbed back into the cart. The driver clicked his tongue and the small horse started to walk off along the street.

Richard wasn't sure where he was. He got to his feet and felt the back of his head which hurt to the touch. The city wall was visible over some houses, as was the church spire, so Richard could form a rough idea of which way Brian's house was. Strongbow would probably be in the church, but he had no intention of complying with either the Countess or Cormac.

Richard found his way back to the house. He poked his head around each street corner to check for Cormac first, and Normans and Welshmen who rode by gave him bemused looks. Traffic became busy, which Richard assumed was because the army was springing into action to prepare for the arrival of the Irish.

He was pleased when he stuck his head around one last corner and the house was just where he thought it should be. He was less pleased that a dozen Irishmen still hung around outside it. However furious Nicholas might be if someone hit him on the head, they were not fighting their way through that many opponents.

Richard walked to the next street instead to try to get to the back of the house. He walked into someone's yard and then clambered over a short wooden fence to get into the yard behind Brian's building. Long grass grew up to his thigh and thistles and nettles stung and spiked his legs. There was no door into Brian's house, but Richard remembered how the church at Yvetot had started to rot below the ground, so he pushed his way up to the wooden walls and knelt down in the weeds. He ignored their stings and started to dig into the earth with the knife Cormac had dropped for him.

Richard dug until his knees ached from kneeling and his hands and shoulder throbbed from exertion. But the wood under the earth was black and flaked off like well cooked salmon. He punched the wood with the back of the knife and a chunk of wet wood fell off. He put his mouth to the gap and whispered Bowman's name.

No one came.

'Bowman,' he said as loudly as he dared.

No one came.

Richard cupped his hands and made a series of owl hoots into the basement of the house.

He heard footsteps. Down the steps someone came, Richard looked through the hole and saw Bowman.

'Over here,' he said.

'I'm surprised to see you, young lord,' Bowman came closer, 'can you dig us out?'

'I don't think so,' Richard said, 'it look me half the day to dig this hole, and it's only big enough for an arm.'

'Well, what are we going to do?' Bowman asked.

'Get me Dermot's letters.'

'Really?'

'Yes, it's our only hope,' Richard said.

Bowman disappeared, then came back clutching the parchment in his hands. He thrust them through the hole, which tore some of the pages.

Richard took them. 'If anyone tried to get in, fight them.'

'With what? The monk's writing quill?'

'This,' Richard pushed the knife through the hole.

'Careful,' Bowman said, 'you nearly had my eye out. Handle first.' He took the knife. 'We will need more than this if things get serious.'

'I'll get more weapons if I can't get help,' Richard said, 'just hold on, I'll be back as soon as I can.'

'Don't get distracted, young lord,' Bowman said as Richard got up, got stung by a nettle, and retraced his path back to the road behind the house.

Richard ran all the way to the church. The doors were barred and he had to catch his breath before he could speak to the guards.

'Strongbow is busy,' one told him.

'Let me in, some Irish are going to kill Normans if you don't.'

The guard shrugged. 'Those are my orders. No one goes in.'

Richard stepped closer. 'Are you sure?'

The guard nodded.

Richard punched him straight in the nose. The guard bent double, clutched his nose and cried out. Richard stepped around him and heaved the doors open. They creaked and let light into the church. Richard's shadow preceded him as he stepped into the expanse of the holy building.

Strongbow and the four Norman knights with him all turned around.

'What are you doing here?' Milo asked.

'My lord,' Richard said, 'I have something you need to see.'

'Approach,' Strongbow said, 'I've forgotten what I was saying now, anyway.'

'He is interrupting, we can't allow it,' Milo said.

'What do you want Richard?' Raymond asked.

Richard approached with the letters in his hand and gave them to Strongbow.

'I can't read these,' he replied.

His bishop took them, read them slowly, then read them again.

The man sighed. 'It would appear that some of the Irish in the city were involved in the plot with the former king.'

'Those Irish are holding my friends hostage,' Richard said, 'if I don't kill you before sunset, they will burn the house they're trapped in.'

'Kill me?' Strongbow pushed himself up from his chair.

'Yes,' the bishop replied, 'and according to this letter, they will send your body parts to each of the kings of Ireland.'

Richard thought that was a nice touch from Brian, although it bothered him the monk had even thought of it.

'Will they now,' Strongbow grew red in the face, 'show those to my wife.'

'This is what we needed,' Raymond said, 'no one will question the accidental death of King Dermot now.'

Strongbow nodded. 'Raymond, deal with Richard's problem for me.'

The big knight nodded. 'Show me the way, boy,' he said.

Richard had to wait as Raymond mustered a body of knights and they prepared their horses. He shouted at a company of Welshmen who walked across the square and they returned a short time later with their bows and bags of arrows.

'I'm going to send a message to the Irish who think to resist us,' Raymond said as he mounted his horse next to Richard.

'We don't have long,' Richard replied, 'it's already starting to get dark.'

'Fear not,' Raymond adjusted his mail around the saddle, 'we'll be there as fast as you can run.'

Raymond shouted something to the archers, who ran off. Then the ten knights and squires with Raymond moved off towards Brian's house.

Richard had to run to keep up, and once they rounded the street and he saw Cormac was with his men, he allowed himself a moment to breathe. He had made it in time, the house was not on fire.

Raymond drew his sword and pointed it at the Irish. 'Kill them all but save the leader for me.'

The knights charged and their horse's hooves clattered against the stones that were stuck in the otherwise hard ground. Hard or not, their attack dug up the road with hoof-sized divots.

The Irish watched for a moment, then most turned and ran. Three of Cormac's men stood their ground, they raised swords and prepared for impact.

Raymond and his knights lowered their lances and skewered Cormac's comrades with no difficulty at all.

The fleeing Irish got little further when the Welsh archers appeared at the bottom of the street and loosed a volley of white-fletched arrows at them. They hit the ground with arrows sticking out of their unarmoured bodies.

The knights ceased their charge as some of the arrows that missed skidded along the earth and went amongst their horse's hooves. They shouted at the Welsh and threatened to ride them down.

Cormac got to his feet, an arrow in his thigh. Two other Irish weren't dead either, although neither had entirely dodged the missiles.

Bowman sprung from the house, Richard's knife in hand, and ran at Cormac. Nicholas, for once without his wolf-pelt, followed closely behind.

'Leave him,' Raymond shouted, 'he's mine.'

Bowman swore even as he ran.

Cormac saw him coming and backed away with his hands in the air.

Bowman ran past him and rammed the knife into the chest

of one of the other Irishmen.

Nicholas launched himself at the other, knocked him to the ground and sat on top of him while he pressed his fingers into the man's eyes.

Bowman used the knife a second time and let the body drop to the street.

Cormac went to run but the Welsh drew back their arrows and he knew he was done.

Bowman pointed the knife at Cormac. 'Do you recognise this?' He asked.

The Irishmen shook his head.

'You gave this to my young lord, and told him to kill our new King with it.'

Cormac's eyes widened in understanding. 'But how?'

Bowman walked forwards and Cormac retreated. The blonde man jumped at the Irishman and grabbed his head by the hair.

Raymond cantered his horse over and pointed his sword at Bowman.

'I'm not going to kill him,' Bowman said, 'I swear it on my own life.'

Raymond stayed his sword.

'I just want to even this man's head up, and settle the score for the children he poisoned,' Bowman said. He sawed the knife down onto Cormac's remaining ear.

His victim screamed and blood seeped down the side of his face. Bowman held him firm despite Cormac's desperate clawing hands. Bowman finished when the ear was fully severed, which dropped to the earth with a splat. Bowman pushed Cormac away. 'He's yours now,' he said to Raymond.

The big Norman laughed. 'I hope the three of you stay in Ireland when this business is done. Life is very interesting when you are around.'

Nicholas's victim howled on the floor with no eyes. Raymond walked his horse over and pushed the stallion onto his writhing body. The stallion stood on him then shifted his weight back. He didn't want to step on the lumpy and moving body, so pawed at it instead.

The blinded man didn't know what hit him as metalled hooves broke his ribs and his nose. One blow dislocated his jaw, and his screams changed to muffled moans instead. Another blow cracked something in his head and he fell still. The horse kept pawing until Raymond pulled him away, streaks of blood mixed with mud from his hooves discoloured the street. The horse walked away and left red shoe-prints behind it.

'These Irish are to serve as an example to others who think to fight for their freedom,' he shouted at the top of his voice, 'we will quarter the bodies of each man here and send them to the kings of Ireland so they shall know the price of defiance.'

Cormac started to beg for his life. Raymond laughed at him, so he started to beg for a quick death instead.

'Men who try to kill kings deserve slow deaths,' Raymond told him.

Richard scratched the back of his neck and wondered if that applied to him, too.

Some of the Welsh looted the bodies, while others came to take a hold of Cormac. Blood poured down the side of his face still, and terror shone from his once confident eyes.

Raymond took him to a tower on the wall, where they climbed to the top with Cormac. Raymond drew his knife and slowly sliced off Cormac's fingers one at a time. Raymond untied his own leather belt and looped it around the Irishman's neck. It was so wide it went around one of the stone crenelations too, so that when Raymond threw him to the outside of the wall, Cormac hung by his neck and stayed there. He tried to claw at the belt around his neck, but his fingers were bloodied stumps and he succeeded only in covering his face and neck in even more blood.

Richard didn't watch him die, because in the time it took him to bleed to death, the blood running down the grey stone wall, the Irish army marched into sight.

THE SIEGE OF
MANY KINGS

The Irish army made its camp far over the river to the north of Dublin. The sound of trees being felled echoed into the city even though the activity itself was out of sight. Richard stood on the walls as trees groaned and fell in the distance, and decided it was more menacing that the enemy were not visible.

The longships came next, their square sails furled as they rowed along the river and disembarked to the east of the city. They moored their ships in the Black Pool that gave the city its name. When Raymond came to check on their gatehouse, he told Richard that the ships had unloaded Norse warriors, a relic soon to fade into the past. They flew banners that Brian said were of the Isle of Man, the Western Isles of Scotland, and maybe the Orkneys. They dragged some of their boats up onto the fields outside the city, but roped the rest together so they blocked the river.

The next day, a third army arrived. The news sounded with the church bells ringing and knights riding their horses to the southern walls, but that army too made a camp in the distance.

Richard spent the nights in Brian's house, wondering how much food Strongbow had managed to get into Dublin. When they awoke on the third day, a fourth army was near the walls to the west.

'How many of them are there?' Bowman asked when they heard the news.

'The army that tried to block us from Dublin in the first place was of four kings,' Richard replied.

'So there's at least one more army due to arrive?' Bowman

prodded the hearth with a stick and angry embers floated up towards the ceiling.

As it turned out, news of only one further army came, on the fifth day.

'However many kings it is now,' Richard said bitterly as he returned to the house with a carefully counted out ration of bread, 'there are thousands of men outside the walls trying to get in.'

'We managed well enough at Baginbun,' Nicholas said from his wolf-lined bed.

'That was a promontory,' Richard said, 'Dublin has walls and we need to defend the whole length. How many men do we have left from the thousand we started from Waterford with?'

No one replied to that because they all knew hundreds had been lost since the landings.

Brian was not in his house because he had been sent out on the second day with the last of Strongbow's messengers. Requests for assistance had been sent to the Normans at Waterford and to Irish allies across Leinster.

'Why don't they attack?' Nicholas asked a few days later as they took their turn to man the wall.

'They don't need to,' Richard said, 'they just need to wait for our food to run out. They probably learnt a lesson from Baginbun, too.'

The next day, when Richard had lost count of them, Cormac's body began to smell. The leather belt Raymond had lashed around the crenelation held firm, so Richard took Sir John's dagger, and when no one was looking, cut through it. It look longer than it should have, the blade now dulled by use, but the body still thudded into the newly cleared out ditch below. It would still smell, but at least it was a lot further away from Richard's nose now.

Once relieved from watch, Richard went to find someone to sharpen the dagger. One small street under the southern walls was full of those in metal trades. The smiths themselves operated outside the walls because their dwellings tended to catch fire, but safer activities were carried out within the city.

Richard found a man and woman who operated a foot powered grinding wheel, and asked them to sharpen the dagger.

Unable to understand each other, they used their hands to ask for a payment of food. Richard instead pointed outside and then made a sign of slitting his own neck, to make the point that his sharpened weapons might help to keep the couple alive by keeping the enemy out. The man held his hand out and a triumphant Richard watched as a keen edge was returned to the blade. He gave them the Little Lord's sword too, that was so marked and chipped that to return a clean edge to it, the sword was shrunk down by almost a finger's width.

Finally Richard tried to find someone to repair the many holes in his mail shirts. It took him all day to find a servant of Strongbow's who sat with a small anvil hammering the rivets shut on a shirt. This man, an Englishman with failing eyesight and a rigid manner that Richard found strangely unhuman, refused to help Richard.

'I have mail shirts from ten men of high birth to repair,' he said, 'and they have all paid me in advance with coins.'

Richard argued for a while but the ring-smith wouldn't concede, so Richard went home.

The following day, Raymond and Milo went around all the army to tell them that the Irish inside the walls were to be rounded up. Traitors lurked amongst them, and Strongbow feared knives in the dark.

Richard trudged off behind Raymond later on as the Welsh herded the natives to the walls to the west.

Strongbow and the bishop seemed to go through them and split them into two groups. One, full of men, was instantly hacked to pieces by the Welsh and Raymond. The rest cried, sobbed, and howled in grief as their sons, husbands and fathers were killed before them.

Their own fate was to be pushed outside the walls and to have the gate locked behind them. They streamed out towards the Irish army camped in the distance, but stopped when the Irish advanced on them and blocked their way. Hundreds of armed Irish pushed them back until they were close enough for the Welsh to waste a few arrows on them.

Caught in the middle, the rejects huddled together as neither side let them move.

As dusk fell, Richard took their bread ration and hurled it over the walls towards the beleaguered and grieving families. The couple who had sharpened his blades crept out and took the bread.

A Welshman on the wall saw them, and loosed an arrow that sunk into the back of the old man. He dropped the bread as he fell, and as it rolled across the grass Richard sighed. Bowman had been right in Aquitaine, Richard always tried to do the right thing, but it always went badly wrong.

Not wanting to see where the second arrow went, and unable to do anything about it, Richard walked slowly away and back to the house.

'Why are you so glum?' Bowman asked him.

'Do I need a reason?' Richard snapped, then relaxed and told him why.

'I hate the Irish,' Bowman said once he was done.

'It's really the Welsh this time,' Richard said.

'Fine,' Bowman replied, 'I just hate Ireland.'

'I would drink to that,' Richard said, 'if we had anything to drink other than water from the well.'

'At least they haven't poisoned it,' Nicholas said.

'Yet,' Bowman would have prodded the fire angrily, but they were out of wood for that, too.

Several weeks later, as the bread ration reduced down to half a loaf for all three of them, sickness came to Dublin.

First a Welsh archer died, his boil-covered body thrown over the wall, but soon others followed.

Richard remembered that Saint Ciaran had died of plague, and was sure he was wreaking his revenge on the Normans for what they'd done to his monastery.

Richard had been placed on night watch, and rested his folded arms on the walls as the moonless sky covered the plains outside the city.

'Brian has been gone a long time,' he said to Bowman.

'Aye, he has,' the blonde man replied, 'it's more likely than not he won't come back.'

'I've got used to him,' Richard said, 'I almost miss him.'

Bowman squinted into the night. 'I can't even see beyond the shanty houses,' he said.

Richard sat down with his back against the wall and gazed over the rooftops of Dublin.

Bowman sat down next to him. There was smoke from only one or two fires.

Nicholas walked up to them with a cup of water. 'This will have to do for both of you,' he passed it to Richard, 'and I have bad news from England.'

'England?'

'The Irish can block our carts, but a single horseman has no trouble riding through their net,' Nicholas replied.

'Well, what's the news?' Bowman asked.

'King Henry has forbidden ships to travel to Ireland.'

'Then how did the message get here?' Bowman said.

Nicholas frowned at him. 'Are you going to let me finish?'

Bowman folded his arms.

'All knights in Ireland must return to England at once or forfeit their lands and be banished forever,' Nicholas said, 'which I thought you should know, Richard.'

Richard put his head in his hands. 'I'd like nothing more than to leave,' he said, 'but how am I supposed to do that while we're penned up here?'

Nicholas shrugged. 'I'm just the messenger,' he said.

Richard felt lost. 'I'm going to die here, aren't I,' he said into his arms.

'I think so,' Nicholas said.

'I can't die here,' Bowman said, 'I'm going to be a father.'

'Shut up,' Richard lifted his head.

A thud of wood on stone came from behind them, on the outside of the wall.

Richard looked at Bowman. 'I told you,' he said, 'I'm dying here.'

Bowman's eyes widened. 'I can't be on the walls, I must live for my child,' he said.

Nicholas bent down and slapped him in the face.

Richard thought he could hear voices and movement from over the wall. 'I think we need to sound the alarm,' he said.

Bowman jumped up at his half-brother with anger in his eyes and nearly knocked him off the wall.

Richard sprung up and turned around, the wooden end of a ladder right in his eyeline as it leant on the wall.

'Irish,' Richard shouted, 'we're under attack.'

All hell broke loose.

Bowman let Nicholas go and they rushed over to the ladder.

War cries were sounded below as other ladders hit the walls and attackers stormed up them.

Richard drew his sword just as the first Irishman appeared on the ladder. His fingers landed on the stone first, and Richard chopped down with his sword. The man screamed and pulled his hand back, leaving the fingers on the battlements.

Two Welsh archers nearby lay on the stone parapet unmoving, and Richard wondered if the plague had taken them overnight. The ladder they should have been able to push off was therefore unattended, and an Irishman with a sword and small round shield jumped onto the walls.

Nicholas ran at him with his head down, no time to draw his sword.

The man stepped back in terror because he thought he was being charged by a black wolf.

Nicholas grabbed him and threw his straight into Dublin, where he landed with a crash onto a pig fence that broke his back.

Richard tried to push the ladder from the wall, but it was now too heavy.

A spear thrust up from the ladder but it missed Richard.

Bowman grabbed it, leant over the wall, and pushed it back down. The spear's owner fell from the ladder as it hit him in his open mouth.

Bowman kept hold of the spear, turned it around and used it to stab the next man on the ladder through the skull.

Nicholas fought at the second ladder, his sword claiming the life of the next man up it.

'We need fire arrows,' Richard said, 'send fire down into them.'

Bowman laughed as his spear mangled a man's fingers and he refused to climb any further up the ladder. 'Fire arrows take an age to prepare, young lord, they are of no use,' Bowman lunged down again and a man cried out in pain.

Richard realised he wasn't even needed now.

'Fire arrows,' Bowman turned from the ladder, 'are only for those who want to show off.'

'Shouldn't you be fighting?'

'They aren't climbing up the ladder anymore,' the blonde man said, 'it's over already.'

Richard peered over the wall and saw Bowman was right. The Irish had left the ladder and made their way back out into the night. He could hear the sounds of fighting from along the wall, and hoped that the defenders had been alert the whole way around.

A horse cantered towards them down inside the city. The face of Milo looked up at them. 'All knights to the east gate,' he shouted, 'the footmen can hold the rest of the walls, hurry.'

'You heard the man,' Nicholas started to pull the ladder up, 'could you help me maybe?'

Richard went and helped him heave the ladder into the city so it couldn't be reused.

Bowman pulled up his ladder all by himself and threw it down into Dublin with dismissive ease. He pulled a splinter from his hand and swore.

They ran around the wall, collecting anyone who understood them on the way.

When they reached the east walls, Richard saw a throng of warriors out in the gloom approaching the city.

Milo had dismounted and marshalled a hundred mail clad knights at the foot of a gatehouse.

Milo ordered the gate to be opened and the Normans poured out. Richard saw his uncle's shield colours in the press.

Raymond stood on the wall above them. He shouted to the Welsh who arranged arrows on the wall in preparation.

The men from the longships cheered when they saw the Normans coming to face them, and formed a tightly packed shield wall. Their big round shields overlapped on each other and iron helmets stuck out above. The warriors held short stabbing spears over the shields, and Richard wondered if they all had mail coats, too.

'They could be a problem,' Bowman watched as the Normans formed a line to match the length of the Norse shieldwall.

'We're only one rank deep,' Richard said, 'they look two ranks deep.' A sinking feeling gnawed at him. At Baginbun, it had been the mailed warriors who had managed to kill at least one of Alan's knights.

Milo, standing in the middle of the line himself, waved his sword forwards.

Out of the Norse wall strode a giant of a man, stripped to the waist and swinging a huge double handed axe. He had long brown hair that came down below his shoulders, and even from far away, Richard could see he was mad.

'What is he doing?' Richard asked.

'Choosing to die easily,' Bowman said.

The big Norse man twirled his axe in a figure of eight and waited for the Normans.

Milo shouted back to Raymond, but he shouted back that the enemy were beyond arrow range.

Milo advanced regardless. The Normans stepped slowly towards the enemy, their own shields interlocked, for it was foolish to run headlong at a shieldwall.

They reached the lone giant with his axe first. The man howled so loudly it rang in Richard's ears, and he heard the crunch as the axe cleaved a Norman shield right down to the metal shield boss at its centre. The axe kept swinging and with a crunch a knight's leg was cut right from his body.

Along their line, the Normans edged towards the Norse, who taunted and banged their spears onto their shields.

The Norse and Normans met with the smashing sounds of shields on shields. Spears and swords danced and fenced above the wall as men aimed at faces while trying to defend their own.

The noise of metal on metal filled the plain, and Raymond turned to Richard and his mouth dropped. 'What are you doing up here? You are supposed to be leading the charge around the back of them.'

'No one told us,' Bowman replied.

'Milo was supposed to,' Raymond tore at his beard in frustration, 'get your horses, and get out of the city. There should be twenty of you, but three will have to do. You need to crash into the back of the enemy before they leave us with no knights.'

Apprehension stabbed Richard's guts and he ran into the gatehouse and down the staircase.

Bowman ran after him, and Richard felt his toe start to hurt again as he went, the weight of his two mail coats and shield sapping his strength little by little.

Luckily, Dublin was not very big. Richard threw his saddle onto his horse, shoved the bridle into his mouth and jumped up on top as quickly as he could.

The three of them rode out of the south gate and out into the open air.

Solis cantered, pleased to be able to stretch his legs, and the cool air of the night felt fresh on Richard's face. They had picked up lances and rounded the corner of Dublin at a full gallop. Richard said a silent prayer that Solis's shoulder wound hadn't festered.

The battle lines were straight ahead. The city and Normans on their left, the Norse engaged with them, and the silhouettes of longships still further to their right. Some fires burnt up on the walls, but the battle took place in blackness.

Bowman and Nicholas were either side of him, but Solis was the quickest and Richard pushed him out into the lead. He brought his lance down over the neck of his horse and pointed it to his left. The Norse line was two men deep, and Richard aimed his lance at the man on the very far left of the enemy line, and Solis and the man behind him.

The Norse, surrounded by the song of battle, never heard the horses.

Richard clenched with the inside of his upper legs and pushed his weight down into his stirrups. He leant slightly forwards and the full weight of his and Solis's bodies went down through the lance to its razor sharp tip. The lance pierced the neck of his target, ripping it open, and Solis's hooves and chest knocked down the man behind him. Richard kept going as he and his horse rolled up the Norse flank. A tangled mess of bodies and spears slowed him down so Richard turned to his right to get away from the enemy.

Bowman turned with him, but Nicholas flew along the back of the Norse with fury.

The Norman knights whose enemies had suddenly been flattened or scattered, roared and charged. Still in their formation, the Normans turned the flank of the shieldwall and started to eat along it.

'Should we go again?' Richard asked Bowman, whose lance was broken just behind the point.

'No,' Bowman said, 'I think we've done quite enough.'

Nicholas charged down the back of the line picking off unsuspecting men with his lance.

'We probably shouldn't leave him alone, though,' Richard said.

'No, young lord,' Bowman said, 'you have children too, he doesn't.'

'You really need to stop that,' Richard turned Solis towards the centre of the battle, where the big man still swung his axe.

The blade, dark coloured in the lack of light, separated a knight's head from his body. Richard had never seen the mail coif around a man's neck broken like that before.

Milo found him and ducked the axe, but his sword merely scratched the man's skin, skin already covered in cuts.

The Norman right flank advanced rapidly now, behind the shieldwall as well as rolling up it. They hacked and slashed at the Norse and they fell, their mail and stout shields only delaying the inevitable.

Richard charged at the crazed axeman as the Norse started to run.

Milo took an axe blow on his shield, which cracked and threatened to split.

Richard lanced a warrior who fled straight into him, then another.

Milo's shield gave way on the next blow, but his sword stabbed up into the big man's stomach, were it stuck.

Undaunted, he raised his axe to cut down Milo who was in no position to step out of its way.

Richard spurred Solis and the stallion pushed a Norseman out of his way with his teeth. Richard swept his lance around and managed to hit the shaft of the great two-handed axe as it started to fall on Milo. As he rode past, the warrior dropped it and a dismounted knight speared him in the chest.

A Norman knight threw himself to the ground to avoid Richard's horse and swore up at him from the blood soaked mud.

Milo retrieved his sword from the huge warrior's guts and use it to finish him off as more knights slashed at him. The mad Norseman went down in a flurry of blows and blood.

Nicholas cantered back over, blood on his horse's chest.

Milo glanced up at Richard. 'What took you so long?'

Richard was aghast and chose to wheel Solis around instead of answer. The surviving Norse were chased by the knights and Bowman, who chased man after man and cut down at their armoured heads until they fell.

Two Normans dragged a warrior over by his shoulders. His mail coat was slashed and his helmet was gone. He had a black and swollen eye so he could only see out of the other.

'King Hasculf,' Milo was out of breath but for the very first time his face almost looked happy.

'De Cogan,' the defeated Norseman looked down at the body of the fallen axeman with a solitary sad eye, 'any man who can defeat Johan the Mad is worthy of my respect.'

'The Mad?' Milo asked.

'He was a berserker. One of the last, in the isles at least,' Hasculf replied.

Milo kicked the battered body just to be sure. 'You made a mistake coming to Dublin, I did not want to see you again.'

'Nor I you,' Hasculf said, 'but Dublin belongs to my people and we shall have it back.'

Milo shook his head. 'Times have changed, your kind are being pushed back into the sea. You might have more armour than the Irish, but you cannot face a Norman army. Only three horsemen, poor horseman at that, caused your defeat.'

'Who's he calling poor?' Bowman said loudly.

'Not now,' Richard said, 'although considering we saved his army, he is being quite rude.'

The Norse King, covered in golden rings and trim, shook his arms free from the knights holding him.

Milo waved them back. 'His people will pay a king's ransom for him, it may be the only coin we make from this whole expedition.'

Hasculf sneered. 'My people will shower you in silver. Maybe even some gold,' he said.

'Finally,' Nicholas said, 'a way to pay my ransom back.'

'Take him into the city,' Milo turned that way himself.

'I enter this time as a captive, but once I've been released I'll come back with a far greater army, and enter as a liberating hero.'

Milo stopped in his tracks.

'We'll slaughter every Norman we find,' Hasculf continued, 'do you think you can defeat a Norse army twice the size of this one?'

Milo still had his sword in his hand, and he flashed it at the King's neck with all the force his shoulders and back could muster. The blade cut through flesh, and remarkably bone, and Hasculf's head toppled onto the grass. His body tottered then dropped like a felled tree.

'No, why did you do that?' Richard moaned.

Nicholas sighed. 'Never mind then.'

Milo looked up at the horsemen. 'We faced this army in the field because we don't have the men to repel it if it attacked the walls. There were supposed to be twenty of you, too. And you were supposed to attack quicker. We lost a few knights because of your delay.'

'Raymond said you were supposed to tell us to mount up, but you never did,' Richard said.

'That was Raymond's duty,' Milo said, 'but either way, the remaining Norse will sail home and the river blockade will be lifted. Do not question me again.'

Richard didn't see any point in arguing so turned Solis towards the walls and rode away from the battlefield.

Their watch duty on the walls for the next few weeks was more quiet as the Irish fell back to the more potent weapons of hunger and disease. It was the former that killed the Irish families stuck outside Dublin's wall, but the latter that ate into the numbers of the defending army. The weather was unseasonably warm and up on the wall Richard could smell Cormac's body below him ripen unpleasantly. On his way to the wall that morning, he'd seen a cart carry the bodies of six Welshman to wherever the plague victims were being thrown, and he was sure he becoming ill himself. Bowman and Nicholas took their watch at different parts of the wall so their duty was lonely and silent.

Richard almost fell asleep on the wall when he saw movement in the distance. The Irish still camped in their various armies slightly away from Dublin, but the movement he thought, came from a single rider.

Dust rose gently from the horse, which wasn't going very fast. If Richard was trying to break the blockade to get in, he knew he'd be at least cantering, but this rider was not. He might have even been walking. Some Welshmen in the tower Richard stood next to started talking, and he heard the sound of a bow being drawn.

The rider approached, definitely only at a walk, and neared arrow range.

Another bow drew.

'Wait,' Richard said.

A head popped up from the tower above and a young man with a confused expression said something in Welsh.

'Don't shoot,' Richard said, 'don't you understand?'

The Welshman shrugged.

Richard shook his head and waved his arms angrily, but the Welshman's head vanished into the tower.

The rider stopped by the gate and an arrow sailed from the tower and struck the ground a few paces away from his horse.

'Stop it,' Richard shouted and ran into the tower and opened the gate himself. He ran down to ground level and stood in the open gateway. 'Come on Brian,' he said, 'quickly in case the next arrow doesn't miss.'

Brian flapped his legs and his horse moved on and Richard smelt its sweat before Brian was close enough to dismount. Richard helped the monk to the ground.

'Thank you,' Brian rubbed his rear and his legs, 'I didn't expect them to shoot at me.'

'What did you expect?' Richard said.

'I don't know,' the monk scratched his cheek, 'I am in such a hurry I didn't think about it.'

'Why are you in such a hurry?' Richard asked, 'are

reinforcements on their way?'

Brian shook his head. 'No, it's better than that.'

'How could it be? Unless the Irish have left.'

Brian grinned. 'I saw something I need to tell Strongbow about.'

Strongbow dropped the cup he'd been inspecting for water, seeing as all other drinks had long since run out. 'Really, monk, are you sure?'

'Quite sure,' Brian replied, 'King Rory and the other kings are all bathing in the shallow water north of his army's camp. Many Irish nobles are there with him, Rory was in the water with no clothes on at all. It was all very sinful.'

'By God's own eyes, this could be our last chance,' Strongbow stood up from his chair in the church.

'The army there were all asleep, I rode right through them,' the monk continued, 'they cared not that I rode towards the city, I think they all drank their fill last night.'

'They could be hungover for hours,' Raymond said from next to his lord, his eyes alight.

'The only benefit of running out of wine and ale is that our men are as sober as newborn babies,' Strongbow smiled, 'and as the Irish are over the hill, they won't see us coming.'

'We'll leave just the sick and injured on the walls,' Raymond said, 'I'll assemble everyone else.'

'Don't use horns,' Strongbow said, 'the first noise the enemy must hear should be our hooves and war cries.'

Raymond nodded and swept out of the church, followed by Milo and the two other knights who'd been with him.

'I thank you for your work, monk,' Strongbow said, 'this is the very moment that Ireland will submit to Norman rule for a thousand years. We are close to rotting away within these walls, the plague will finish us all if this sally fails. While everything rests on the prowess of our knights, on our victory, you young monk, you will be the sole reason for it.'

Brian's eyes, which had started brightly and with energy, dimmed as he realised the implications of the news he'd so happily brought.

Richard put his hand on his shoulders and turned him

away from Strongbow. 'Don't worry about it,' he said, 'just concentrate on praying for us as we attack.'

The attack that would decide the future of Norman Ireland would be a full frontal assault. The Norman force that mustered in front of Dublin's walls was split into the customary three divisions. Milo commanded the rearguard with twenty knights and forty Welshmen, while Strongbow took the main division with forty knights and two hundred archers.

Bowman looked along the line of Raymond's vanguard with a meagre twenty knights and groaned. 'Is this it? There's only forty of the Welsh with us, how are we supposed to rout a whole army?'

'I think Saint Ciaran's punishment is showing pretty clearly,' Richard said, 'this looks like less than half the men who we had at Waterford.'

Archers started to climb up onto the backs of the knight's horses, because Strongbow had ordered them to ride into battle and they couldn't do so alone because there were no longer enough horses for them.

Solis had thinned and Richard had shoved some extra horsehair into the pads under his saddle to try to keep it fitting properly. A long scar ran down the horse's shoulder that would forever remain without hair, but otherwise the stallion felt happy to be outside. He pawed the ground and refused to quite stand still.

An archer heaved himself up behind Richard and he smelt sweat and wool from him. The man's bow poked Solis and the stallion snorted in annoyance.

'This is the idle hour of the afternoon,' Raymond shouted from the centre of his twenty knights, 'but we shall not be idle today. Today we will free ourselves from our Irish oppressors and claim Ireland for ourselves and our descendants. Our lord has tasked us with finding King Rory and killing him. Nothing else matters, that is your purpose.'

'Great,' Bowman muttered, 'we'll just kill another king, shall we?'

'If we're going to hell for one already,' Richard said, 'what difference is another?'

Bowman laughed as Strongbow rode out in front of the army on his grey Italian warhorse. He turned to face them, and although far away, his booming voice carried to Richard.

'An Irish Archbishop carried an offer to me this last week from High King Rory,' he said, 'he offered me the rule of Waterford and Dublin if I knelt before him and limited our ambitions to these two places. What do you say, you men who have followed me through rain and sun, ambushes and victories, do we submit to an Irish King?'

The army shouted no, or at least the Normans who understood him did.

'Then we shall ride today for ourselves, God can take the Irish kings and even the King of England. Damned them all, who are they to order us, we men who have forged our own path? The battle ahead is daunting and our enemy is a seething mass, a multitude who will defend themselves, but what is death to men like you? Death is just a moment between this life and eternal life, it is only to be feared by those who fear that when they die, that all has perished with them. But it has nothing to fear for us, those who bring glory with them through all time. Immortal valour is ours, now ride, ride into their camp and kill them all, those who dare to oppose us.'

The army cheered and Richard gripped his lance tightly, feeling a burning in his being that he could describe as elation.

Raymond ordered the vanguard to march and they moved off in a line across the plain and towards the hills.

'If I die,' Bowman shouted as the horses pushed into a canter at the foot of the first hill, 'look after my daughter.'

'Look after her yourself,' Richard replied as Solis started to ascend the slope. At the top of it, the twenty knights came into view of King Rory's army. In the long time they'd had in camp, the Irish had built wooden shelters with canvas roofs that looked almost as good as houses. Fires drifted up all around the valley that stretched out before them, with carts parked up in one area and hundreds of small horses eating piles of cut grass in another.

Raymond pointed his lance at the centre of the camp where the valley reached its lowest point and a stream flowed into a shallow pool.

Richard could see tiny figures in the pool, but around the rest of the camp there was precious little movement.

'They're all asleep,' Nicholas shouted from the other side of Richard.

There were no guards, either, as the vanguard raced down the slope and the alarm was finally raised within the camp. The Irish army lurched slowly into life. As they cantered towards it, Richard saw men stick their heads out of shelters, and start to run back and forth. The surprise part of the attack had worked.

The horses had started their canter early, but they were all eager to be in open ground and had pent up energy to expel. Their charge, as lances lowered and the camp grew closer and closer, was irresistible. Raymond's lance skewered two Irishmen at the same time, a feat that singers would sing about for hundreds of years, as Welshmen shot arrows from the backs of horses as they went. Richard didn't remember them hitting much, and the approach to the stream was a blur of horses, lances and wooden shelters.

Rory's guard hurried to form up into a body in front of the pool as the King himself pushed his way through the water. Raymond's horse was at the front of the vanguard which was now scattered behind him.

Solis chased his horse closely but had to grind to a halt when Raymond did the same to offload his Welsh archer. The one behind Richard slid off and they started to pour arrows into Rory's guards.

Bowman arrived and deposited an archer of his own. Nicholas appeared from another direction and without anyone else on his horse.

'What happened to yours?' Richard asked.

'He got in my way,' Nicholas replied and pushed his horse into line next to Richard and Bowman.

'No time to waste,' Raymond cried, 'it's all or nothing, attack!' His horse put its head down and started quickly towards Rory's guard.

Richard put his legs onto his horse, and at the moment Solis took his first step a lance point ripped into the mail on Richard's left shoulder. Even before the lance and its bearer flew by, Richard knew who it was.

Luke cantered between Richard and Nicholas, through a gap that wasn't big enough for him. Richard felt his left leg get carried forward away from him and a twinge of pain burst out from his knee.

Nicholas swore as Luke's shield bashed into his lance and knocked it from his grasp. Richard thought about lowering his lance at his uncle and chasing him, but Raymond was half way to Rory's guard already, and thanks to his uncle's attack, only Bowman had gone with him.

Richard decided to swallow his urge for revenge and cantered after Raymond and Bowman. The two of them charged the Irish guard, who were four men deep, and cut their way into their ranks.

They only made it three ranks in before their horses were stopped by the weight of enemy numbers. Richard and Nicholas joined the attack moments later and Richard's lance jarred as it dug into flesh and was ripped from his armpit. The guardsmen in their haste wore no armour and were unprepared for battle, so their numbers only counted for so much. Richard saw Rory, completely naked, run away from them out of the pond. A short Irish spear hit Richard's shield as another ran off his forearm and into his chest. Richard spurred Solis and the horse burst through out of the guard just as Raymond did the same.

'He's escaping,' the big Norman shouted as Rory threw himself onto a horse lacking even a bridle, and clung on to its mane for dear life as it galloped north and away from harm.

Richard turned to see the Welsh join the fray. Nicholas wasn't on his horse anymore, instead he stabbed and slashed and cut at the Irish until between them the whole guard was dead.

'We were so close,' Raymond sat on his horse looking at the cloud of dust Rory had left behind, 'and now we're all dead men.'

Milo and his rearguard cantered by, cutting down fleeing men, a task they continued out of the valley and up the next hill.

Bowman spat blood onto the grass. 'Where were you? If we'd all charged, we'd have got to the King.'

'My uncle got in the way,' Richard said, 'if it wasn't for him we'd have been beside you.'

Raymond, his face red, turned to Richard. 'The only reason I won't cut your head from your body right now is that you're the reason my head is still on my shoulders in the first place. But you've ended Norman rule in Ireland.'

Richard opened his mouth to argue, but what was the point? Rory was gone.

'We might as well make sure this army is finished,' Raymond shouted to anyone who could hear, 'chase them down, kill as many as you can.' He charged off with his sword in hand.

'I saw,' Nicholas walked over, 'he lost me my lance. We should kill him for that.'

'We should,' Richard replied, 'if the other Irish armies don't kill us first.'

Bowman shook his head. 'I can't believe how close we came, should we slip away and ride to find some coastal village with a fishing boat we can steal?'

'I don't know,' Richard said, 'do you know how to sail?'

'No.'

'We wouldn't get far,' Nicholas replied, 'if the Irish have any sense they'll be on their way to swarm us now.'

Richard cast his eyes around the camp. Smoke plumed up from hundreds of the shelters as the Welsh set them on fire, and the horsemen had nearly pushed all the way through the camp. The scattered Irish ran on foot up the hill to the north, but Milo's rearguard pursued them closely and their hopes looked bleak.

'Shouldn't we join in?' Nicholas looked around for his own horse.

Richard shrugged. 'What's the point? We'll check the camp for survivors and wait here for everyone else to get tired.'

And get tired they did. The Norman horsemen chased the Irish into the hills until the sun was halfway back down to the horizon. Knights came back in twos and threes, complaining that their sword arms were dead and their horses exhausted. They all drank from the pond where King Rory had taken his bath, and once Raymond returned Richard followed him back slowly towards the city.

'There will be stories about this battle,' Bowman said once they were halfway back, 'I've never seen so many killed in one place before.'

'And the stories will be about how we nearly caught the King, if it wasn't for me and my uncle,' Richard said bitterly.

'Raymond may well want to keep that quiet,' Bowman replied, 'but look over there.'

Richard followed his finger over the plain to a cloud of dust. 'What is it, is the enemy coming for us?'

'I think they're going away,' Bowman said in disbelief, 'one of the Irish armies is leaving.'

Strongbow sent out riders who eventually confirmed that all of the Irish armies were leaving. Too many of its commanders had perished in the sally, and those that survived had lost their appetite for war and decided to go home. The slaughter of the day stunned even the most hardened of the Normans, and crows circled the field for days afterwards, their numbers dwarfed only by the rats that grew fat on the bloated corpses. But even though the High King had escaped them, at the end of it all, Dublin was in Norman hands. As Richard fed their horses from hay taken from the Irish camp that evening, he at least knew that food and drink was on its way. The enemy around them had departed and left the battered, tired and weak Norman army alive, and although it was barely alive, alive it was. And as Richard felt relief that his uncle hadn't in the end caused their destruction, a ship docked on the riverfront. A ship carrying a message from the King of England.

PAYMENTS

It seemed that everyone had turned out to see what the ship had brought. Some of the army was engaged in ferrying captured supplies from Rory's camp back into Dublin, but everyone else was hungry and hoped that the vessel brought them fresh supplies.

'Strongbow looks nervous,' Bowman said as they stood in the crowd as a boarding plank connected the tall-masted ship with the riverside. The new King of Leinster stood to welcome whoever disembarked but his fingers scratched at his sword pommel as he waited.

'You?' Strongbow said loudly when the same messenger walked down the plank who had brought him King Henry's command to call off the invasion back in Wales.

The messenger in his red tunic held a rolled up parchment in his hands, the red royal seal on it clear even from where Richard stood.

'Are we all about to be declared traitors and outlaws?' Richard asked partly to himself.

'I think the King already did that,' Bowman said.

Strongbow ripped the seal apart and read the message.

'Well?' Raymond asked before he was finished. The big Norman's red cloak was still wrapped around his shoulders, but the little of it that remained was shredded and barely reached his waist.

Strongbow lowered the letter and gazed off into space, his face a lighter white than before.

'Well?' Raymond asked again, 'how bad is it?'

'He's coming to Ireland, Raymond,' Strongbow replied quietly, very quietly.

'To hang us all?'

Strongbow turned to the crowd that waited in silence to hear their fate. 'The King of England has sent me terms,' he shouted, his voice lacking its usual power, 'we are to surrender Waterford and Dublin to him if I wish to keep the crown of Leinster.'

As the message was translated to the Welsh, the Normans complained loudly of surrendering Dublin, the city they had just come so very close to losing. Once they quietened, the newly informed Welsh made the same complaint.

Strongbow held up his arms for silence. 'The King demands that I hand over all my lands in Wales, England, Normandy and France,' he continued.

'He's robbing you,' one knight cried. The Normans jeered again.

Strongbow took a breath. 'Those are his terms. But the King is sailing to Ireland with the royal army.'

The onlookers fell quiet as the implication sunk in.

'We couldn't hope to defeat the royal army, even if we dared march against the royal banner,' Richard said.

'No,' Bowman said, 'we have what, half a thousand men left? And half of them are sick. We have less than a hundred knights, fewer fit horses, and we've seen King Henry's army, he can afford however many mercenaries he pleases.'

Strongbow looked around the faces who looked back at him with worry. 'I have always been a loyal subject of the King of England.'

Bowman snorted and had to clap a hand over his mouth to stifle his laughter.

Strongbow noticed and his eyes shone fury at him. The new King's normal vigour returned to his voice. 'I am loyal to England and I will not seek battle with my King. I will agree to his terms to save you from having to fight and die against an English army. That is my loyalty to you, you brave men who fought for me. I will no longer put you in danger, so I will pay homage to King Henry for Leinster and hand over the cities.'

Conversation broke out amongst the gathered army.

Richard closed his eyes and said a prayer for he had no wish to be caught up in what would be a full rebellion against the crown if things went badly.

'Strongbow's turned the King's mastery over him into his own victory,' Bowman said.

Brian breathed a sigh of relief next to him. 'The violence has ceased,' he said happily.

'As a sign of goodwill to the King,' Strongbow continued, 'this army is now disbanded. All those who fought will receive payment for their service, come to the church today and each man will be given what he is owed.'

'Finally,' Bowman said.

Richard nodded. 'Nicholas will be pleased, I'll go and tell him.'

The King's messenger looked as relieved at Strongbow's decision as everyone else, but he still retreated back into the ship rather than onto Irish land. Out of the ship walked a party of monks, most of whom wobbled and clung on to each other for balance.

'Ah,' Brian cried, 'monks of Rome to fill the monasteries of Ireland.'

'Rome?' Richard asked.

'England,' Brian answered, 'but you know what I mean.'

The party of monks disembarked and spoke to Strongbow and Raymond, neither of which looked remotely interested.

Behind the monks came some clerks, and behind them some nuns.

'They kept their promise,' Brian almost jumped up and down, 'the old ways will be gone within a generation.'

'I'm glad you're so happy,' Bowman said.

'Now I can leave Ireland,' the monk replied, 'with my task complete.'

'What about all the death and destruction you caused?' Richard asked.

Brian looked over to the river. 'I can leave Ireland now.'

Richard thought the monk was just looking for excuses to leave his troubles behind, but as he didn't mind his company that much, he left him alone.

Brian turned back to the nuns and Strongbow bowed to one of them. 'It is an honour to host you, Lady of Newstead,' he said.

'God be praised,' Brian's eyes widened, 'we have been blessed by a saintly presence. God shines his approval on our actions.'

'Newstead?' Richard repeated the word over in his head.

'Richard,' Bowman put a hand on his shoulder.

'I've heard that before,' Richard replied, 'I just can't place it.'

'Richard,' Bowman repeated, 'you haven't just heard of it before, you've been there before.'

Richard's eyes fell on the nun who Strongbow had bowed to. His mouth dropped open.

'That's your sister,' Bowman said.

Brian turned his head slowly to Richard. 'Your sister is the Lady of Newstead?'

'Apparently,' Richard replied.

'I knew I was drawn to you by divine providence,' the monk said, 'this was all part of the Lord's plan.'

'Calm down,' Bowman said.

'What's Adela doing here?' Richard asked.

'Claiming Ireland for the true church,' Brian said.

'Go and ask her,' Bowman suggested.

Richard walked towards her and Strongbow looked at him questioningly. 'What do you want, boy?'

'This is my sister.'

'Richard?' Adela asked with surprise across her young face, 'what are you doing here?'

'Me? What are you doing here?'

'You're the brother to a saintly nun?' Strongbow started to laugh, 'that's brightened an otherwise mixed day.'

Adela bowed to Richard. 'Many monks and nuns in England have been invited to cross the sea and spread Christianity amongst the pagans here. We had not thought to accept until the Martels sold our nunnery to a merchant who wanted it for his house.'

'It is just another plot by the King to encroach on my power here,' Strongbow said, 'he only will have invited those who will do his bidding to Ireland.'

Adela didn't look concerned. 'It gladdens me to see you well,' she told Richard.

'I don't know about well,' he replied.

'You're missing a finger and something happened to your face,' she peered at the scar across his eye.

'One was bad luck and one was a bad friend,' Richard

explained.

Strongbow laughed. 'This one is a true warrior of God,' he said, 'but come, Richard, you need to line up with everyone else and receive your payment.'

The King of Leinster slapped him on the back and started to go back to the church.

'I have my sisters to see to,' Adela said, 'I will seek you this evening, be at the church.'

Richard agreed and went back with Bowman to find Nicholas so that they could learn what their efforts had been worth.

It turned out that it wasn't just Richard and his companions who were keen to find out what they were going to get for their troubles. Four hundred men crowded the square outside the church where they pushed, shoved, and sometimes fought each other to get to the doors. Raymond and some knights stood by those doors and let in only a few men at a time.

Richard, along with Bowman and Nicholas, were let in with Milo because they wisely chose to follow him as he cleared a path for himself through the clamouring masses.

When the church doors slammed shut behind them, the quiet was welcome.

'I feel like a dog waiting for his dinner,' Bowman stood with folded arms as Milo approach Strongbow. The new King of Leinster then appointed Milo as the governor as Dublin itself, at least until the King arrived, as well as giving him some lands to the south of the city. The grumpy looking Norman knight seemed pleased with this and left almost smiling.

'You three,' Strongbow said as Richard and his comrades approached. He turned to a clerk who held a list up to him and squinted at the lines on it.

'Who am I fooling,' the King laughed, 'I can't read it. All three of you have served me well and I would be greatly honoured if you all stayed in Ireland as landed knights in Leinster. Although you,' he looked at Nicholas, 'will have to lose that wolf-pelt, those bishops will never stop complaining to me otherwise.'

'I like it,' Nicholas said, the wolf draped around his shoulders even though his mail shirt was in Brian's house.

'We were hoping for coin,' Richard said.

Strongbow groaned. 'You know I have you down for quite a lot of land in the north of Leinster, you'd be a great landowner. Equal to Milo, actually.'

Richard thought about it, Adela would probably be sent to that area, too.

'Young lord,' Bowman poked the back of his calf with a foot, 'you have land, a wife, and children in Normandy. Which you are planning on returning to, remember?'

'He's right,' Richard said, 'I can barely manage one small village so I don't think I am the man you're looking for. Besides, the north will probably be attacked by the Irish soon enough, I would rather not have lands there.'

'That's why I want you there, all three of you,' Strongbow said, 'you're proven native-killers.'

'We came for coin,' Richard said, 'so we must humbly refuse the very generous offer of land.'

'Show me my hoard of gold, and you're welcome to scoop an armful up,' Strongbow chuckled to himself. His clerk looked at him unamused.

'I can't run an estate here and one in Normandy,' Richard complained, 'I'm not even sure I can look after my family's lands in England, let alone here.'

'If you kill your uncle,' Bowman added.

'The choice is yours,' Strongbow said, 'you can take vast tracts of rich lands, or you can sail home with nothing but memories. And I know who your uncle is, he was the first into Dublin and there will be no killing of him in Ireland, I forbid that. Order must be maintained.'

'I need something for Nicholas to pay his ransom to me,' Richard said, 'that was the whole reason we came to Ireland in the first place.'

Strongbow looked up to the rafters of the church. 'What am I supposed to do to help you? I have nothing to give you except land, which you do not accept. An act, I should warn you, that seems a lot like ingratitude.'

Richard realised there was nothing to be gained from either this conversation or Ireland. Hopefully the last of Dermot's rings that Nicholas had kept back would fetch a decent price in

England.

'This was a waste of time,' Bowman said, 'all of it. I'm going home.' The blonde man turned his back on Strongbow and marched out of the church.

The King decided to ignore him but Richard thought it best if he left too. He grabbed Nicholas and dragged him out of the church.

'Maybe I want to become a Irish lord?' The Martel knight said.

'You can do whatever you like once that ring has been sold.'

They re-entered the square and the crush of knights almost pushed them back into the church. Raymond barged into them and opened an escape route.

'I want to stay in Ireland,' Nicholas said, 'how else will I ever carve out a name for myself?'

'You want a name? You want stories told about you?' Richard asked, 'neither of those put food on the table.'

Nicholas wrenched himself free from Richard and started to run out of the square.

'You'll be wanting to catch him,' Bowman said, 'he's wearing the ring. If we never see him again then we'll have lost the only thing of value to come out of this whole sorry story.'

Richard couldn't agree more and started to run after Nicholas.

'I told you not to trust him,' Bowman shouted after them.

Richard chased Nicholas down a street that was full of the monks from England, as well as the rest of the army who had been collecting supplies from Rory's camp. Nicholas was much faster, and Richard only caught him up when he found him lying on the floor, out cold. Standing over him, and holding the precious golden ring up to the sun, was uncle Luke.

'That's not yours,' Richard shouted and ran at his uncle.

Luke looked back down, realised who was coming, and sprinted away himself.

Richard glanced down at Nicholas, but alive or dead there would be little he could do for him, so he followed his uncle. He felt his legs burn as he ran, he ran more than he had in a long time, powered by rage. Finally, he thought, it was the right time to end the feud.

Luke ducked into an alleyway, jumped a pile of broken

pottery and turned down the next street that ran back towards the church.

Richard followed and his toe started to hurt again, which angered him because it had been feeling mostly better.

Luke led him right back to the church where he pushed through the crowd until he banged straight into Raymond's back.

The big Norman whirled around with anger in his face. His sword was already drawn from threatening the unruly army, and he pointed it at Luke's unarmoured chest. 'Stop,' he commanded.

Luke breathed heavily but wasn't going to argue with Raymond.

Richard almost collapsed to a halt and really wanted to rub his toe. 'He stole something from me,' he cried.

'What did he steal?' Raymond asked.

Richard began to answer but instantly realised that the truth would lead to a confiscation of the ring. At best. 'My lands, and I need to kill him,' Richard said.

Raymond's patience had been drained by the army's inability to queue nicely, and his face darkened. 'This feud ends, before you nearly get me killed again. I've had enough of it. A full judicial duel, by the letter of the law, will happen at dawn. You will both fast for the rest of the day under supervision of other knights, who I'll be picking. Then at dawn, you'll fight so God can reveal who has the right of this matter. At dawn, by the Black Pool, and to the death.'

Richard spent the rest of the day in a dark room with one of Milo's knights standing beside him. While the sun shone through the window outside Richard's thoughts were mixed and rapid, but once the sun had set his mind began to slow. Everything had happened so fast, one minute he was chasing a wayward captive knight for a golden ring, and then the ring was gone and he was going to face his uncle in a fight to the death. Not very long ago, that thought would have terrified Richard, but as he ran his finger along the indent of his scar, he feared it not. He looked down at his missing finger, which he still felt, and wondered if he would be short of a few more soon. He spent some time thinking about how many fingers he would be happy to lose in a victorious fight, then banished such silly thoughts from his mind. The dawn would bring his chance to avenge his mother, and as he increasingly believed, his father too. As a faint glow of light appeared from the window, Richard felt surprisingly at peace. He remembered Strongbow's words before the sally, that death was just a moment between other lives, and he accepted it. Besides, he knew Luke was guilty, so why should he doubt God's justice?

Richard's tranquillity lasted until the doors flew open and the world flooded back in.

'Are you ready?' Raymond asked.

'I am,' Richard replied.

'Good,' the big Norman grinned, 'because it's happening now whether you like it or not.'

The Black Pool was deep and wide, so wide it was used as a port for ships. It had a peaty smell as water rushed from one river in the direction of the main river to the north of Dublin. The ground beside it was damp and the air smelt salty. Four wooden posts had been driven into the soft ground and a rope tied between them to form a square arena for the combat. Raymond led Richard out to it, where Luke already stood next to Gerold. The older man handed Luke his sword belt.

Bowman and Nicholas stood with Adela on the opposite side of the square, Bowman holding his weapons for him.

'Each man can have their sword, shield and a knife,' Raymond said, 'there are no replacement shields and no one is to hand either man new weapons of any sort. This is a family dispute and no one else is to intervene on pain of death. However bad it looks for your man,' Raymond looked between Bowman and Gerold, 'you stay your hands or I'll chop them off.'

Bowman nodded and approached Richard to tie his sword belt around his waist. 'Here you are, young lord,' he said as he belted Sir John's dagger on as well because he could see that Richard's hands were ever so slightly shaking.

'Thank you,' Richard looked over towards Nicholas, 'I'm surprised he's here.'

'Apparently he didn't really mean to run away,' Bowman held up Richard's battered shield, 'he thinks he's coming back with us to Normandy.'

Richard took the shield and slung it around his neck. The straps used for foot combat where in a different place than those used on horseback, which were much dirtier and torn.

'You really need a new shield,' Bowman said.

'I know.'

'No talk of giving me your horse if you lose?' Bowman asked.

Richard smiled and shook his head. 'Firstly, I wouldn't give him to you, and secondly, I'm not going to lose.'

Bowman clapped him on both shoulders. 'That's the spirit.'

Luke was already in the arena behind a shield of the same colours as Richard. Neither man wore armour, so the duel would be of a different nature than had they been protected.

Raymond looked between them. 'I expect we probably should have a priest present to say some words of some sort, but we shall begin. To the death.'

Richard glanced at his sister and was pleased to see she remained impassive and still. She nodded back at him, her arms inside a large dark cloak.

Luke stepped forwards with his shield up to his eyes and his sword concealed behind it.

Richard cursed Sir Wobble for never having taught him to fight properly, and copied his uncle.

Richard's shield had chunks missing along its top and Richard had a bad feeling his would disintegrate first. He stepped closer to his uncle. When men who are used to wearing armour fight without it, they fight further apart and take fewer risks, so the two combatants moved in and out of striking distance as they circled each other like wolves.

Richard took a big step forwards just to see what his uncle would do.

Luke stepped sideways and cut through the air where Richard would have been if his step hadn't been a feint. That was good, Richard thought, he could counter that.

'The boy is calm,' Luke said, 'but soon he'll be hot with temper like his father.'

Richard stepped forwards again but this time Luke took a step backwards and Richard couldn't use the counter he'd wanted to.

'But the boy is predictable, just like his father,' Luke lunged forwards and pushed at Richard with his shield. His sword appeared from over the top of it and it flashed at Richard's eyes. He had to duck it and he felt the blade move through his hair as he almost fell backwards before recovering himself.

His uncle laughed. 'The boy defends like a weak child. He has the footwork of a leper.'

Richard sensed his own annoyance build and realised that was what his uncle wanted. He tried to ram his worn shield into his uncle's face and cut over the top of it. Luke's sword flashed up to parry the attack and his shield pushed into Richard and half put him off balance.

'The boy doesn't even have his own ideas,' Luke said as they circled each other again.

'Stop talking,' Richard said, 'you're just wasting my time.'

'The boy speaks the truth,' Luke replied, 'for he has precious little time left to waste.' He cut at Richard and the sword cleaved off part of the thin leather covering of his shield.

Richard sidestepped but wasn't close enough to strike.

'The boy is but a shadow of the father.'

Richard grunted and ran at his uncle. Their shields clashed and Richard tried to cut around both of them this time. Luke did the same and both cut each other's left shoulders, but only glancing blows.

Luke laughed. 'The boy fights like he never learnt how, but then his father did abandon him very young.'

'What did you do to him?'

'Me?' Luke circled Richard and tried to walk him onto the square's rope, 'he was in sufferable, he talked down to me. He deserved his fate.'

'What was his fate?' Richard jogged out of the corner he'd nearly been pushed into.

'To die with the Templars of Jerusalem, broken and in pain.'

'What happened?'

Luke started to circle the other way and Richard felt the eyes of his companions and sister on his back.

'The boy asks questions he knows nothing of,' Luke replied.

'I'm not a boy,' Richard knew his anger grew, 'I've taken castles for one King and been the death of another, you are

351

nothing to me.'

'Death of a king?' Luke's eyebrows furrowed and Richard took his chance.

Richard darted left into his uncle but then went right and tried to get around his shield. The Little Lord's sword arced around and he put all his effort into the swing. Except Luke had moved just enough that it only caught the rim of his shield and they both stepped apart unharmed and out of breath.

'Was that all the boy has?' Luke grinned behind his shield, 'was that his grand plan?'

Richard said nothing because it was. His uncle's shield, gently curved around his body, loomed at him like an impenetrable barrier.

'The boy despairs.'

'I should have killed you in the alleyway in Waterford, a dishonourable death for a dishonourable man.'

'The boy is a coward,' Luke walked towards Richard.

'You're the one who ran,' Richard stood his ground and watched for his uncle's sword to appear from out behind his shield.

Luke tried to stab Richard in the face, an attack that flew out from behind his shield like a crossbow bolt.

Richard ducked it and ran out of the way, out into the centre of the square. He saw Bowman behind Luke, holding onto Nicholas's shoulder, and Adela standing as still as stone.

'The boy even ducks,' Luke let out a snort of derision, 'the rumour is that the boy can't even keep a hold of his sword.'

Richard flexed his grip on the Little Lord's sword and marvelled how it was still in his hand. A thought dawned on him that even with the sword in his hand, he would never defeat his uncle with it. Luke had fought on battlefields across the world, there was no battlefield ploy that would fool him.

Then Richard had an idea, he would have to do something no one would do on a battlefield. He walked towards his uncle.

'Don't drop your sword,' Luke sneered.

Richard ran at him then did something that would either win the day or get him killed. He threw the Little Lord's sword at his uncle's head.

Luke's eyes widened and he swung his own sword up to

intercept it. Steel clashed loudly with steel as the flying sword spun off the combination of Luke's shield and sword and into the wet ground of the square. But Richard had already dropped to the ground and had Sir John's dagger in his hand. He drove the newly sharpened blade into Luke's foot and the dagger dug deep into the grass and earth beneath it.

His uncle yelled and tried to step backwards. The impaled foot tore itself at the dagger, but Richard held it so firmly that Luke's momentum threw him backwards into the ground by the rope as his foot stayed pinned to the earth.

Richard pulled the dagger out and plunged it down at Luke. The dagger sunk into his thigh just before Luke brought his shield round and cracked Richard in the side of the head with it.

Richard reeled away with black spots and flashing lights in his eyes, then scrambled to his feet. He swayed for a moment before his eyes focused on his uncle who was up on one knee, but the leg with the two wounds disobeyed him and he could go no further.

Richard's head spun so much he tasted acid in his mouth but he swallowed it down and adjusted his shield. It wasn't over.

Luke pulled his shield in front of himself too, but he looked down at his thigh, which Richard knew would be bleeding. 'I can wait for the bleeding to kill you,' Richard said, 'which would be a fitting end.'

Luke cried out in frustration, his howl echoed around the Black Pool, and with a huge effort he forced his leg to stand him up.

Behind him, Bowman groaned and put a hand on his sword.

Adela's hand left her cloak and stopped Bowman's as she shook her head at him.

Luke took one slow step off the rope towards Richard.

Richard's vision was clearing but he wasn't sure he'd see the next attack in time.

Clear or not, Richard saw a flourish of Adela's cloak behind Luke, and the sun glinted on something silver. Something silver that Richard recognised.

The candlestick that he had used to escape from Keynes and saved his life with, the candlestick that he later gave to Adela, caught the sun again as she swung it at the back of her uncle's head. The silverware, solid and still stained by his blood, cracked the back of his skull and his eyes rolled up and went white.

'No,' Richard shouted, for an intervention was a death sentence.

Luke's body dropped dead where it was.

Adela took a step backwards and nodded to Richard. 'He was my uncle, too,' she said.

Everyone, shock and horror on their faces, looked to Raymond.

The big Norman looked down at the body and over to the newly red candlestick. 'That was unconventional,' he said.

'You can't kill her for that,' Richard felt tears brewing.

Raymond chuckled. 'Rules are rules and I did say this was a family affair and no one else could intervene. Although, I suppose she is family so she technically did not break that rule.'

'Really?' Richard couldn't help himself asking.

'Why not?' Raymond shrugged, 'everything that happens is God's will, or so the priests keep telling me.'

Nicholas pushed Bowman off his shoulder. 'Can I have my ring back?'

'This ring?' Raymond held his hand up, on which the big golden ring sat on one finger.

The Martel knight nodded.

'Seeing as our King Strongbow forbade the killing of that man,' Raymond pointed the ring finger at Luke, 'I am accepting this ring as payment for not telling him about it. I'm the Constable of Leinster now, you know. I will grant the three of you passage back home though, so if you feel wronged, consider the ring the price of that safe passage.'

Bowman put a hand on his half-brother's arm. 'Let it go,' he said.

Richard looked down at the body of his uncle and up to his sister. 'Why in God's name did you bring the candlestick with you?'

Adela tipped her head imperceptibly to one side. 'My voices told me to bring it to Ireland to stand as the centrepiece of our new nunnery. They told me to bring it here this morning and that it was God's will.'

Raymond snorted behind Richard.

'They've just stopped,' she continued, 'I don't hear them now.'

Richard walked over to her, discarding his shield on the way. 'We're free now,' he said, 'our mother's spirit is free, too.'

His sister nodded. 'I know I told you not to seek vengeance, but God did say an eye for an eye.'

Richard felt very tired, and suddenly very hungry. 'Do you want to stay in Ireland?'

She nodded. 'I do. And you must not.'

Richard agreed, he had a feeling Raymond wanted rid of them now anyway.

'It's over,' Raymond shouted at the knights he'd brought with him, 'take the square down and let us go. Oh, Richard.'

'Yes?'

'Before you go, you need to get rid of that body,' Raymond turned and left them.

Bowman stepped over the rope. 'You had me worried there,' he said, 'I'll throw the body into the Black Pool for you.'

Bowman bent down and started to slide the shield off.

'Hold on,' Richard squatted down by his uncle and picked up a foot, 'I knew it, he's wearing my father's spurs.'

Richard unstrapped the buckles and released the pair of golden spurs from the dead man's feet. He stood up and they twinkled in the morning sun.

'Do you think he killed father?' Adela asked.

'I don't know,' Richard said, 'but I'm going to find out.'

Bowman picked up Luke's arms and shouted over to Nicholas. 'Come on, grab his feet.'

Nicholas did and they carried the body over towards the water.

'Do you think he'll float?' Nicholas asked.

'He's guilty,' Bowman said, 'so probably.'

They hurled the body into the dark water, where it splashed loudly all over both of them.

Bowman sighed. 'That's your fault, you should have thrown him further.'

'My fault?' Nicholas replied, 'we had half each.'

The body resurfaced and floated away face down. 'Told you,'

Bowman said.

'What now?' Nicholas asked as he tried forlornly to shake his tunic dry of the black water.

Richard looked at his sister. 'I think we should throw the candlestick into the Pool, then go home.'

'No,' Nicholas said, 'that's the only thing of value we have left.'

'It doesn't belong to you so you can't pay your ransom with it. You'll have to earn it another way,' Richard said, 'which means we'll have to find Sir Wobble and see if we can make a fortune on the tournament circuit.'

Bowman walked over to him. 'At least as a knight I can join in now,' his smiled beamed from ear to ear.

Nicholas wanted to argue but didn't have any better ideas. 'I hate Strongbow,' he said, 'I never want to hear that name again.

Richard grinned. 'You remember Sarjeant wanted to brew another type of cider?'

Nicholas nodded.

'I know what I'm going to call it, we'll name it after the King of Leinster.'

The Martel knight shook his head. 'If you do I'm never going to drink it.'

Bowman laughed as Richard looked at his sister. 'Do you want to throw it?'

Adela presented the stained candlestick to him in both hands. 'I think you should, it will mean more from you.'

Richard grasped the silverware. It was cold in his hands and he turned it over slowly. He'd come a long way since being that frightened child at Keynes, but it was time to close that chapter of his life. Richard walked to the Black Pool and took a deep breath of the salty, peaty, air. He wasn't going to miss Ireland or his uncle. Richard mustered all his might and hurled the candlestick through the air in the direction of Luke's floating corpse. It spun as it went, bounced off his head one last time, and with a final splash it was gone. Black ripples spread out across the Pool as Richard turned his back on his uncle and everything he had inflicted on him. Tomorrow was a new day, and Richard had a plan.

HISTORICAL NOTE

The Norman invasion of Ireland is still a sensitive subject, at least on one side of the Irish sea. Strongbow's invasion kicked off a series of events that would drive the course of Ireland's history right up to the present day. All of those troubles, divisions and problems have their roots in the events covered in this book, events that are not well known in England. The ten knights and seventy Welsh archers who landed under Raymond le Gros and defended the promontory fort at Baginbun Head where the thin end of the wedge. Historical sources describe how Raymond and his tiny band fought off the Irish, and even how they used a herd of cattle to overrun the enemy and drive them away. Raymond apparently also mutilated seventy captured Irishmen and hurled them from the clifftops, an act that I feel set the tone of the English involvement in Ireland.

The brutality and controversy of the Norman invasion makes writing fiction around it potentially problematic. I chose an approach that would show the Anglo-Norman prejudices of the Irish, warts and all, with very little input from the Irish side, because I wanted to convey the world from Richard's view. His view that would have been based on tales of the pagan Irish, their savagery and lack of civilization. The Normans looked down on the Irish and their different customs, some of which had a basis in fact. The Irish rode smaller horses than the Anglo-Normans did, and did so without the use of saddles. They sometimes used bridles, but sometimes steered their horses with only the use of an iron or wooden rod, the appearance of which in a horse's eyeline would make it turn the other way. This made them comparatively useless as heavy cavalry, but meant their actual riding abilities had to be a degree higher than anyone using a saddle, and therefore they were potentially effective as missile cavalry.

It might seem outlandish, but some Irish did scorn armour in battle because it was seen as cowardly, an idea that we can find in England in the Iron Age, when it was the Roman's turn to deride the English for doing it. Gerald of Wales, a cousin to Raymond le Gros, left us a record of the invasion that sees the natives as little more than barbarians, but gives us fascinating details to go on that are better than anything an author could ever make up. For instance, the house built on a post outside the walls of Waterford that was cut in two to bring it down, is mentioned in Gerald's account, and even fits in with the archaeological record of Waterford. That is apparently how the Anglo-Normans actually got into the city. Likewise, the Irish ambushed Strongbow's army as it made painful progress through the Wicklow Mountains. During this, they put up screens between trees to block the Norman cavalry, showing that however backwards the Normans might have thought they were, the Irish were by no means tactically inept. The staggering loses and defeats they suffered at the hands of a much small invading army might not cover them in glory, but they were up against knights in mail armour riding on the backs of horses larger than their own. These knights would appear to their Irish opponents as nothing short of superheroes, almost impervious to weapons, strong and relentless.

Despite this, the Irish did mount a fierce resistance at both Waterford and Wicklow, but lost Dublin to a surprise assault by Raymond and Milo while Strongbow was busy arranging a truce. Dublin was a Norse settlement, and their population would have been identifiable as such. Even their houses had a different construction to the native Irish, although whether the Anglo-Normans noticed they were a separate people is another question. The raid on Meath, where monasteries were brutally plundered was an act designed to undermine High King Rory, an act that would not have endeared the invaders to the locals. It is hardly surprising that Rory mustered an army of many kings and went to take Dublin back. The Norse fleet that joined in was historical, and John the Mad, a berserker, was involved in the first of two attacks on the city that for this book I merged into one to save repetition. It seems odd to find a berserker, seemingly a relic of a bygone age, taking his drugs and fighting bare-chested as late as the twelfth century, but again the evidence is there. This was something I nearly left out because it seems so out of place in a world of knights and castles, but I left it in because the truth is often stranger than fiction. King Hasculf was the original governor of Dublin, and Milo did behead him after he boasted that he'd be back with a bigger army once his ransom had been paid during that first attack. This interesting mix of old Norse culture and knightly ransoming convention is fascinating, but it also shows how desperate Milo must have been at a time when their lives hung in the balance. The way in which the siege was lifted is likewise as stated in the historical record. Probably bored by the amount of time they had been camped outside the city, Rory was reported to be taking a leisurely bath while his army relaxed in the afternoon. Strongbow marshalled his army and gave a speech not far from the words I gave him, at least if you believe someone recorded his actual words accurately at the time. The Normans charged out, with four hundred men and archers riding on the rumps of knight's horses, and roundly slaughtered the Irish. Raymond is written as having skewered two men with one lance strike, and Rory escaped naked from his bath. Defeated, but not fatally, Rory was still never able to retake Dublin. The defeat was so complete that only one of the Norman army was wounded, and the other Irish armies gave up and went home.

The invasion was never a forgone conclusion, and as the army made its way up the country in those early weeks, the atmosphere must have been anxious. King Henry had sent a messenger forbidding Strongbow to set sail from Wales, but once he was safely ensconced in Dublin, the King had to do something about a man who now also wore a crown. The deal he made with Strongbow in this book is the one they made historically, and the King did cross over to Ireland to stamp his authority on it. From then on, the Normans spread out but never managed to fully conquer the whole land. Over time the Norman lords began to take on some customs of the Irish, and a cultural exchange took place that made it an even more complicated place.

King Dermot was the man who invited Strongbow in with the promise of marriage to his daughter Eva, a move for which he is rightly blamed for the English involvement in Ireland. His death was ruled as natural at the time, but Strongbow certainly benefited most from his passing. Dermot spent a long time trying to persuade Strongbow to sail with him in the first place, at one point writing to him. 'Neither winds from east nor west have brought your much desired presence.' But one can only wonder that although Dermot and his family might have desired an Anglo-Norman presence, the rest of Ireland did not.

Next up - Book Four in The Legend of Richard Keynes series:

Knight Errant*

*Out soon!

But if you can't wait, investigate the author's non-fiction work:

The Rise and Fall of the Mounted Knight

www.clivehart.net

Printed in Great Britain
by Amazon